MW01284038

HAREM GHOSTS

PRINCETON SERIES ON THE MIDDLE EAST

Cyrus Schayegh and William Blair, Editors

HAREM GHOSTS

WHAT ONE CEMETERY CAN TELL US ABOUT THE OTTOMAN EMPIRE

Douglas Scott Brookes
and
Ali Ziyrek

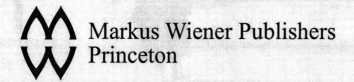

Markus Wiener Publishers
Princeton

Copyright © 2016 by Markus Wiener Publishers

All rights reserved. No part of this book may be reproduced or transmitted in any form or by any means, whether electronic or mechanical—including photocopying or recording —or through any information storage or retrieval system, without permission of the copyright owners.

Cover photo: The Sultan Mahmud II Tomb Complex, circa 1880
Cover design: Noah Wiener

For information write to:
Markus Wiener Publishers
231 Nassau Street, Princeton, NJ 08542
www.markuswiener.com

Library of Congress Cataloging-in-Publication Data

Brookes, Douglas Scott, 1950-
  Harem ghosts : what one cemetery can tell us about the Ottoman Empire /
Douglas Scott Brookes and Ali Ziyrek.
     pages cm
  Includes bibliographical references and index.
  ISBN 978-1-55876-610-5 (hardcover : alkaline paper)
  ISBN 978-1-55876-611-2 (paperback : alkaline paper)
  1. Mahmud II, Sultan of the Turks, 1784-1839—Tomb. 2. Cemeteries—Turkey—Istanbul—History. 3. Mausoleums—Turkey—Istanbul—History. 4. Istanbul (Turkey)—Buildings, structures, etc. 5. Cemeteries—Social aspects—Turkey—Istanbul—History. 6. Harems—Turkey—Istanbul—History. 7. Istanbul (Turkey)—Social life and customs 8. Turkey—Social life and customs--19th century. 9. Turkey—Social life and customs—20th century. 10. Turkey—History—Ottoman Empire, 1288-1918. I. Ziyrek, Ali. II. Title.
  DR562.B76 2015
  956'.015—dc23
                            2015018229

Markus Wiener Publishers books are printed in the United States of America on acid-free paper, and meet the guidelines for permanence and durability of the Committee on Production Guidelines for Book Longevity of the Council on Library Resources.

Mortui vivos docent

—ANONYMOUS

Sultan Mahmud II

Contents

Sultan Abdülhamid II

Foreword

It is a pleasure indeed to contribute a foreword to the book that will, at long last, introduce the magnificent mausoleum of Sultan Mahmud II to the world at large. Since 1840 countless visitors to Turkey's metropolis have passed this beautiful building and its garden graveyard without, it seems to me, realizing the gems of architecture and culture that await discovery within its dignified walls. Now, over a century and a half after the tomb arose on the heights above the Golden Horn, we have a guide that unlocks the secrets it holds, thanks to my friend Dr. Douglas Brookes.

I have long felt an attachment to the Mahmud II Mausoleum because this is where so many of my family have been buried since the middle of the 19th century. Sultan Mahmud II is the ancestor of all the current members of the Ottoman family as at one time he was the sole male member of our dynasty. He is my direct ancestor through both my parents. Buried beside him are his son Sultan Abdülaziz, his grandson Sultan Abdülhamid II, and his wife the fascinating Empress Mother Bezmiâlem, whose good works continue to benefit the people of Istanbul today—including the school just behind the tomb, overlooking it. Numerous members of my family are buried in the tomb and its garden including my mother's brother, H.I.H. Prince Mahmud Namık, who was interred in the mausoleum in 1977. It should be noted that subsequent to the exile of the Imperial dynasty in 1924, not only were the male members of the family not allowed to return to their homeland, even their remains were not allowed to be buried on Turkish soil for a further 50 years.

It is particularly gratifying now to see the care devoted by the Turkish authorities to preserving this monument where not only members of the Imperial Family, but also leading lights of the country's government and culture, lie for eternity. Most recently, it was quite moving to witness the huge crowds that accompanied my cousin, H.I.H. Prince Osman Ertuğrul, to his rest here in 2009.

May the reader savour this pleasurable journey through the portals of the Mahmud II Tomb and into the splendid Ottoman past!

H.I.H. Prince Osman Selaheddin Osmanoğlu
June 2015

Acknowledgments

This book is a joint effort. It began ten years ago when the co-authors conceived the idea of a brief guide to the Mahmud II Tomb Complex to assist the many locals and foreigners who visit the tomb each year. From that modest beginning, as the mausoleum and its garden graveyard gradually revealed the spectacular insights they hold for understanding High Ottoman culture, the brief guide morphed into the book you are reading.

Ali Ziyrek of the Istanbul Directorate of Tombs wrote the architectural analysis of the tomb that served as seed for the project, facilitated research about the tomb, and provided the present-day photographs. He offers heartfelt thanks to family and to work colleagues for their support.

Douglas Scott Brookes researched and wrote the text in its final form, translated into English the Ottoman inscriptions and poetry as well as the quoted excerpts from Arabic, French, German, and Turkish, and composed the biographies of those buried here. He sincerely thanks Edhem Eldem, whose writings have greatly expanded our understanding of Ottoman cemeteries, Hamid Algar and Fred Donner, who lent valued insights on Arabic inscriptions in the garden graveyard, and H.I.H. Prince Osman Selaheddin Osmanoğlu, who graciously lent photographs from his family collection.

Introduction

Amid the hordes of excited tourists and enterprising locals who flock nowadays between Istanbul's Topkapı Palace and Grand Bazaar, the more curious may pause for a moment to consider the rather enigmatic gray building that looms above them on the northern side of Divan Yolu Boulevard, the "Council Way" that has formed the main artery of the city since antiquity. To the tourists, its pleasing lines may seem somehow familiar, after the otherness of Topkapı or Aya Sofya or the Bazaar, while to most of the locals pursuing their business here it will simply announce *something old*. Those who venture up its short steps, invited by the pleasing architecture at home anywhere in Europe, pass beneath the elegant portals to find themselves suddenly transported from the melee outside into a welcome garden of peace, stippled from wall to wall by the most astounding, imposing, and densely packed marble sculptures. Only with a moment's reflection will those not particularly versed in Ottoman culture realize that this garden of calm and beauty with the strange sculptures is in fact a cemetery. They have entered the Sultan Mahmud II Tomb Complex.

Let us establish at the outset that this tomb complex is rare anywhere in the world: a royal mausoleum, for monarchs and their families, whose garden evolved into the paramount burial site for figures of national importance, all at the very heart of the city, literally steps from the busiest of thoroughfares. Not for nothing did the local English-language newspaper describe the place in 1883 as "the Ottoman Westminster Abbey," for British residents in the then-capital of the Ottoman Empire would recognize in this eternal resting place of royalty, cultural luminaries, and statesmen the local exemplar of their own national pantheon, on a smaller scale.

Like most graveyards, this one too stands willing to reveal a great deal about the culture that produced it, in this case the splendidly flowering High Ottoman society in its long last bloom, between 1840, when the mausoleum opened, and the end of the Ottoman Empire in the 1920s. If one can read the signposts it offers, that is, for that culture and its intricate language—at any rate to all but the handful of cognoscenti who love them both—are as dead as the inhabitants of these graves. And so, this book: to guide not only those who visit this gracious edifice and its grounds, but those whose curiosity that magnificent yet distant and elusive culture piques.

Why the title *Harem Ghosts*? Because all the inhabitants of the mausoleum grew up in or resided in the Imperial Harem, as we shall explain, while nearly all those at rest in the garden resided in their own private harems.

We shall begin our digging in this cemetery with the surprising tidbit that of the 176 persons buried at this eminent site, four died by suicide and seven were murdered.

Notes on the Text

The Turkish epitaphs are sprinkled here and there with Arabic words or phrases, all of them Koranic quotations or religious invocations. To impart the sense of this language shift to the reader, translated Arabic words or phrases are in italics.

Translations from the Koran are taken from Arberry 1974.

Turkish personal and place names are given in Modern Turkish spelling, except in quotations, which retain the spellings in the original quote. Turkish words not found in a good English dictionary are italicized at first occurrence in the text. Pronunciation of Modern Turkish letters is as in English, with the following exceptions:

c = j
ç = ch
ğ = not pronounced, but extends the length of the preceding vowel
ı (undotted i) = the "i" in *bit*
i (including capitalized dotted i) = "ee"
ö = the "er" in *her*; same as French *eu* or German *ö*
ş = sh
ü = "ee" pronounced with rounded lips; same as French *u* or German *ü*

Words appearing within brackets (as opposed to parentheses) are the translator's additions, not appearing in the original text.

Interestingly, the tombstones and palls contain errors rather more often than one would think: misspelled words, or a clearly wrong day, month, or year. Some of these may be attributed to the stonecutters, who could not correct a gaffe once committed in stone, at least without throwing out the whole piece. Other errors, especially in birth and death dates of Imperial princes, remain frankly inexplicable.

Tombstone dates offer up their own challenge, as one sometimes cannot tell to which calendar the date refers. In such cases the translation assumes the Hijri calendar—the Muslim lunar calendar. Other tombstone dates, though, are clearly from the Rumî ("Anatolian;" also called Malî, "financial") calendar, the Ottoman solar calendar adopted in 1840 and based upon the Julian calendar, but with Muslim years. Then again, the Gregorian calendar, universal then as now in Western Europe and North America, pops up periodically in the graveyard, especially after its adoption by the Ottoman Empire in 1917. With all these calendars in simultaneous use in Ottoman lands in this era, it's little wonder confusion reigned about dates!

Just to stir the confusion pot a bit, we have the fact that the lunar Hijri year runs shorter than the solar Gregorian year, which yields anomalous situations when one tries to be accurate about dates. For example, our Princess Atiye died at age 26 per the Western calendar, but 27 per the Muslim. For this reason, ages given in Western newspapers could easily differ from ages incised on tombstones, but both could be correct.

Image Credits

Ali Ziyrek is the photographer of all present-day photos in this book. Where known, photographers of historical photos are (by subject): Sultan Abdülhamid II, William Downey; cover photograph, Abdullah Frères; Mehmed Pasha (Cypriot), Abdullah Frères; Prince Ömer Faruk, Kenan Reşid; Readers of the Koran, M. Iranian; Safvet Pasha, Papazyan Frères; Tomb along gaslit Divan Yolu, Abdullah Frères; Tomb earliest photo, James Robertson. The image of Sultan Abdülaziz's funeral is from *The Graphic*, 24 June 1876; that of Abdülhamid II departing the tomb is from *Illustrazione Italiana*, 1 October 1876.

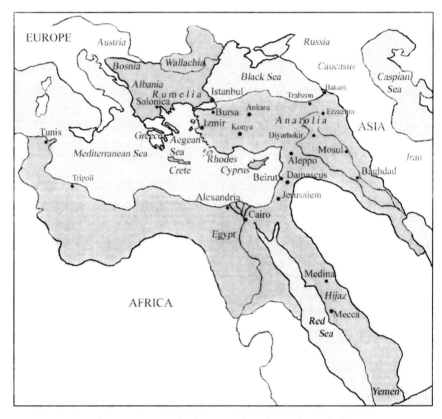

The Ottoman Empire in 1840, when the tomb was built.

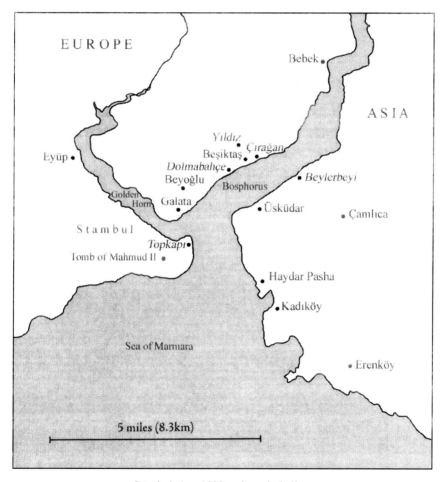

Istanbul circa 1900; palaces in italics.

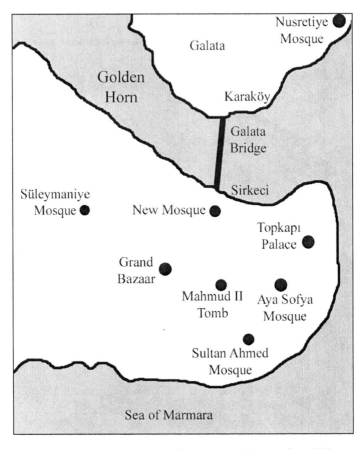

Stambul (the historical center of Istanbul) and Galata circa 1900.

CHAPTER 1

THE MAHMUD QUANDARY

No one really thought Sultan Mahmud II was dying. Still only fifty-three years of age, and monarch for longer than most of his subjects could remember, this vigorous man had quashed all opponents and wrought dramatic changes to strengthen the Ottoman Empire. Surely he had decades yet to continue his forceful reign. And so the sudden death of the great reformer, defeated at last by tuberculosis at the country home of his sister Princess Esma on 1 July 1839, quite shocked his subjects, not least because it came in the middle of the disastrous war with his Egyptian viceroy, Muhammad Ali.

> The Sultan had been for some time ailing, but the accounts daily received of him from his kiosk . . . whither he had removed for a change of air, were so far from being such as to lead to the suspicion of his approaching dissolution, or even of his disease being of a dangerous character, that up to Thursday last, I may say, his again resuming his usual occupations and amusements was from day to day looked forward to with the greatest confidence. On that day, however, Dr. Millingen, physician to His Late Highness's sister, was sent for. . . . On Sunday evening he again sank, and expired on Monday morning. . . .
>
> The sudden and unexpected announcement of the Sultan's death was such as it would not be easy to describe: regret, consternation, and fear were alternately depicted in every countenance.[1]

Unforeseen as it was, the monarch's sudden demise presented the Imperial Court with the immediate quandary as to where to bury his august remains. Mahmud's son and heir, the new sixteen-year-old sultan Abdülmecid, quickly took what was surely the counsel of his father's advisers and ordered the remains interred in the spot where, contemporary newspaper accounts agreed, the deceased monarch "during his lifetime . . . had himself pointed out as the place where he proposed erecting his mausoleum."[2] This was the private garden of what had been the winter residence of Mahmud's sister Esma, but which the Princess had deeded to Mahmud just the year before his death, probably at his request. Straddling the ridge that runs horizontally through the center of the old city, at the time of Mahmud's death the site commanded magnificent views over both the Sea of Marmara to the south and the Bosphorus to the north.

The wish was an unusual one, since with the single exception of Abdülhamid I, whose mausoleum lies next to a medrese or religious school, all royal tombs erected in the Ottoman capital since the city's conquest by the Turks in 1453 had stood in or near the courtyard of a great Imperial mosque—indeed the courtyard of the monarch's own mosque, if he had built one during his reign.[3] But there was no mosque here.

Furthermore, Mahmud had built his own soaring and gracious mosque, the Nusretiye, along the banks of the Bosphorus just north of the city, near the barracks of the Tophane artillery corps. He had his reasons for building where he did, namely to cultivate the allegiance of the artillery for his impending showdown with the rebellious Janissaries. Given the mosque's symbolic ties to his victory (thus its name, *Nusretiye*, "victory") in that struggle—the defining triumph that enabled the later successes of his reign—Mahmud's mosque would have made a fine site for his tomb. But the Nusretiye Mosque lies outside what foreigners called *Stambul*—the city's historic heart, the walled-in peninsula between the Golden Horn, the Bosphorus, and the Sea of Marmara—and the tradition of burying monarchs at or near the city's Imperial mosques meant that all Imperial tombs lay squarely within Stambul. Erecting his tomb at his mosque would have broken this tradition. His deep and wrenching changes to Ottoman society notwithstanding, that much of an iconoclast Mahmud (or his heir Abdülmecid, who in the end bore responsibility for selecting his father's tomb site) was not.

Sultan Mahmud II, pointing the way toward progress.

And so the reforming Sultan's burial location conformed completely with tradition on the one hand, being in Stambul. But on the other hand, as a freestanding tomb *not* connected to a mosque it signaled a break with royal tradition, and complemented the reforming zeal that characterized Mahmud's personality and reign. Placing his tomb squarely in the then-heart of town, along its busiest thoroughfare—even encroaching onto the sidewalk, with steps that almost challenge passersby to approach the large windows and contemplate his clearly visible catafalque within—also perfectly complemented Mahmud's intentional reorientation of the Ottoman monarch from aloof figure secluded in the palace to involved player very much in the public arena. It's probably why Mahmud wanted to be buried on Divan Yolu in the first place.

Contemporaries noticed the break with the past that Mahmud's burial site represented:

> Ordinarily the turbé, or funeral chapel, of the founder is placed near the mosque he has built; but contrary to this custom, the turbé of Mahmoud is, characteristically, placed in a special edifice, of a modern architecture, very slightly Orientalised, and in quite another quarter of Constantinople.[4]

In line with the Muslim custom of burying remains as soon as possible after death, Mahmud's funeral took place the day he died, since he passed away in the early morning hours. Brought downhill by carriage from his sister's villa at Çamlıca on the Asian shore of the Bosphorus, the corpse was conveyed across the Bosphorus by oared royal barge, to the accompaniment of the ceremonial salvo of artillery fired each minute to announce the accession of a new monarch. Once the barge landed in Stambul at the entrance to the Golden Horn, the remains were transported by carriage uphill to Topkapı Palace, as royal tradition demanded, for washing and enshrouding.

> By ten o'clock the body of the defunct sovereign had been removed to the seraglio [Topkapı Palace]; by twelve, his son and successor, Sultan Abdul Medjid, was proclaimed; . . . and at five o'clock in the afternoon the funeral procession moved from the palace.[5]

From Topkapı the procession headed west along Divan Yolu Boulevard to the former garden of Princess Esma—the first of some 140 funeral processions that over the next century and a half would follow this route to this destination. Of course no tomb yet existed in the garden to receive the royal body in its shroud, so simply into the ground it went, the site marked by an opulent Imperial tent pitched over the spot.

Western writers marveled at the simplicity of an Ottoman sultan's funeral, the first to take place in thirty years:

Now, however, the lamentations really commenced, and the interment of Sultan Mahmoud was, indeed, a scene which some of the so-called loyal European nations should have witnessed. Divested of all the pomp which attends such ceremonies throughout more civilized countries [*sic*], sorrow alone, in all its bitterness, accompanied his body to the grave. The bier on which his body was carried, supported on the heads of the Capouji Bashis ["Head Gatekeepers," important functionaries at Court], was simply covered by shawls; and among all the ministers and officers of the household not a dry eye was to be seen; crowds of his subjects, weeping from the genuine feelings of their hearts, filled the streets on every side, and the air was actually rent by the piercing shrieks of the women who thronged to approach, for the last time, the person of their lamented sovereign. The procession had not far to go to the place of interment, but a few months since selected by himself, when he little thought how soon he would occupy it. It was in the centre of the city, close to the ancient hippodrome, having been formerly the site of one of his sister's palaces. The notice was too short for even the rubbish to be cleared away, and the body was simply put in the ground, and a tent pitched over it, till such time as a mausoleum suited to his rank can be created to replace it.[6]

By contrast, the nineteenth-century Ottoman historian Lûtfî Efendi reported Mahmud's death and funeral in the considerably more dignified tones typical of Ottoman historical writing, particularly when mentioning the Imperial Family:

In the villa of his noble late sister the Princess Esma, in Çamlıca, toward morning on Monday the 19th of Rebiülahir 1255 [2 July 1839], at the age of 55 [in Hijri calendar years], he proceeded gracefully to the Garden Pavilion of the Hereafter.

His Majesty had been suffering for one year from internal ailments caused by various distresses, but as this development was attributed to the strain of the many matters claiming his attention, requisite medical treatments were not attended to. When he began to exhibit signs of weakness, the Chief Physician and various additional palace doctors examined him, whereupon they concluded that he suffered from inflammation of the lungs. Believing a change of air beneficial, he ordered that he be moved to the garden of the villa of his noble sister the Princess Esma, resident in Çamlıca, noted as it is for pleasant water and air. Nonetheless, his malady grew critical, and over a period of fifteen days the weakness of the Imperial body became ever excessive, so that at length he must lay his head onto the pillow of prostration. By command of God the Most High, he completed the numbered breaths of life and laid aside the tumultuous travail of rule, whereupon his victory-filled soul ascended to the lofty stages of Paradise. . . .

Just before sunrise, the mercy-embellished remains of [the new sultan Abdülmecid's] late illustrious father were brought down by carriage from the aforementioned villa to the pier at Haydar Pasha, and from there conveyed by caique of seven banks of oars to Topkapı Palace. There before the ablution fountain near the Chamber of the Noble Mantle the obligatory washing and enshrouding of the corpse were carried out, after which as is the custom the remains were conducted in procession for burial and concealment at the location set aside for building a tomb, within the gardens of the Princess Esma villa along the Divan Yolu.

Several poets composed the line of verse, *Han Mahmud'a makam ola makam-ı mahmud* ["May a lauded station be the station of the khan Mahmud," a clever pun in the original], as a chronogram on his death. . . .[7]

At the time, your unworthy author was employed as collator of documents in the offices of the newspaper *Takvim-i Vekayi*, and on that day I went to Aya Sofya in the company of my colleague, the proofreader Karsızâde Hoca Cemal Efendi. From the Imperial Gate [at Topkapı Palace] to the site of the noble tomb, men and women from every class of society filled to overflowing the streets and neighborhoods of Sultanahmed and Aya Sofya, where the darkness of the clouds of mourning and sorrow

enshrouded earth and sky. Fully forty-seven years have passed
since I saw the coffin emerge through the Imperial Gate—held
aloft by a thousand and one hands of the crowd, who were standing, bewildered, in astonishment and grief, calling out *Allahu
Ekber* ["God is Most Great"]—and yet their anguish remains
clearly before my eyes. The shrieks and wails of the many thousands who had gathered there, *Padişahım bizi bırakıp nereye
gidiyorsun?* ["My Padishah, where are you going, leaving us"]
rose to the heavens, because he had reigned for nearly a full
thirty-two years and bequeathed a great number of glorious
deeds, so that all the people felt of him a most compassionate
father. . . .

His Majesty Sultan Mahmud Khan having never once failed
to carry out the procession to mosque each Friday, on the Friday
two days before his death he ordered a minbar placed in the an-
teroom of the chamber in which he had passed the night at the
villa at Çamlıca, and thereby attended Friday prayers, which
displayed to the congregation present both his strength of character and his piety.[8]

Quite soon a tall fence went up around the garden as a temporary pro-
tective measure for the fresh grave with the tent over it, although typically
the garden would have had some sort of wall around it already. The tent—
not just any tent, but an elaborate Imperial pavilion that sultans inhabited
on military campaigns, and which had long symbolized royalty in Ottoman
culture—continued the custom of erecting a tent over a sultan's grave until
his tomb could be built.[9] Nor was that tomb long in coming, in this case.
On 5 July 1839, four days after the burial, in one of the first acts of his
reign Sultan Abdülmecid issued orders for the construction of the mausoleum complex that would properly house his father's remains here in
what had been until recently the garden of the new Sultan's aunt, Princess
Esma.

We must pause for a moment to consider this Princess who had sacrificed her villa to her brother in this way, as not many would relish the
thought of a large burial chamber erected beside what had been one's home.
But Esma was close to Mahmud, and so presumably willing to relinquish

her property for her brother's sake. Moreover, she possessed several homes throughout the capital, so that forgoing this one didn't exactly put her out. Surely too Mahmud had explained to his sister his wish to build a family mausoleum on the site, so that the Princess saw sacrificing her garden for an eventual tomb as not only meritorious on her part, but also prudent preparation of what could serve for herself one day sooner rather than later, given that at 60 she was of an age to consider such things. If so the Princess's sacrifice served her well, as only nine years after her brother she too was, in her turn, laid to rest within the tomb in what had once been her own garden.

We have one eyewitness account of the site shortly after Mahmud's death. The Prussian army officer Helmut von Moltke, who spent four years in the Ottoman capital as military adviser during Mahmud's reign and who had met the Sultan, informs us in his memoirs that when he visited the gravesite two months after the monarch's death, the tent still stood over the grave, as it would until the walls and roof of the new building were complete.

One would think that identifying the architect of such a major building in the Imperial capital would be a straightforward matter. The famed Garabed Balian, of the Balian dynasty of Armenian architects in service to the Ottoman court throughout the nineteenth century, has traditionally been credited in the secondary literature with designing the Mahmud II tomb. In recent years, though, controversy has arisen as to whether the Balians did indeed design the buildings traditionally attributed to them, or whether they contributed as assistants or subcontractors but not lead architects. Lacking, as we are, a register from the government architecture office of the day, say, stating unequivocally who served as lead architect on which projects, we are left with the unsatisfactory task of drawing conclusions from the evidence on hand.

Not helping our task is the paucity of government archival records and newspaper accounts of the tomb dating from the period when it was built. The very few that we have mention only Abdülhalim Efendi, head of the government's Directorate of Imperial Buildings, and describe him as *Bina Emini* (Construction Superintendent), overseer of the tomb project. But no mention of Mr. Balian, in either the archival records or the contemporary newspapers, as involved in the project in any way, or as attending the open-

ing ceremony, or in the list of recipients of awards upon its completion—
rather odd, all that, if he were the lead architect—even while mentioning
(in the newspaper account when the tomb opened) the two brothers
Ohannes and Boğos (of the Armenian Dadian family, also high in state
service) as assistant *kalfa*s (master-builders) in the Imperial Buildings office
who earned awards for their work on the tomb project.[10] Yet nowhere in
the contemporary records is Abdülhalim Efendi called *architect* either. Are
we left to assume that *Bina Emini* included the function of architect? Possibly, but that too seems doubtful.

And so we may never know for certain who designed the complex. Yet
recent research on 19th-century Istanbul architecture[11] has pieced together
clues that surely serve us here, too: one, teams of non-Muslim *kalfa*s indeed
worked as designers on the grandest state projects in this era, alongside the
Bina Emini who was charged with administrative oversight; two, Mahmud
II's abolishment of the centuries-old Imperial Architects' Office in 1831—
only eight years before the tomb project—threw the state architectural hierarchy into confusion that lasted for years, decades even, with the abolition
of old ranks and structures obscuring who was in charge of what; three,
Garabed Balian enjoyed the Sultan's confidence in his skills, learned at the
hands of his father Krikor (d.1831, architect of numerous grand imperial
edifices), leading to a virtual Balian monopoly on state architectural design
and construction in Istanbul throughout the century; four, decorative motifs
typical of later Balian buildings clearly appear in the Mahmud II tomb; and
five, the Ottoman archives are notoriously silent when it comes to attribut-
ing credit for architecture in this era.

Putting all these clues together, it seems most logical to attribute design
of the tomb complex to Garabed Balian as a kind of architect-contractor.
Yet the project was clearly a dual effort, with Balian engaging master craftsmen (probably mostly Armenians, as was the case later in the century) to
execute the designs developed by his team of architect-*kalfa*s, while Abdülhalim Efendi exercised oversight of the project in the effort by the Directorate of Imperial Buildings to retain some measure of control.

Let us pause briefly to consider both gentlemen. Gifted in fashioning
dignified and graceful designs for stone buildings that incorporated both
Ottoman and Western decorative elements, the prolific Garabed Balian
(1800-1866) designed numerous government structures across the Imperial

capital, from schools and factories to churches, mosques, and Imperial residences. The Mahmud II Mausoleum Complex constitutes his only foray
into tomb architecture, and predates by more than a decade his most famous
work, Dolmabahçe Palace.

Meanwhile, the venerable Abdülhalim Efendi was temporarily excused
from his position as head of the government's Directorate of Imperial
Buildings in order to concentrate all his efforts on the tomb,[12] receiving appointment to the project only three days after Mahmud's death. A practicing
architect since 1798, Abdülhalim Efendi had trained in his youth with the
European architects brought to Istanbul by Sultan Selim III, which attests
to his close familiarity with the European architectural styles executed here
at this tomb. Abdülhalim Efendi also supervised repairs on the immense
Mosque of the Prophet in Medina in 1847. Retiring in 1852, he died in
Istanbul in 1855.

Whether one credits Balian or the *kalfa*s he delegated to the project, or
both, the architect(s) (quite probably with design input from Abdülhalim
Efendi too) fashioned the mausoleum complex above all in the European
neoclassical *Empire* style then very much in vogue in official Ottoman
architecture, and which distinguishes the tomb from the neobaroque of later
works built in the capital, most spectacularly Dolmabahçe Palace. Alongside the European neoclassicism, the architect(s) added elements from
traditional Ottoman architecture and art, as well as from the baroque and
rococo that preceded neoclassicism in Ottoman architecture. By articulating
in stone this fusion of European practices with Ottoman tradition, the complex erected in honor of Mahmud II, who consciously borrowed European
ideas and grafted them onto the structure of the Ottoman state, wonderfully
expresses the very essence of the reforming Sultan's reign.

At the same time the design perfectly articulates the spirit of Mahmud's
son and heir, since only four months after commissioning this tomb the
new sultan Abdülmecid launched the Tanzimat era, "reorganizing" (the
meaning of the word) the Ottoman state by borrowing ideas prevalent in
European democracies and incorporating them into Ottoman culture. And
so the architectural synthesis of Ottoman and Western European design in
Mahmud's tomb constitutes the first representative of what came to be
called the Tanzimat Style in Ottoman architecture.[13]

As mentioned, work on the complex proceeded largely without leaving evidence for later researchers in the government's archives. Thus we have only the briefest of tantalizing tidbits: the order to the Arsenal to construct carts for hauling large stones to the tomb construction site; and the two orders specifying extremely large quantities of copper and of lead to be provided to the site by the Imperial Mint, the lead no doubt for sheets to line the domes and the roofs of the two buildings on site.[14] Planning and construction of the building lasted a bit over one year—a remarkably short time that testifies to the speed with which goals can be met when the Director of Imperial Buildings is detailed to the project exclusively, along with the Balian practice of delegating design work to multiple master craftsmen and thus keeping construction moving along multiple fronts—so that the new structure opened its doors on 12 October 1840.

The tomb along gaslit Divan Yolu Boulevard in the 1880s. The decorative band around the center of the tomb ties it to the arcade wall and unifies the whole complex.

CHAPTER 2

MORE THAN A TOMB

What began as a tomb quickly evolved, in the architect's design (and henceforth for simplicity's sake we shall assume Garabed Balian as the only one architect), into a complex of buildings designed not just to house royal remains, but to discharge the dynasty's duty of benevolence toward its subjects.

If we turn our eyes to contemplate the facade of the complex facing the street, we see how, appropriately enough, the architect has designed the royal mausoleum to overwhelmingly dominate the entire site from its corner position. Faced with subtly elegant grayish-white marble, the impressive structure stands in the shape of an equal-sided octagon, the customary form of elite Ottoman tombs. Yet within this familiar shape the architect has pierced each facade (excluding the entrance facade) with a single tall window, rounded at the top, in a clear architectural break with traditional Ottoman tombs that typically featured two stories of windows within rectangular frames.

Meanwhile the building's lofty, lead-plated dome falls firmly within the Muslim architectural tradition of capping tombs with domes—at least, tombs of the elite. The Mahmud II dome is one of many in this historic quarter of the city, and echoes them, while lending the building height and dominance to attract and impress the viewer. Most spectacularly, the eye-catching gilt metal device atop the tall pinnacle that crowns the dome draws the eye even as it resists ready understanding of what it is, at least to the contemporary viewer. A moment's contemplation reveals it to be a resplendent, multi-rayed sun cradled within a recumbent crescent moon. Although in 1840 the Ottoman Empire did not yet possess an official coat of arms (that would come later in the century), sun and crescent moon motifs had served for centuries as symbols of the Ottoman monarchy, and serve here

The earliest known photograph of the tomb, from 1856.
The original finial adorns the great dome, while the cobblestones of
Divan Yolu Boulevard flow up to the entrance gates, conveniently forming ramps.

to proclaim this building an Imperial edifice, announcing that we are in the
presence of Ottoman royalty. Creating visual interest, the pinnacle is not
set parallel to the street facade of the site—as one might expect—but instead forms a 45-degree angle to it, since the device also indicates the direction of Mecca, toward which the heads of the dead are turned, and
toward which visitors to the tomb would pray.

Contemporary illustrations tell us this is not the original finial atop the
tomb's dome. The original device resembled the two-horned finial atop the
water kiosk (described below), only larger. Sometime between 1856 and
1876 the current sun-and-moon device was installed. Was the rather generic
two-horned device thought insufficiently royal or dramatic? It certainly
failed in both categories, compared to its eye-catching successor. Or was
the original destroyed in a lightning strike or other untoward event, and
this newer device simply happened to be on hand? We can only speculate
as to the reason, since no evidence has surfaced to explain the change.

Continuing the Imperial identification of the complex through its exterior decorative program, the sun-and-crescent motif reappears along the frieze under the tomb eaves, within escutcheons supported by swords and capped by a burning torch—neoclassical symbols of power and enlightened knowledge, respectively. Three other sun designs adorn the grillwork at the tomb windows and along the courtyard wall, one a simple oval emitting straight rays, the other a circular device of eight triangular rays that hints at evolving into a star (the final form it would assume in national symbolism), and the third a classic sunburst within the arched opening at the top. Completing the Imperial solar program, sunbursts emerge from clouds within the archway atop each of the two entrance gates, in a rococo treatment quite possibly unique in Ottoman architectural decoration. Yet another Imperial device adorns the iron gates, within diamond-shaped frames: arrows and quivers, the symbols of military strength that we have noted inside the tomb. Finally, elegantly carved in marble between the lines of verse over both gates is the oldest and most recognizable Imperial symbol of all: the *tuğra* or royal cypher incorporating the name of the reigning sultan, here proclaiming to passersby that this is an Imperial edifice and—for those

The sun-and-crescent motif within the frieze.
By the 1880s the device evolved into the familiar star-and-crescent emblem.

The sun, symbol of the Ottoman
monarchy, points the direction to
Mecca in the rooftop device that
replaced the dome's original finial
sometime between 1856 and 1876.

Sunbursts, quivers, and swords:
the tomb's iconographic program
continues in the iron entrance gates
into the complex.

rare literati versed in deciphering tuğras in all their intricacy—that it was
built during the reign of Abdülmecid. All these devices would appear in the
elaborate Ottoman coat of arms that finally made its official debut in 1882.

Placed together here at Mahmud's tomb, the Ottoman symbolic array of
suns, moons, swords, quivers, torches, and tuğras harmonizes with the decidedly European design elements (pilasters, Ionic capitals, and keystone
brackets atop the windows) to express in architecture that reform and revitalization of the Ottoman state could occur through knowledge (adopted
largely from Europe) and power (reestablishing Imperial authority throughout the empire). Altogether, the decorative program serves to glorify and

honor the deceased monarch who cherished and pursued these ideals during his lifetime.

Stepping back again to consider the site from the street, one's eye alights upon the tomb in its monumental dignity, yes, but then follows the next most captivating element: the high courtyard wall, an arcade in marble and iron grillwork whose rounded arches, as in the tomb windows, subtly echo the curves of the dome. So does the small dome over the water kiosk—the stall for distribution of free drinking water to the public, in the center of the arcade-wall—as well as the white marble globe of the water fountain at the far right corner of the wall. The architect has oriented the domes and the globe along a diagonal axis that begins at the gleaming brass finial atop the tomb, bisects the water kiosk finial, and ends at the globe. Balian's masterful arrangement plays off the horizontal line of the arcade-wall to create an intriguing visual triangle, pleasing to the eye and happily unifying the components of the site when viewed from the street.

Asymmetrical this virtual triangle is, and far more interesting than if the architect had placed the tomb at the center of the site. Beyond the visual interest, though, the unexpected placement of the three major structural components (tomb, water kiosk, and fountain) underscores the message of

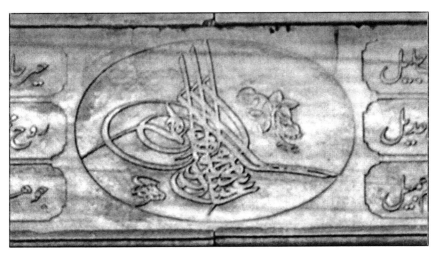

Sultan Abdülmecid's tuğra (cypher) in the center of the verse
over the eastern entrance gate tells the visitor who built the complex.

benevolence that the Imperial House sought to impart to its subjects here, for while the tomb dominates the site visually, it does not occupy central position along the street facade; that honor goes to the water kiosk, while over at the corner the water fountain offers itself readily to passersby. The dynasty has not just buried its dead here, it has provided life-giving water to its people. Over the entrance gates, the elegantly calligraphed twin verses (see chapter 3) celebrate this dual nature of the site as worthy repository for Imperial dead and as beneficent provider of water to the community, even while carrying out their expected task of praising Sultan Abdülmecid for having commissioned the complex.

Water and Piety

In an age when only the wealthiest homes could boast of running water piped to them, constructing kiosks for the distribution of drinking water constituted a meritorious act in Muslim culture for those who could afford to do so. Conscious of their duty to use their God-given wealth for acts of piety, the Imperial Family led the way in constructing water kiosks and fountains across the capital city.

The dome above this round kiosk, with its ornate metal pinnacle of two horns in mirror image of one another—as mentioned above, a not-uncommon device for adorning important roofs in Ottoman architecture—sheltering a sun device between them, echoes the roof treatment of the mausoleum in a way that pleasingly ties the two structures together.

In the early decades of the tomb, before the city installed water lines, attendants staffed the kiosk inside the structure, behind the grills, dispensing water and perhaps fruit drinks in metal cups attached by chains to the marble counter. Inside, the dome interior is ornamented with flower bouquets in relief, repeating the motifs inside the mausoleum.

Projecting into the garden behind the kiosk stands a structure with two small rooms flanking a central hall that leads to the kiosk. The east-side room served as workspace for the kiosk attendants and the tomb sextons, while the west-side room (on the mausoleum side of the central hall) served as a clock room, manned by two timekeepers. As at a mosque, the purpose of the clock room and timekeepers was to determine for visitors to the mau-

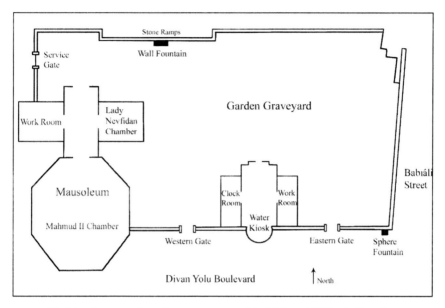

Tucking the mausoleum into one corner of the Mahmud II Tomb Complex
left plenty of space for its pleasant garden.

soleum the time for performing the daily prayers. The post of timekeeper
at an Imperial tomb being quite a prestigious one, the first Head Timekeeper
to be appointed to the tomb came from the senior ranks of dervishes of the
Mevlevi order of Sufis. This talented sheikh, Ahmed Eflâki Dede by name
(*Dede*, "grandfather," being the honorific title for senior sheikhs), fit the
post well since he had previously served as Court Timekeeper to Mahmud
II, inspiring the witty couplet

> By finger the clock he powers, Eflâki Dede
> Halting yet setting appointed hours, Eflâki Dede

and evolving into the greatest Turkish clockmaker of all, whose charming
masterpieces (most of them musical clocks) adorn Topkapı and
Dolmabahçe Palaces today.[1]

Meanwhile, the water fountain along the exterior wall, at the corner of
Divan Yolu Boulevard and the old Babıâli Street, complemented the water

The sphere atop the tomb's public water fountain has attracted attention—and pranksters—since the Complex opened.

kiosk in supplying water to the neighborhood in the days before indoor plumbing. It surpassed the kiosk in utility, by providing water at any time whereas the kiosk would have been manned at certain hours only.

On a small scale, the white marble sphere at the fountain harmonizes with the whole of the front facade by echoing the domes over the mausoleum and the water kiosk as well as the rounded arches atop the grillwork in the walls. From nineteeth-century photographs we see that the sphere was originally carved to show the continents and lines of latitude and longitude in relief, a true globe. And so today's plain sphere is clearly a replacement, its diagonal fracture dating to 2002 when would-be thieves succeeded only in cracking it when it fell.

If a globe in neoclassical architecture in Europe originally symbolized the rational world-view of the Enlightenment, it is highly doubtful that many in the Istanbul audience of this building when it opened would have understood this origin of the device, or responded to it as such. What they *would* have known, however, was that the use of such a globe constituted a decided novelty in the architecture of the Ottoman capital, proclaiming Sultan Mahmud's tomb as something new and different from his predecessors' tombs, or in fact from any other building in town.

And finally, the water program of the mausoleum complex contains yet another fountain: at the back of the garden, along the former retaining wall of Princess Esma's villa. We don't know when this elegant white marble fountain was built—did the Princess commission it for her then-private garden?—but its neoclassical lines and motifs of quivers and suns strongly

The elegant marble fountain in the garden, against the stone retaining wall
of what had been Princess Esma's villa.

suggest it belongs to the design program of the mausoleum. If indeed the
latter, then it probably served the dual purpose of refreshing tomb visitors
while providing gardeners a source from which to water the garden's flower
beds.

　　All in all, then, in both architecture and decoration the overall effect of
the complex upon the viewer is to boldly proclaim itself *dignified, elegant,*
and *European-inspired.* The few concessions to Ottoman-ness in the complex remain the shape of the tomb and its traditional dome, the stone wall
pierced with grillwork, and the decorative program of traditional Ottoman
motifs and calligraphy. Distinguishing this building from countless others
like it in Christian Europe, together these elements create what amounts to
an Ottoman variant on the *Empire* style in neoclassical architecture.

The garden graveyard, looking toward the western entrance gate along
Divan Yolu Boulevard. To the right, the square apartment for Sultan Abdülmecid's
use when visiting the tomb; now the Lady Nevfidan Chamber.

Catafalques and Palls

Leaving the garden to enter the mausoleum, the visitor notices that two
rooms flank the short interior corridor leading to the main chamber. The
room on the western side of the corridor was and is ostensibly work space
for the sextons of the mausoleum complex, while that on the eastern side,
with windows overlooking the garden, debuted as a private apartment for
use by the monarch (or probably any member of the Imperial Family)
during royal visits to the tomb. But in 1855 the latter room was given over
to royal burials as well. This is the Lady Nevfidan Chamber, housing
catafalques of Imperial Harem ladies as well as three children of the monarchs interred in the main chamber, and named for Mahmud II's Senior
Consort, the first person interred within it. More discreetly, in Ottoman
days it was called simply *Başkadın Efendi türbesi*, "the Senior Consort

Tomb Chamber." In this room the paneled vault ceiling—most likely a remnant of the space's design as a royal apartment—includes elegant plaster reliefs of bouquets in vases adorned with garlands. The motif is European in its treatment here, but continues the long tradition of flowers as a favored form of decoration in Islamic architecture.

At the far end of the corridor one enters the principal chamber, with its eighteen catafalques that mark the eternal resting place of Imperial Family members and consorts. Each catafalque takes the traditional Ottoman shape of elongated box with sharply pitched "roof" that tapers slightly from head to foot. Built of wood, the catafalques are empty, serving but to mark the burial place of the deceased in crypts below the flooring. Each is covered in a made-to-fit pall, in the most splendid examples dark velvet worked exquisitely in the traditional Ottoman art of raised gilt embroidery. For important male personages, a fez in the style they would have worn in life adorns the head of their catafalque (only males wore fezzes). The fez atop

The main tomb chamber, with its catafalques of (left to right) Princess Atiye, Empress Mother Bezmiâlem, and Sultan Mahmud II.

Mahmud II's catafalque is especially significant because as part of his reforms, Mahmud introduced the fez into the Ottoman Empire to replace the
traditional turban for all men except religious figures.

Grills made of intricate silverwork or inlaid mother-of-pearl, both traditional Ottoman arts, surround the catafalques of the most prominent Imperial Family members here. The elaborate grill that formerly surrounded the
catafalque of Mahmud II, however, has been placed in museum storage.

Calligraphy forms a major element of the interior decorative program,
as one would expect in a Muslim tomb, given the central place of calligraphy among Islamic arts. Here the celebrated calligrapher Mehmed Haşim
Efendi (d. 1845) has bequeathed for our admiration exquisite examples of
his work in the *Celi Sülüs* style, of which he was master. The calligraphic
program begins in the corridor leading to the principal chamber, greeting
visitors with the dynamic inscription over the chamber doorway, in marble
highlighted with gold and green paint, the latter color especially symbolic
of Islam. It is the Koranic invocation—and thus in Arabic, of course—
In the Name of God, the Compassionate, the Merciful. Inside the chamber,
the eye rises to the eight small green medallions (one for each angle of this
octagon) that bear the names of God, the Prophet Muhammad, the first four
Caliphs of Islam, and the Prophet's grandsons Hasan and Husain. Between
the medallions, oval niches mimic the oval windows to help draw the eye-
sight upward, toward heaven; within the niches, quivers symbolize military
might, Mahmud's goal in founding his new army to replace the Janissary

Elegance and simplicity: calligrapher Haşim Efendi's Koranic
invocation over the interior doorway into the tomb.

Corps. In the tradition of the Pantheon in Rome, recessed squares adorn the dome, the plaster ornamentation combining classical garland motifs with fan-like rays of the sun, the traditional symbol of the Ottoman monarchy that serves to emphasize who is buried here.

Where dome meets wall, the spectacular band of calligraphy encircling the room renders, in gold leaf letters over green, the entire Chapter 67 of the Koran, "The Kingdom," with its fitting affirmation of faith and of God's mercy. Little noticed by visitors because of its position well above the line of sight, the band constitutes a masterpiece of artistry, in complexity of composition and elegance of execution, bequeathed by Haşim Efendi to the ages. Continuing downward, over the doorway the master's no-less-intricate legend consists of verses 26 and 27 of Chapter 55 of the Koran, "The All-Merciful," with its lines so appropriate for a tomb, "All that dwells upon the earth is perishing, yet still abides the face of thy Lord, majestic, splendid." Striking indeed is the absence here of any kind of tile decoration in the Ottoman tradition, such as the exquisite Iznik tiles that adorn the interior of most other Imperial tombs constructed since the 1500s. Also deliberately absent from the decorative program are the stained glass

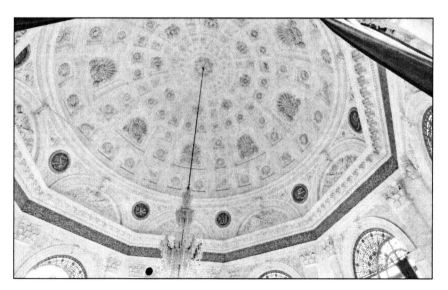

The paneled dome with sunburst motifs and name-bearing medallions, above Haşim Efendi's magnificent band of Koranic calligraphy encircling the room.

Haşim Efendi's dramatic panel above the interior doorway begins
at the lower right corner (with the Arabic word *kullu*, "all," كل),
flows up and down in waves, and ends at the upper left.

windows, alfresco painting, and arabesque woodwork present in traditional
Imperial tombs. Instead, like the outside decoration, the interior decor at
Mahmud II's tomb is quite up to date for 1839, which is to say overwhelmingly European in flavor. Here the predominant color is white, as opposed
to the rich blues and reds of tilework and stained glass in traditional tombs.
With this, Mahmud's mausoleum serves as the first and the last example
of European decoration in royal Ottoman funerary architecture, since the
two royal mausolea built in Istanbul subsequently—those of Mahmud's
son Sultan Abdülmecid and his grandson Sultan Mehmed V Reşad—
reverted to traditional decor. In death as in life, Mahmud stood out as one
of a kind.

The magnificent crystal chandelier suspended from the dome harbors
its own mystery. From the Ottoman newspaper account when the tomb
opened in 1840 (quoted at the end of this chapter) we know that the tomb
was built with a suspended chandelier. We just can't be sure it's *this* chandelier. One unproven assumption is that the current crystal chandelier was
installed years after the building opened, replacing the original hanging
lamps—that is, if one can believe the American source from 1855 who describes those original lamps for us, rather impudently: "The tomb of Sultan
Mahmoud is a little hexagonal chapel, with gilded bronze lamps suspended
from the ceiling, quite like those in our restaurants."[2] But judging from the

failure of the article's author to note the tomb is octagonal, not hexagonal, we remain unsure how much credence to grant his description of the lamps, and wonder whether he means the small glass oil lamps (still extant) in the corners between the windows, although those lamps hang from wall brackets, not the ceiling.

The superb crystal chandelier in the Mahmud II Chamber; Queen Victoria's gift?

Deepening the mystery, the inventory of the tomb's artifacts carried out in the 1940s tells us, but without providing any documentation of provenance, "The prior inventory book states that this chandelier was a gift to the tomb from Queen Victoria of England." It is possible that Queen Victoria presented the chandelier during the tomb's construction, since she was already on the British throne at the time, and if so then this spectacular lamp is original to the tomb. Causing one to hesitate, along with our inability to locate archival records in either Turkey or Britain proving the luster's provenance, is the fact that the contemporary Ottoman newspaper accounts when the tomb opened do not mention the chandelier as a gift from the Queen of England, yet one would expect they would, most certainly, as a matter of pride. Did she present it later, say in the 1850s to mark the two countries' alliance in the Crimean War, or in 1867 when Sultan Abdülaziz visited her in London? We do not know.

Further stirring the pot, a second tradition holds that the French empress Eugénie presented the chandelier to Abdülaziz during her state visit to Istanbul in November 1869.[3] But a newspaper description of the tomb before the Empress's visit describes the chandelier already in place:

> The conical ceiling was richly ornamented with moulded flowers and wreaths in white plaster, and from the centre was suspended a splendid chandelier of glass, which was unnecessary by day, as the apartment was full of light from the plain glass windows, protected on the outside by gilded gratings.[4]

Still, Sultan Abdülaziz had visited both the French and British monarchs during his state tour to Europe in 1867, so it is possible that one of them presented the chandelier to him then.

While we may not be certain whether the French Imperial Court presented the chandelier, we *do* know that Empress Eugénie visited the tomb. The *New York Herald* of November 11, 1869, tells us the Empress's sightseeing while in town included the usual mosques and the Grand Bazaar and that "On her way to the latter she examined the mausoleum of Sultan Mahmoud II. . . . Thousands of people had assembled by the wayside to see her, and as she passed the long lines of Turkish females, all dressed in the richest attire and gayly colored cloaks, they actually cheered her."

The 1940s inventory of tomb artifacts also states—again without documentation of provenance—that the two gilt wall clocks that flank the entrance were gifts of Napoleon III, the Empress's husband. Whether gifted upon Abdülaziz's visit to France in 1867 or during Eugénie's visit to Istanbul in 1869, or at some other time, we do not know—but the clocks cannot be original to the tomb since Napoleon III did not come to the French throne until some ten years after the tomb opened. It is true that documentation has not surfaced to verify an Imperial French origin for the clocks, yet there is no particular reason to doubt the inventory's claim. What we can state for certain is that the clocks are of European manufacture, since they use Roman numerals whereas an Ottoman clock would have used Arabic.

In 1893 the American writer Mrs. Clara Waters visited the tomb and recoiled at the chandelier:

> The only thing disturbing is a large, cut-glass chandelier, such as one sees in a modern ballroom, and I could but wonder whether it were put there when the tomb was built. . . . It looks more as if Abdul Aziz might have brought it from Paris, and given his father's tomb as bizarre and mongrel an air as he imparted to much else in his city on the Bosphorus.[5]

Quite the contrary, Madame! In presenting the chandelier to the tomb—if indeed he did so—Sultan Abdülaziz would have considered his gift a means to honor his deceased father by enhancing the latter's resting place. To today's eyes the gorgeous chandelier adds an air of grace that softens the room and by its very European nature serves as yet another symbolic tribute to the deceased Mahmud II, who had sought to combine European ways with Ottoman tradition.

Furnishing a Tomb

The cheerful gallimaufry of artifacts that originally adorned the tomb's interior, warming and tempering it, appears in photographs from the era as well as in travel writings, including that of the Italian author Edmondo de Amicis in 1874:

The interior walls are ornamented with bas-reliefs and decorated with carpets of brocaded silk. In the middle rises the sarcophagus [of Mahmud II; at the time the only sultan yet interred here] covered with beautiful Persian shawls; and upon it is a fez, emblem of reform, with its erect plume sparkling with diamonds. Around the sarcophagus is a graceful balustrade inlaid with mother-of-pearl, which encloses four silver candelabra. . . . Rich mats and carpets of various colors cover the floor. Here and there upon elegant lecterns sparkle precious Korans, written in letters of gold. In a silver casket there is a long roll of muslin covered with minute Arabic characters, traced by the hand of Mahmoud, when a prisoner in the old Seraglio, before ascending the throne. He ordained that this record of his youth (a copy of the Koran) should be preserved near his tomb.[6]

Even earlier, the French writer Gautier, at his visit in the early 1850s, depicted both Mahmud's special fez as well as the Koran the Sultan calligraphed as a youth:

The Sultan-reformer has, upon his coffin, instead of the classic and traditional turban, the innovating "fez" of the Nizam [the new army Mahmud established], starred with a superb agrafe of gems. There is also shown, to those who visit his tomb, a transcript of the Koran, made by this calligraphic prince, during the tedious leisure hours of the long captivity which preceded his accession to the throne.[7]

In the 1890s the American writer who disparaged the chandelier did, however, compliment the sumptuous artifacts that graced the room, including the draperies:

The biers are covered with richly embroidered velvet, that of "the Reformer" being purple. At the head is his fez, with diamond aigrette and plume. There are shawls of extreme value thrown across these biers. Those of the Sultan and Sultana [the Empress Mother] are surrounded with mother-of-pearl railings,

Readers of the Koran make use of the bookrests presented to the tomb by members of the Imperial Family. The square plaque on one such opulent bookrest reads, "From Her Highness the Illustrious and Virtuous Princess Esma, Honor Upon Her." And so Princess Esma donated not only the land to build the tomb but also artifacts to adorn its interior.

while Koran-stands richly inlaid with silver and mother-of-pearl and massive candlesticks in silver are in profusion. The Korans here are very fine, and are held sacred. The cupola is decorated with stalactites of gold and delicate cornices, while silk damask hangings soften the light.[8]

Writing in 1906, the French travel writer H. Barth tells us that the Order of Osmanî adorned the catafalque of Sultan Abdülaziz, who had founded it—an act with precedence, as Abdülaziz himself had decorated the catafalque in Bursa of the dynasty's founder, Osman I, with the breast star of the Order in 1862. This and other artifacts formerly in the mausoleum but now in museum storage include candlesticks, Imperial patents, Persian shawls, a covering for the gate at the Kaaba in Mecca emblazoned with the Imperial cypher of Mahmud II, a work of calligraphy drawn by Sultan Abdülmecid, a splendidly calligraphed Koran presented by Abdülhamid II, the exquisitely framed elegy composed by Şerif Pasha at the death of his wife Princess Emine (see the Princess's biography in chapter 5), and elegant bookrests presented by Imperial Family members, including Princess Hibetullah and Princess Esma, both of whom were eventually buried in the mausoleum.

One artifact presented to the tomb in September 1840, even before it opened to the public, was the banner of İbrahim Pasha of Egypt, the flag having been captured in the recent battle between the Ottomans and their rebellious Egyptian vassals and then donated as a kind of war trophy "to hang in an appropriate window in the Padishah's father's tomb," so the archives tell us.[9]

Not surprisingly, most of the artifacts within the tomb were gifts of the Imperial Family, as donations to the charitable foundation that oversaw the tomb. Such donations constituted a meritorious act in the eyes of the religion and culture. Alas, the pious gesture did not necessarily protect the artifacts from theft. As one example from the archives tells us, in February 1901 the police officer Hasan Efendi received the Medal of Honor for his role in recovering the shawl that had been stolen from one of the catafalques in the tomb.[10]

In Foreigners' Eyes

Set as it is among famed buildings near and dear to the heart of the Istanbul tourist, the tomb has always attracted foreign visitors, including journalists who noted for their readers the surprising airiness and comfort of the mausoleum:

> The burial place of Mahmoud II, Sultan of Turkey, is a circular building of white marble, very elegant, with a lofty dome. . . . Many windows and much light pervade this vault, and all the decorations are as rich and showy as any private house. The effect was pleasant, the desolate chill and gloom of such places being all done away with.[11]

The tomb's unexpected homeyness struck another early Western observer, who nonetheless managed a solid dose of just plain cheek to accompany his plentiful misinformation:

> To the left I beheld a building in the most sumptuous style of Turkish architecture. . . . Peeping through the grating, I saw a kind of front parlor laid with matting, and from the ceiling, daubed with floral designs *in tempora* by some Italian decorator, hung two or three tawdry chandeliers. A common English eight-day clock in a mahogany case stood silent in one corner. The horologe had need be mute there. The place was a tomb; and as I peeped I saw a number of biers rising perhaps five feet from the ground . . . and at the head of one bier I could dimly see a faded fez cap with a plume and an aigrette which glittered with the sheen of diamonds. Beneath that sarcophagus moulder the remains of Sultan Mahmoud II, the great reforming Sultan who slew the Janissaries, and strove to Europeanize Turkey, leaving to his son Abdul Medjid, his grandson [*sic*] Abdul Aziz, and the other Caliphs whom you wot of, the hideous legacy of the Eastern question. Mahmoud lies here ; and around him slumber the Sultana Valideh, his mother [*sic*], his sisters, and five of his daughters. They and the dumb English eight-day clock sleep

very tranquilly together. But surely they should put a sundial in this sepulchre. The rays glinting through the gilded lattices might have played strange tricks with the gnomon.[12]

The American humorist Mark Twain called at the tomb in 1867 on his way through Europe to the Holy Land, and left his impressions in his amusing book, *The Innocents Abroad.* As was his wont, Mr. Twain, popular for his irreverence as much as his folksy and flowing writing style, spared no one in the book, certainly not the Turks:

> We took off our shoes and went into the marble mausoleum of the Sultan Mahmud, the neatest piece of architecture, inside, that I have seen lately. Mahmud's tomb was covered with a black velvet pall, which was elaborately embroidered with silver; it stood within a fancy silver railing; at the sides and corners were silver candlesticks that would weigh more than a hundred pounds, and they supported candles as large as a man's leg; on the top of the sarcophagus was a fez with a handsome diamond ornament upon it, which an attendant said cost a hundred thousand pounds, and lied like a Turk when he said it. Mahmud's whole family were comfortably planted around him.[13]

Other Western newspapers reflected the usual anti-Turkish prejudices of the day with distortions probably accepted by readers as fact, but which tell more about the culture that produced them than the culture they purport to describe. From today's perspective the articles veer into the absurd (the sultans were buried with "many tons" of gold and precious jewels), the ignorant (two infant sons of Princess Emine buried here had been strangled by their grandfather), or, in at least one account, the laughable:

A Sultan's Joke

An accident which occurred soon after the accession of the present Sultan [Abdülmecid] shows that in some respects, at least, he is not disposed to follow up the strong traditions of his race. At the beginning of his reign the Ulema was resolved, if possible, to prevent the new Sultan from carrying out those reforms which had been ever so distasteful to the Turks, grating at once against their religious associations and their pride of race, and which recent events had certainly proved not to be productive of those good results anticipated by Sultan Mahmoud. To obtain this object, the Muftis adopted the expedient of working on the religious fears of the youthful Prince.

One day, as he was praying, according to his custom, at his father's tomb, he heard a voice from beneath, reiterating in a stifled tone the words, "I burn." The next time that he prayed there the same words assailed his ears—"I burn" was repeated again and again, and no word beside. He applied to the chief of the imams to know what this prodigy might mean, and was informed, in reply, that his father, though a great man, had also been, unfortunately, a great reformer; and that, as such, it was but too much to be feared that he had a terrible penance to undergo in the other world. The Sultan sent his brother-in-law to pray at the same place, and afterwards several others of his household; and on each occasion the same portentous words were heard.

One day the Sultan announced his intention of going in state to his father's tomb, and was attended thither by a splendid retinue, including the chief doctors of the Mahometan law. Again during his devotions were heard the words, "I burn," and all except the Sultan trembled. Rising from his prayer-carpet, he called in his guards, and commanded them to dig up the pavement and remove the tomb. It was in vain that the Muftis interposed, reprobating so great a profanation, and uttering dreadful warning as to its consequence. The Sultan persisted. The foundations of the tomb were laid bare, and in a cavity skillfully left among them, was found—not a burning Sultan, but a dervish. The young monarch regarded him fixedly and in silence, and then said, without any further remark or the slightest expression of anger, "You burn? We must cool you in the Bosphorus." In a few minutes more the dervish was in a bag, and the bag immediately was in the Bosphorus.[14]

Pride of the City

With its strikingly different looks both inside and out, the tomb set an unexpectedly confident note in the gloom of 1840 Istanbul, engaged as it was
in the ongoing military struggle with the Governor of Egypt. Newspapers
heralded the grand new addition to the capital's architectural riches, the
government's official gazette *Takvim-i Vekayi* ("Calendar of Events") invoking spectacular internal rhyme, alliteration, and lofty vocabulary that
would dazzle the literati and leave the average citizen perplexed, all to tell
its readers that the exalted mausoleum opened in the presence of Sultan
Abdülmecid himself (who must have been in a good mood since a daughter
had been born to him the day before, as the gazette announced in the para-
graph preceding the tomb story). The royal visit included the traditional
prayers recited and animals sacrificed, and appropriate gifts distributed to
Abdülhalim Efendi for his brilliant work in overseeing construction and to
Haşim Efendi for his magnificent calligraphy adorning the interior.[15] In far
more readable language, its rival newspaper *Ceride-i Havadis* ("Journal of
Events") deemed the new mausoleum praiseworthy indeed:

> The tomb of His Majesty the Paradise-dwelling Sultan Mah-
> mud, under construction near the Burnt Column on Divan Yolu,
> has been completed through the skill of Abdülhalim Efendi, who
> was charged with the project under Imperial auspices. It opened
> on the Kandil Day of 15 Şaban the Noble [12 October 1840, one
> of the four days whose evenings are sacred, hence minarets are
> lit, traditionally with oil lamps, the meaning of *kandil*], and His
> Majesty our Padishah Abdülmecid Khan honored the tomb with
> a visit that day. From the corner of the street that leads to the
> Covered Bakery, the structure extends toward the upper reaches
> of Divan Yolu, where the mausoleum itself has been erected at
> a corner. Along the lower side of the complex, toward the quar-
> ter of Divan Yolu, a clock room and an elliptical water kiosk
> have been built, with four rooms projecting in a row behind the
> walls of the tomb garden above Divan Yolu, for the sextons, the
> timekeeper, and the water kiosk attendant.
>
> The exterior of the mausoleum is quite beautifully adorned

in pure white marble all of a piece, its windows tall, its entry-
ways and railings superb and gilded, its oval water kiosk quite
handsome. Inside the inner door to the mausoleum and overlooking the tomb garden, a most ornate and cheerful room has
been created for His Majesty's use. Before the windows within
the garden walls, a pretty fountain formed from a single piece
of white marble has been placed, over it a globe of the earth,
again of marble, and traced with geometrical designs.

The portals beside the mausoleum and the water kiosk are of
beautiful and artful iron grillwork, the curves of their surmount-
ing arches drawn with suns placed over clouds, lending them an
especially different sort of beauty. Above the Mausoleum Gate
and the Water Kiosk Gate, each with a carved tuğra, chronogram
verses on a green background have been inscribed, reading:
[the two verses are presented here; see "Gates of Rhyme" in
Chapter 3].

As one enters through the Mausoleum and Water Kiosk
Gates, flower beds within boxwood borders have been planted,
with delicate, white-painted grillwork placed along the exterior
walls for jasmine to wrap around. The interior of the mausoleum
has been outfitted with lovely curtains and superb small carpets.
His Late Majesty's catafalque pall is of deep violet velvet with
coat of arms and quite exquisite embroidery worked in pure silver thread, its forwardmost side also worked in silver thread that
reads in fine Sülüs script: [the pall inscription is presented here;
see "Sultan Mahmud II" entry in Chapter 4]. A heavy, jeweled
aigrette with a sun motif engraved at its center has been attached
atop the fez at the head, and fine shawls are spread over the pall,
all surrounded by grillwork of superb mother-of-pearl, with
eight large silver candlesticks set out around the catafalque. Suspended most elegantly from the center of the dome is a superb
chandelier, while in each of the corners formed between the windows hangs a beautiful oil lamp. Three fine astronomical clocks
have been placed in the clock room, and the cups for the water
kiosk have been beautifully fashioned in the shape of semi-
globes.

The result is a most excellent tomb, the likes of which have never been seen in the Well-Protected Domains [the Ottoman Empire]. For as long as he [Mahmud] is at rest here may Almighty God grant our Sovereign Lord and Padishah [Abdülmecid] long terms of life and ordain that in his royal days culminating in success, his realm and nation prosper and flourish. Amen.[16]

And so the new mausoleum took its place among the architectural jewels with which the Imperial Family adorned the capital in the century-long last flowering of the monarchy. Far more than just a royal tomb, by providing water to the public, as well as a place of respite, reflection, and prayer in the heart of the city, and then, as we shall see, a garden to honor eminent commoners at their deaths, the Mahmud II Mausoleum Complex constituted yet another manifestation, in stone and mortar, of the ideals of order, justice, maintenance of religion, charity, and generosity that for six turbulent centuries defined the bond between Turkey's Imperial Family and the peoples over which they reigned.

— CHAPTER 3 —

THE CEMETERY AS WINDOW

There's something about cemeteries that both attracts and repels. But in the midst of this stimulating mixture, perhaps their greatest appeal is the chance they offer to learn. For what seems at first merely a house for the dead soon reveals itself to the curious contemplator as a vibrant window onto the society that made it. At the Mahmud II Tomb Complex, the window opens onto Ottoman culture at the top ranks of society, in what turned out to be the final decades of the 600-year-old Ottoman monarchy.

The Consummate Sepulchre

Death has no gloom for the philosophical Orientals!
—Miss Julia Pardoe, 1839[1]

Miss Pardoe's slight exaggeration aside, tombs in Europe and America do tend to be dark, cheerless, and neglected places hardly welcoming of visitors, whereas Ottoman culture favored spacious and airy tombs bathed in plentiful natural light, at least for tombs of royalty and high dignitaries. And so an Ottoman author mentioning burial chambers would as a matter of course attach an adjective or phrase describing the effect: "the light-filled tomb," "the illumined grave," "the radiant sepulchre." The exemplar of the radiant tomb stretches far back into Islamic cultural history, and we see it gloriously at work in the Mahmud II Mausoleum, whose neoclassical architecture lent itself especially to large windows that brought the ideal of the luminous sepulchre to new heights.

Along with the natural illumination, prominent Ottoman tombs tended toward attractively decorated interiors fitted (as here) with curtains at the windows and carpets on the floors, as if visitors were expected, as indeed they were. For Ottoman culture considered tombs of the great to be places of pilgrimage, for paying one's respects to the deceased but also as efficacious locations for prayer, for reading and reciting the Koran, and for soliciting intercession of the deceased in securing the granting of a wish. Tombs of dervishes, preachers, and teachers served particularly well for this purpose, but so did the tombs of renowned warriors and certainly, the tombs of monarchs.

Reflecting the importance of tombs in the culture, the monarchy incorporated sepulchres into its panoply of royal rituals. At his accession, each new sultan received a sword girt about his waist (in lieu of a coronation, since the Ottoman monarchy did not use crowns) not at the palace, but inside the tomb of the Prophet's standard-bearer Eyyûb Ensari, just outside the city walls along the Golden Horn. Following the girding ceremony, on his way back to the palace the new monarch called at one or more tombs

Abdülhamid II departs the tomb on the day of his sword-girding ceremonial
at the beginning of his reign, September 1876.

of his ancestors, for prayer and paying respects; the completion of the Mahmud II Mausoleum in 1840 added another possible such venue, and so we
see Sultan Abdülaziz calling here in 1861, and Abdülhamid II in 1876, to
pray at the tomb of their father/grandfather (respectively) on their sword-
girding day.

Throughout his reign, the monarch, or his mother, or other members of
the Imperial Family, engaged men whose profession it was to publicly recite
the Koran at Imperial mausolea, particularly on days of special religious
significance, and in this custom too the mausoleum of Mahmud II proved
no exception. As but one example from the archives, we have an Imperial
consort of Abdülhamid II paying in 1901 for professionals to recite, before
an audience at the tomb, Süleyman Çelebi's famed Nativity Poem, on the
anniversary that year of the Prophet's birth.[2]

If these larger and more significant tombs were meant to be visited, then
custodians had to be engaged to look after the buildings. Thanks to archival
records, we know that the Ministry of Imperial Pious Foundations employed
up to four sextons—in Turkish *türbedar*, "tomb-holder"—at any given time
at the Mahmud II tomb complex. Besides keeping the tomb tidy for visitors,
sextons ensured the buildings and their furnishings remained in good repair,
and supervised the gardeners (another respectable position on the Ministry's
payroll) who kept up the grounds, and the attendants who distributed water
to passersby from the kiosk. The archives contain copious requests over the
decades from sextons for funds to repair the buildings in their charge or
renew the furnishings.

As with other government employees in the rank-conscious Ottoman bureaucracy, sextons were designated by seniority (Senior Sexton, Second
Sexton, etc.; gardeners and kiosk attendants were similarly ranked by seniority), and given rooms for their use on the premises during working hours.
As a highly respectable position on the government payroll, the job was ea-
gerly sought after. As but one example, the archives tells us that upon hear-
ing of the death of a sexton at the Mahmud II tomb on 28 September 1861,
a certain Said Efendi, instructor of Persian at the school for government officials, petitioned that very day for the post.[3] His application began with the
formulaic phrase most such petitions employed: "The post of sexton at the
noble mausoleum of His Majesty the Paradise-dwelling Sultan Mahmud—
may his grave be pleasant unto him—having become vacant. . . ."

To carry out its cultural role, except in times of disrepair this building was open to visitors for a small entrance fee to support the complex and its custodians. The custom continues today of this tomb providing a quiet space for reflection and prayer, a welcome place of refuge from the boisterous city around it.

The Path to the Tomb

Whatever their differences in life, grandees honored with interment in the garden here shared strikingly similar funerals. Unless they resided in Stambul and died at home, nearly all made their final voyage from their home by Bosphorus steamer (occasionally, in oared caique)—within their coffin of course, the remains having been ritually washed and wrapped within a shroud (as the religion requires) at home. Echoing the rise of national identity over the nineteenth century, beginning around 1890 the coffins of the eminent men buried here would typically be draped in the Ottoman flag (which itself took shape some forty years previously), adopting the custom of nationally significant funerals in Europe.

At the Sirkeci jetty, beside the Golden Horn bridge, attendants transferred the casket onto a horse-drawn carriage for conveyance uphill to Aya Sofya Mosque, accompanied by officers of the government and the palace, along with male relatives, and an honorary escort of gendarmes and police preceding and following the procession. At the conclusion of the brief funeral service in the courtyard of the mosque, the cortege continued the short distance along Divan Yolu Boulevard to the tomb complex. Entering the garden through either gate, the corpse was laid within the grave opened for it, with the enshrouded head positioned to face Mecca.

As one typical example recorded in the government archives, the funeral on 26 November 1894 of Süreyya Pasha, Senior Secretary in the Yıldız Palace Chancery, began with the transport of his coffin by steamer from Dolmabahçe Palace to the pier at the mouth of the Golden Horn. From there a horse-drawn carriage conveyed the Pasha's remains uphill to "the noble mosque of Aya Sofya," attended by "a great many officials and courtiers and dervishes and readers of the Profession of God's Unity," including cabinet ministers and "numerous Imperial troops, policemen, gendarmes, and

The funeral procession of Sultan Abdülaziz approaches the mausoleum, June 1876.

city police forming a guard of honor." Following the funeral service the coffin was conveyed from Aya Sofya for interment "in the private sepulchre prepared at the noble mausoleum of His Majesty Sultan Mahmud, whose abode is Paradise."[4]

During the monarchy, funerals of Imperial Family members followed the same path, except that in line with Court tradition, remains of the three monarchs and the Empress Mother interred here were washed and enshrouded not in the villa or palace where they died but rather at the Chamber of the Noble Mantle at Topkapı Palace. Nor was a public funeral service held at Aya Sofya Mosque, as with commoners. Instead, for princes, princesses, or concubines the funeral took place in the privacy of the deceased's residence, while in the case of monarchs and the Empress Mother it was conducted by the Şeyhülislâm before the Gate of Felicity, the entryway into the Third Courtyard at Topkapı Palace.

As part of the dynasty's traditional concern to display benevolence to its subjects, at an Imperial funeral attendants distributed alms to the poor.

Deciphering Ottoman Tombstones

With their lanky human-like form, Ottoman tombstones stand apart not only in Islamic culture but among funerary monuments worldwide. What we see in the Mahmud II tomb garden is the evolution of Ottoman tombstone design, by the early nineteenth century, into something grand indeed, fit for an Imperial site. Here the flat stones of older and less prestigious cemeteries have become twin cylinders (or occasionally rectangles), headstone and footstone, rising from elegant sarcophagi that serve not to house the body—which Islamic custom dictates must be interred in the earth—but to mark the site of its burial.

The stonework conforms to traditional Ottoman taste in public art. With the culture's discomfort at public (as opposed to private) statuary, sarcophagi here lack the Christian cemetery's statues, busts, reliefs of human figures, angels, or personifications of Death. Here and there the tops of headstones sport the eye-catching fez for men (or turban for religious dig-

The crowded garden graveyard, a veritable museum of sculpture.

Typical tomb in the garden graveyard: that of Münir Pasha, Grand Master of Ceremonies at the Imperial Palace.

The tasseled fez of a gentleman and the star-and-crescent symbol of the Ottoman Empire embellish the headstone of General İbrahim Derviş Pasha.

nitaries), and flower bouquet for women. The distinctive headgear treatment for men attests to the origin of these late Ottoman tombstones in anthropomorphic grave markers of a much earlier age.

But most stones dispense with headgear and launch straightaway, at the top, into the traditional invocation—in Arabic—to direct the reader's thoughts to God. This might be simply the word *He*, or a phrase incorporating one or more of the Most Beautiful Names of God as mentioned in the Koran, quite frequently *The Eternal One* or *The Creator*, or occasionally the Koranic excerpt *Every soul shall taste of death* (3:185). Below this Arabic invocation (if it exists; including it was a matter of choice) the epitaph, in Ottoman Turkish except for the handful of Arabic inscriptions for religious figures or Arabs, records the ranks and positions held by the deceased, appropriately enough for a prestigious graveyard of influential folk whose position in life earned them burial in it. Quite a few of the epitaphs are in rhyming verse, and the vast majority request of the visitor a recitation of the Fatiha, the short opening chapter of the Koran customarily recited for the dead. The families of those buried here, then, would typically have hired three professionals for the tombstone, if they wished to ensure the finest of commemorations: the poet who composed a fitting verse for the epitaph, the calligrapher who rendered the verse stylishly (the finest calligraphers producing delightfully intricate designs meant as works of art rather than easily read fact sheets), and the stonecutter who executed the calligraphy with grace, elegance, and, one hoped, no errors.

The cleverest poets took the epitaph a step beyond mere recitation of biographical data, by including within the last line a chronogram—the mathematical literary device that began appearing in Ottoman verse probably in the late fifteenth century.[5] The penchant for chronograms so apparent in this graveyard reflects not just the position of poetry as the supreme literary form in High Ottoman culture, but also the culture's delight in subtle puzzles, here hidden within the poetry to entice readers to explore beneath the surface and mine the verse for multiple layers of meaning. Each letter of the Ottoman alphabet carries a specific numerical value, which meant that a poet could with care construct a line of verse in which the sum of the values of the letters equaled a certain date the poet had in mind. For this reason what we prosaically call in English "composing a chronogram" is more evocatively in Turkish, *tarih düşürmek*, "dropping a date," or *tarih yazmak*, "writing out a date," or *tarih söylemek*, "speaking a date." Besides commemorating deaths, chronograms might be commissioned or voluntarily composed to mark any number of noteworthy occasions, including declarations of war or peace, marriages, promotions at work, the arrival of seasons or the new year, building a house, or even when a young man first grew out his beard.[6]

The poet usually preceded the chronogram with a line in which he named himself, rather as a way to alert the reader that a chronogram is coming. As one example in our graveyard, for the tombstone of Safvet Pasha the poet Münif composed a lengthy rhyming verse culminating in these two lines:

With tears of grief write out his date, Münif:
"To this world bade Safvet Pasha farewell"

The last line—in Turkish, *dâr-ı dünyâya vedâ' eyledi Safvet Paşa*—is Münif's chronogram, yielding these numerical values for each letter (reading from right to left as in Ottoman script):

$$(80 = 5+10+1+10+50+4) \text{ دنيايه } \quad (205 = 200+1+4) \text{ دار}$$
$$(81 = 70+1+4+6) \text{ وداع}$$

$$(576 = 400+6+80+90) \text{ صفوت } \quad (55 = 10+30+10+1) \text{ ايلدى}$$
$$(304 = 1+300+1+2) \text{ پاشا}$$

Ali Sâib Pasha's epitaph adorns his headstone, above the rococo ornamentation that elegantly frames the chronogram composed upon his death.

Adding the values together, 205 + 80 + 81 + 55 + 576 + 304 = 1301, the year of Safvet Pasha's death in the Muslim calendar.

Sometimes the poet couldn't think of a line that totaled the sum he needed, or a rhyme for the final word of the chronogram that would reach that sum, or else he elected to entertain his reader further by rendering solution of the chronogram one step trickier. On these occasions when the chronogram misses the target date, the poet includes a clue in the preceding line to inform his reader how to arrive at the desired total. Tip-offs among our tombstones vary. In some, the words "bejeweled" or "with jewels" subtly instruct the reader to count only the letters with dots (seventeen of the thirty-one letters in the Ottoman alphabet contain dots). Others bear a phrase that gently leads the reader to the correct computation: "I recited the Ihlas thrice" (referring to the Koranic chapter of that name) counsels the reader to add three to the total in order to reach the intended date.

Contrary to what one might expect, only the commoners buried in the garden received chronograms on their tombstones. The embroidered palls over the catafalques of royalty within the mausoleum provide essential factual data, along with religious honorifics, but never rhyming verse or chronograms. These were left for poets to record for the ages in printed or handwritten texts—a medium far easier to manipulate than gilt embroidery.

Gates of Rhyme

It may strike us as quaint, since poetry is usually not so much a part of daily life nowadays, but to Ottoman eyes a grand building was incomplete without rhyming verse to adorn it, explain it, and honor it. Tombstones have already shown us the exalted status of rhyming verse in High Ottoman culture, and in further reflection of poetry's lofty rank, the builder of a significant edifice would not only engage carpenters and masons but would also commission a poet to compose verse specifically for the site. And so one sees poetry upon mosques, palaces, schools, hospitals, libraries, bazaars, public baths, soup kitchens, and certainly tombs. At our tomb, the six carefully composed stanzas over the twin entrance gates into the garden flowed from the pen of the celebrated Ziver Pasha (1793-1862), in effect the Ottoman poet laureate of his day, whose literary talents led to commissions to adorn a good number of state buildings constructed during the reigns of Mahmud II and Abdülmecid.

The rhyming poems sparkle with stately vocabulary that would stump the average Turk then as now. The verses over the western portal translate as follows:

> May the Everlasting Source of our Help grant the monarch of
>   the age
> Long life blessed with victory and majesty.
> To his sultanic forebears his person indisputably
> Constitutes felicitously a scion most excellent.

That noble king a mausoleum built
As tomb for his father, Sultan Mahmud,
A lofty tomb that like heaven
Became forever abode to the inhabitants of Paradise.

As the Fatiha and Ihlas are recited, may God
Render cheerful the soul of the khan Mahmud.
O Ziver, my chronogram is set with jewels:
"The tomb of Mahmud Khan, the mansion of the heavens."

—1255—

The *Fatiha* ("Opening"), the first chapter of the Koran, and the *Ihlas* ("Sincerity"), the 112th chapter of the Koran, are recited on numerous occasions and various locations, including at tombs.

As we have seen on tombstones, so too poetry composed for Ottoman buildings typically included a chronogram woven into the last line. This verse is no exception. The poet has placed the phrase "set with jewels" immediately before the chronogram as our clue to count only the dotted letters when deciphering it, whereby we arrive at the total of 1,255—the Islamic calendar year in which Mahmud II died, appearing immediately below the chronogram (as was the custom) and thereby helping readers solve it.

Ziver Pasha's elegant verses, calligraphed by Yesarizâde's deft hand and flanking Sultan Abdülmecid's tuğra, distinguish both portals—this verse adorning the eastern gate.

Above the eastern portal the verse translates:

> Source of the water of life, the noble King, the just
> Imperial Majesty Abdülmecid, Shadow of the Glorious Lord
>   God,
> That King's flowing beneficence has become his pure quaff.
> If bountiful recompense be fitting, it gushes like water.

> For the noble soul of his glorious father, that King
> Brought to life at this site a water kiosk without peer.
> Should the soul of Sultan Mahmud drown in mercy, he has a
>   place,
> His tomb is the garden of Paradise, his water kiosk a heavenly
>   spring.

> O God, as the thirsty take drink of water here,
> Let the beautiful water of benefaction ponder the soul of Sultan
>   Mahmud.
> The munificent Ziver has moistened with luster the jewel of my
>   chronogram:
> "The beautiful water kiosk has found a Kevser for the soul of
>   Sultan Mahmud."

—1256—

Once again, amid his many allusions to water in this delightful verse, so appropriate beside the water kiosk, the poet Ziver has dazzled the reader with his composing skill by devising a charmingly suitable chronogram for the last line (invoking the river Kevser, which flows through Paradise). With the traditional love of classical Ottoman poets for layers of meanings, the penultimate line can also read

> The munificent Ziver has moistened with luster
> the dotted letters of my chronogram

as a clue that one is to add up the values of only the dotted letters within it. Obeying these instructions, we arrive at the sum of 1,256—the Islamic calendar year in which the tomb was completed.

Following the verse is the line in Arabic (as similar lines traditionally are in Ottoman verse):

> Yesarizâde Mustafa İzzet calligraphed these lines.
> May God spare them both.

in which the calligrapher asks God's blessing for both himself and the poet. The line tells us that the calligrapher was the accomplished Mustafa İzzet Efendi (1776?-1849), known simply as Yesarizâde or "son of Yesari" after his father and teacher, the famed calligrapher Yesari Mehmed Esad. In the verse inscriptions we see the so-named Ottoman Ta'liq script, which Yesarizâde himself designed and developed after around 1800 from the Ta'liq style of Persian calligraphy, and which subsequent Ottoman calligraphers adopted due to its especial elegance and subtle dynamism.

Along with designing his many works of calligraphy that adorn mosques and government buildings throughout Istanbul and the provinces, this famed and talented artist taught numerous students, among them leading calligraphers of the next generation. Sultan Abdülmecid himself took lessons from this doyen of calligraphers, earning the certificate that professional practitioners of the art bestowed upon pupils who mastered their technique.[7] One imagines that on his visits to this site the monarch felt a measure of satisfaction at seeing the exquisite work of his old teaching master adorn the entry portals to his family's tomb.

Yesarizâde's prolific artistry hides the fact that throughout his career as a calligrapher he worked in the judiciary, rising to serve as the highest-ranking judge in the empire. His son, the musician Necib Pasha, is buried in the garden graveyard.

The Ottoman Career Ladder

When delving beyond the elaborate tombstones and sarcophagi to discover the stories of the people buried here, the reader of their biographies is struck by the differences between how a young man made something of himself in late Ottoman society, and how a young person does so today.

One startling contrast is how many future Pashas (the title accorded the highest-ranking statesmen and military officers) launched their working careers at tender ages—as teenagers, or even younger. These boys typically finished the lower levels of formal schooling, but then directly began work as apprentice in whatever government office would take them in. The apprentice learned from his seniors on the job, supplemented by teachers who came into government offices to instruct the youths in what they needed to know for their work.[8]

The second striking feature apparent from the careers of our older grandees is the traditional Ottoman path for recruiting conscripts into government service. In this patronage system, a young boy entered the household of a great man, either placed by his family or purchased on the slave market. Both of these paths are visible in the careers of the men buried here. Once in his patron's household, the boy would be taught what he needed to know in order to prove useful in life, and when his superiors judged his service in the household complete, he would be placed in government service, to rise on his merits and thanks to the connections of his patron. The idea, of course, was for these young men to remain loyal to their patron, proving of use to him wherever needed. The system was old and well-tried by the 1800s, the century that witnessed its decline due to the introduction of state-run schools, part of the reforms introduced so assiduously by our tomb's primary occupant, Mahmud II.

Another impact of that century's reforms that we see in the lives of the men buried here is the hierarchy of ranks that the Ottoman state developed in this era for civil servants. The ten ranks of civil officialdom paralleled the system of military ranks, even to devising military-style uniforms for the upper echelons of civil officials to wear on duty. Given the prestige of this graveyard no one holding a rank below the top three is buried here:

1. *Vezir*, "Vizier," the traditional Islamic title for highest-ranking government officials
2. *Bâlâ*, "Exalted"
3. *Ulâ Evveli*, literally translating rather awkwardly as "Primary First," but rendered more happily as "First Rank, First Class" by contemporaneous English speakers

Having reached the very top of the civil hierarchy, statesmen of Vizier rank—along with their equivalent in the army, Field Marshals—could use the title *Pasha* following their name, while those below had to content themselves with *Efendi*—a distinction we find carefully preserved on the stones and in the biographies.

Alongside the ranks and titles, one notes the importance attached to the orders and decorations a man received. Since these trinkets served as nothing less than physical marks of the official esteem in which the deceased was held, obituaries typically recorded carefully not only the decoration (Ottoman or foreign), but which class of the decoration the holder bore. Abdülhamid II in particular expanded the array of Ottoman orders, decorations, and medals, bestowing them bountifully as part of his program to inspire loyalty to his person. And so the biographies of the deceased here dazzle with mention of the highest Ottoman orders, the *Mecidî* (or *Mecidiye*, founded by and named for Sultan Abdülmecid in 1852), the *Osmanî* (or *Osmaniye*, "Ottoman," founded by Sultan Abdülaziz in 1861), and the *İmtiyâz* (the "High Order of Distinction" founded by Abdülhamid II in 1878), as well as the highest-ranking medals *İftihâr* ("Glory"), *Liyâkat* ("Merit") and, bearing the same name as the order, *İmtiyaz* ("Distinction").

Reviewing the biographies of the gentlemen interred here, one notes the surprising preponderance of military commanders who also served, even simultaneously, as bureaucrats: generals appointed as governors of provinces, typically. Given the vast spread of the empire, and the limited number of graduates from the Civil Service Academy, it made sense to press military men, with their presumed experience in management, into double duty as servants of the state.

Simultaneously one notes the bewildering frequency with which eminent statesmen rotated in and out of their positions—many postings lasting but a few months, hardly long enough to get one's bearings. This too formed part of the suspicious Abdülhamid's strategy for prolonging his reign, by not allowing his men to set down roots in any one post and so pose a potential challenge to his rule.

Harem Living

The life stories of the princesses, concubines, and harem supervisors interred in the tomb and garden tell us much of the structure of, and changes to, the harem system—that mainstay of Ottoman palace life that for centuries has fascinated writers, readers, artists, and musicians worldwide but which in practice was far less titillating than in the popular imagination.

Simply put, if the patronage system was designed to supply males to fill the offices of the state and the military, the harem system served as its counterpart to supply females to staff the household sections of the palaces and ensure the propagation of the dynasty. Below the Imperial Family, society's leaders—including the governors, generals and admirals, and top-ranked statesmen buried here—adopted the harem system in their own mansions, although on a far smaller scale than at the palace, and only if they had the money and the inclination to do so. But let us be clear: the vast majority of families throughout the empire consisted of one husband and one wife only. Harems were only for the extremely wealthy, and due to both changing attitudes and the staggering costs in what was a weak and impoverished economy, by the end of the monarchy in 1924 practically the only harem still in existence in the Ottoman Empire was that in the Imperial Palace itself.

To outsiders unfamiliar with the culture, the words "Imperial Harem" meant the group of women assembled for the Turkish sultan's sexual use, and like as not raised a decided dollop of lascivious interest accompanied by a wink. But to an Ottoman, the words commanded respect. They meant two things: one, the concubines in the monarch's entourage; and two, the wing of the palace where these ladies and their royal children resided. Black eunuchs guarded the Imperial Family in the palace harem and carried out administrative tasks, while the large number of serving women (officially slaves) saw to the daily tasks in keeping the palace running. Much like an army, in order to ensure discipline the harem system evolved strict courses of training, standards of conduct, and ranks of hierarchy, all scrupulously

observed. From among these female servants came the few women promoted—based upon the aptitude they had shown in their work—to leading
positions of power, wealth, and influence as supervisors of the Imperial
Harem. From the servants' ranks too came the few women chosen—based
upon their beauty and accomplishments—for conjugal relations with the
monarch or (after around 1850) adult princes.

In line with Islamic law for any Muslim male, Ottoman sultans could
take four wives. Once appointed to this rank by the monarch, these harem
ladies received the title *Kadın*, "Lady," which is better translated as "consort" rather than "wife," since in Court practice formal marriage ceremonies
between sultans and concubines (even "wives") almost never took place,
at least until the mid-nineteenth century. Like everyone else at Court, the
four Imperial Consorts were ranked in order of precedence, with the Senior
Consort figuring as the highest-ranking lady of the Imperial Harem, second
only to the monarch's mother herself if the latter were alive.

Beneath the four consorts in Court hierarchy came the other concubines,
in two tiers: the higher-ranking *ikbal* ("fortunate one") and the lower-rank-
ing *gözde* ("chosen one"), the latter not ranked by precedence although the
former were. Upon the death of a consort or *ikbal*, her "sisters" (as they
called one another) below her moved up one notch in rank.

In theory there was no limit to the number of *ikbal*s and *gözde*s a sultan
could take, but in practice they were few. Of monarchs in the era of our
tomb, Mahmud II appointed eighteen ladies as consorts or concubines, Abdülmecid twenty-five, Abdülaziz five, Murad V ten, Abdülhamid II thirteen,
and Mehmed V and Mehmed VI four each. Of these seventy-nine ladies,
eight consorts and three *ikbal*s are buried in our tomb's two chambers. Reflecting the great prestige of this cemetery, as far as we know no *gözde* was
buried here, as their lower rank did not warrant it.

With very few exceptions, Imperial consorts and concubines of the nineteenth and twentieth centuries were in origin Circassian, the Muslim people
of the Caucasus. Like nearly all the women in Court service, they had been
sold into slavery at a young age (despite the prohibition against selling fellow Muslims into slavery) and purchased or presented as gifts to the palace.
Once in royal service they received a new name from the sultan, if they
didn't have one already. In many cases the parentage of these Circassian
women remains unknown, so that tracing the maternal lineage of an

Ottoman sultan quickly runs into a brick wall.

Unlike male members of her family (at least until the late nineteenth century), a princess of the House of Osman underwent an official marriage, arranged by the monarch. As affairs of state, these marriages constituted lavish affairs widely reported in the press, with the groom typically a high-ranking statesman or military officer (or his son) whom the sovereign wished to honor greatly by presenting an Imperial princess in marriage. In turn, the prospective bridegroom had to divorce any wife or wives he may have had already, and was not allowed to take concubines. Nor could he divorce his royal wife, although a princess could—and many did—divorce her husband.

In Ottoman custom the throne passed through the male line only. In order to limit the size of the Imperial Family, children of a princess (herself by definition the daughter of a sultan or prince) were considered of the blood-royal, but grandchildren of a princess were commoners, although prestigious ones.

The harem system, in which male members of the dynasty took concubines of indeterminate lineage whom they may or may not have married, underwent rapid decline in the early years of the twentieth century. The change was part of the ongoing adoption of European royal practice by the Ottoman Court, and followed the path blazed by the Royal Family of Egypt, which abandoned the harem system in the 1870s in favor of one wife for each prince.

The problem for the Ottoman Court was, if the men of the family were now to marry other royalty, as did European princes, whom might they marry? Given that the royal bride must be not only of course Muslim, but Sunni Muslim (which eliminated princesses of Iran), the field narrowed down in practice to only two possible candidates (unless one chose to look outside the empire, which no one seems to have done, yet): princesses of Egypt—former vassals but now quasi-autonomous royalty, with the advantage of mixed Turkish/Balkan/Circassian descent like the Ottoman dynasty and speaking Turkish—or their own cousins in the Imperial Family. And so the first such wedding took place in 1919, when the Ottoman prince Abdurrahim married Princess Emine of Egypt, followed in 1920 by the groundbreaking nuptials of Prince Ömer Faruk (buried in this tomb) and Princess Sabiha, the first marriage between members of the House of

Floral designs typically graced women's headstones, as in the grapevine for Ferahnüma Usta, Supervisor of the Imperial Harem. The royal sun atop the stone marks her exalted status in service to the Imperial Family.

Osman in its six-hundred-year history.

The field of candidates inadvertently expanded further after the collapse of the empire in the 1920s, as the enduring prestige of the deposed dynasty led the new royal families in the successor kingdoms of Albania, Iraq, and Jordan also to seek marriage alliances with the House of Osman. Further afield, two of the dynasty's princesses married Muslim princes of India.

Since then, further echoing the evolution in European royal practice, today's Turkish princes and princesses marry whomever their heart, not the dynasty, dictates.

— CHAPTER 4 —

THE DYNASTY IN THE TOMB

Mahmud's mausoleum continued the Ottoman dynastic tradition of building a tomb for a monarch or an Empress Mother and then, as space allowed, using the building to bury subsequent monarchs and other members of the Imperial Family, as well as Imperial concubines.

Three monarchs are buried in the Mahmud II Chamber, the main room of the mausoleum: Mahmud II, his son Abdülaziz, and his grandson Abdülhamid II. Of the remaining fifteen persons interred in this room, twelve are princes or princesses or their children, while three are harem ladies (two

Topped by fezzes, the catafalques of the three monarchs buried here:
(from the left) Mahmud II, Abdülaziz, and Abdülhamid II.

consorts and one ikbal) of the three sultans interred here, one lady each.

Eleven persons—all Imperial Family members or consorts/concu-bines—lie at rest in the Lady Nevfidan Chamber, the former royal apart-ment off the entry corridor that in 1855 was remodeled into a burial chamber for Imperial Harem ladies. By regulation the House of Osman considered these ladies adjuncts of the dynasty, rather than full-fledged members of it. The exceedingly rank-conscious Ottoman society held this side chamber to be a fitting tribute to these esteemed ladies, and it is cer-tainly symbolic of the high station they occupied in life: close to the blood-royal, but not exactly part of it.

Harem ladies whose son ascended the throne, on the other hand, were most definitely honored as full members of the dynasty, as attested by their title *Valide Sultan*, "Empress Mother" (literally "Princess Mother"), the only harem ladies to bear within their title the royal term *sultan* (which royalty of both genders used). Their unique status as mother of a monarch earned them interment in the main chamber of this building.

Why, then, is only one Empress Mother buried here? Because Court cus-tom called for an Empress Mother to be interred in the tomb of her husband, the father of her regnant son, unless she had built a tomb of her own. And so Mahmud II's widowed consort the Empress Mother Bezmiâlem, mother of Sultan Abdülmecid, was laid to rest here upon her death in 1853, during her son's reign. Her fellow consort-of-Mahmud-II, the lady Pertevniyal, mother of Sultan Abdülaziz, built her own tomb elsewhere in Stambul and lies there. Then, the mothers of the subsequent four sultans, until the end of the sultanate in 1922, were all consorts of Sultan Abdülmecid. Had they lived to see their sons inherit the throne (in the event, only two did), they would have been buried at Abdülmecid's or their own tomb, not here.

Finally, the only other possible such candidate before the end of the monarchy, the mother of the last ruling member of the House of Osman, Caliph Abdülmecid II, died in 1895 when she was still "only" Second Con-sort of the late Sultan Abdülaziz. And so she was buried in the side cham-ber, but had she died during her son's reign in 1922-1924 she undoubtedly would have been laid to rest in the main chamber.

And so the side chamber functioned originally rather like a harem sec-tion of the mausoleum: for burials of a sultan's ladies, near to but separate from the dynasty, whereas princesses of the blood-royal and mothers of monarchs could be buried in the main chamber. That said, if this was the rule at first, it was relaxed over the decades, since three individuals of the blood-royal came to rest in the side room while two later concubines lie in the main chamber.

The following persons, interred within both the main and the side chambers, are listed alphabetically by name within the categories that distinguished them in life: Royalty, and Imperial Concubines. Following the name is the location of the grave on the accompanying map; M1-M18 are in the Mahmud II Chamber and N1-N11 are in the Lady Nevfidan Chamber.

Only personal data on the catafalque palls (if such data exists; some palls lack personal data) has been translated. Koranic verses or religious formulae have not been translated, unless the latter appear within the personal data.

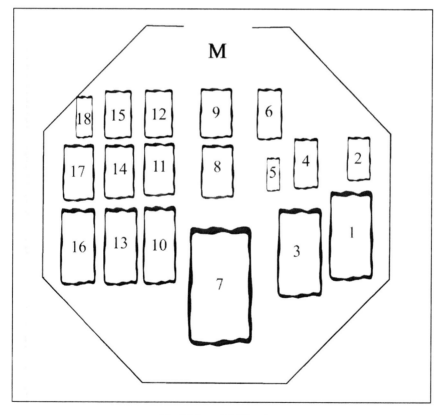

The Mahmud II Chamber.

The Lady Nevfidan Chamber.

Royalty

Sultan Abdülaziz. M3

The younger son of Mahmud II, by the lady Pertevniyal, Abdülaziz was born in 1830 in the seaside villa at Eyüp of his aunt Princess Esma—a testament to the close ties between his father and his father's sister. When he was but nine years old, his father died and his older half-brother Abdülmecid became sultan, whereupon Abdülaziz became the Veliahd, a position he held for twenty-two years.

In contrast to his consumptive brother, Abdülaziz was physically strong and active, managing an excellent farm on the Asian side of Istanbul, hunting, and sailing. But the virile prince also showed artistic talent, producing drawings of considerable accomplishment, and studying and composing Turkish and European music all his adult life.

Abdülaziz acceded to the throne at his brother's death on 25 June 1861. His physical strength and sportsmanship, his love of popular Turkish theatre, and his unaffected dress and behavior endeared him to the Istanbul

populace. He announced plans to
reduce palace expenditures and de-
velop the Ottoman economy.

Sultan Aziz, as he was more familiarly known by his subjects,
also wished to see his empire and
Europe. In 1863 he became the first
sultan since 1517 to visit the Ottoman province of Egypt, while
from June to August 1867 he
toured Western Europe—the first
(and last) reigning Ottoman sultan
to do so. Accompanied by his son
Prince Yusuf İzzeddin and his
nephews the princes Murad and
Abdülhamid, Abdülaziz's visit created a sensation in France and
Britain. Along with lavish banquets
and formal state visits to Emperor
Napoleon III and Empress Eugénie
in France, Queen Victoria at Wind-
sor, and Emperor Franz Joseph in
Vienna, in a gesture typical of vis-

Abdülaziz around 1870, wearing the
distinctive fez that he adopted
and that adorns his catafalque.

iting monarchs yet nonetheless rife with a bit of irony, the Sultan of the impoverished empire donated £2,500 "to be distributed to the poor of
London," as *The Times* reported on 27 July 1867.

The sights of Paris, London, and Vienna inspired the Sultan to transform
his own capital city into something approaching them in splendor. Forsak-
ing his earlier resolve to avoid debt, Abdülaziz began borrowing to finance
cherished building projects, including imperial residences suitable to the
modern royal life the Sultan witnessed in Europe. His new palaces of
Beylerbeyi and Çırağan incorporated the glory of European royal residences, and in the former he entertained Empress Eugénie upon her visit
to Istanbul in 1869. His reign also saw the founding of military and civilian
schools, colleges, and the university, in addition to railway lines, tramway
lines in Istanbul, and new industries throughout the empire.

On the personal level, Abdülaziz continued to compose music in the European fashion, including waltzes and songs of considerable merit, and nourished his love of art by commissioning paintings from European artists he invited to Court. His preferred style of low-cut headgear (visible on his catafalque here) became popular throughout the empire as the "Aziziye fez," named for him. By his five harem ladies Abdülaziz fathered thirteen children, of whom nine survived into adulthood.

On the political stage, Abdülaziz's reign saw the rise of government men educated in the schools his father established—well-trained bureaucrats who came to believe they should share in running the state. These "Young Ottomans" began to oppose what they saw as the monarch's despotism and profligacy. The 1875-76 revolt in the Balkan provinces prompted the leaders of this group to act. Citing what they called the Sultan's oppression, wasting of public funds, and inept leadership, a core group of cabinet ministers deposed Abdülaziz on 30 May 1876, transferring him and his harem from Dolmabahçe Palace to house arrest at Topkapı Palace. A slave girl in the harem of his successor, Sultan Murad V, described the scene in Dolmabahçe Palace that day:

> From the monarch's apartments we could hear women wailing in anguish, along with the appalling sound of breaking glass and chandeliers. The elderly kalfas bowed their heads in acceptance of what fate had decreed, signaling to one another with their eyebrows and eyes as if to say, "Ah, this world, for some it's heaven, for others it's hell. Yesterday they were happy and blessed with good fortune, today the world is their prison. Whatever they're doing now they have a perfect right to do. This should serve as a warning never to think one can achieve mastery over this fickle world."
>
> Two royal barges, one behind the other, pulled away from the quay at the Imperial apartments. Oared boats filled with soldiers swiftly took up position around them. Sultan Aziz and his sons the princes Yusuf İzzeddin and Mahmud Celâleddin sat in the first barge. Ten minutes ago he was Padishah, now he was nothing. His magnificent physique had shrunk in those ten minutes; now it seemed almost the body of a child. The ex-Sultan was

bending forward, as if he did not want to see the world anymore. It was the same with the Princess Mother and the other ladies in the second barge. One can guess the chaotic circumstances under which they had left, since they obviously hadn't time to veil themselves properly but had only wrapped shawls around their heads. This painful scene, which served as a warning to us all, lasted not more than a few minutes.[1]

After some days, at his own request Abdülaziz and his family were transferred to the Fer'iye Palace along the Bosphorus. Disconsolate, on the morning of 4 June 1876 the deposed monarch committed suicide with the pair of scissors he asked his mother to lend him to trim his beard. He was 46 years of age. As Abdülaziz had not built a tomb of his own during his reign, no doubt expecting to live many more years, his shaken successor Murad V ordered his remains interred here in his father's mausoleum, in a funeral the evening of the day he died.

Once the committee of palace and foreign doctors and leading religious figures had examined the corpse, the ex-Sultan's remains were conveyed down the Bosphorus to the pier at the entrance to the Golden Horn. One eyewitness described the corpse's arrival at the quay below Topkapı Palace:

> We were awaiting the body in the Yalıköşkü [the palace's seaside villa along the Bosphorus]. The deceased's remains arrived by steam launch, laid out upon an exposed thin mattress and covered over by a white curtain, with a black shawl draped over that. The palace eunuchs lifted this mattress bearing the body and placed it on a door, in order to carry it. But because the door was too narrow, the sides of the mattress hung over the edges. Also the shawl did not cover the whole body and had partially slipped down, and so since no one could tell whether they were carrying the body feet first or head first, I lifted a part of the covering where it had slipped and saw that it was being carried correctly [i.e., head first].[2]

From the jetty, the coffin was transported by carriage uphill to the Chamber of the Noble Mantle at Topkapı where, in line with Court tradition, the

monarch's corpse was washed and wrapped in the burial shroud. From Topkapı the casket was carried the short distance to the Mahmud II Mausoleum. As fate would have it, then, Abdülaziz was both born and buried
at properties owned at one time by his aunt, Princess Esma.

One can but marvel in sheer admiration at the organizational skills of
the Ottoman palace, charged with staging a royal funeral within only hours
of the ex-Sultan's death; no doubt officials drew on the Court's centuries
of experience in the matter. As reported in the foreign press:

> The procession started from the Palace of Top Capou, and was
> headed by a military band, but no music was played until the
> return, next came a guard of honour, which was followed by the
> grand dignitaries of the State on horseback. Nearly two hundred
> Ulemas and Softas [theological students] chanting verses from
> the Koran immediately preceded the bier. The coffin was an im-
> mense wooden box of that shape usually employed in Turkey,
> and was covered with small, but handsome, Persian carpets, the
> ex-Sultan's fez being placed at the head. The body was borne
> by eight infantry soldiers, with side arms only. An immense
> crowd, composed of all classes of the Mahomedan population,
> followed the procession and lined the streets, which were
> guarded by sentries placed at intervals, with arms reversed.[3]

In tribute to the deceased monarch, the poet Sâdi Bey penned an elegy with
the refrain:

> Weep, people of the world, weep for the martyred Shah,
> Let mourners shed bitter tears of regret.[4]

and the monarch's poetess sister Princess Âdile composed her rhyming
"Elegy to the Late Sultan Abdülaziz Khan," in which each stanza ends with
the defiant lines:

> May the world mourn and weep dearly for Abdülaziz Khan,
> Assist, O God, his blessed body, painted in crimson blood.[5]

while irreverent children in Istanbul sang the ditty that translates as:

> They put me off the throne
> Across the Bosphorus blown,
> Into Topkapı thrown.
> Awake, Sultan Aziz, awake,
> The whole world weeps for your sake.[6]

Despite the detailed reports by foreign doctors summoned to examine the corpse the day of the Sultan's death, all of whom agreed Abdülaziz had died by suicide, rumors circulated in Istanbul and the European press that the Sultan had been murdered by the conspirators who overthrew him. The tribunal ordered several years later by Abdülhamid II convicted several of the conspirators of murdering Abdülaziz, although the impartiality of the tribunal remains highly dubious.

PALL

His Majesty Sultan Abdülaziz, son of the Ghazi Sultan Mahmud Khan, *may God settle him in the Paradises of the Heavens.* Felicitous date of birth, 15 Ş. [Şaban] 1245 [9 February 1830]. Imperial accession, 16 Z.a. [Zilkade] 1277 [in error for 16 Zilhicce 1277, 25 June 1861]. Death, 12 C.a. [Cemaziül'evvel] 1293 [5 June 1876]. Reigned 16 years, 4 months.

Sultan Abdülhamid II. M1

In her memoir *My Father, Sultan Abdülhamid*, Princess Ayşe described her famous parent in complimentary terms:

> My late father was of medium height. His beard was dark brown in color, as was his hair, which ran thick around the sides of his head but had thinned out on top. He had the prominent nose that served as the distinguishing feature of the House of Osman.
> His eyes were a hazel hue between green and blue and framed between eyelids naturally outlined in black, with a glance

markedly intelligent and sensitive. His eyebrows were not bushy—manifesting another trait of the Ottoman dynasty. His open and broad forehead revealed his intelligence. His lips were neither thick nor thin, and his face tended toward white and pink. His body was even whiter than his face, almost the color of ivory, with a bit of hair on his chest and arms. His hands were of average size and shape, as were his feet.

He possessed a fine voice, rich and strong, so that one enjoyed listening to him as he spoke. He could express his thoughts and intentions in a wonderfully clear and refined way, and his movements reflected the dignity and pleasant courtesy of an emperor. In a word, he exhibited the quintessential features of the House of Osman.[7]

The young Prince Abdülhamid in Britain during the 1867 state visit of his uncle Sultan Abdülaziz. Practically the last official image of him since he never allowed his photo to be taken once he came to the throne.

Son of Sultan Abdülmecid by the lady Tirimüjgân, Abdülhamid was born 21 September 1842. At age 9 he lost his mother to tuberculosis, whereupon following palace custom he was given to another of his father's consorts to raise, the lady Perestû, who had no children of her own. In later years Abdülhamid would say, "My poor mother left this world at such a young age, but still I can picture her. I could never forget her; she loved me very much. When she took sick she used to have me sit opposite her and content herself with gazing into my face, for she couldn't bring herself to kiss me. May God rest her soul."[8]

In his youth Abdülhamid studied the usual subjects for an Ottoman prince—Ottoman history, politics, economy, geography, Arabic, and Persian—but also took lessons in French. He sailed, swam, and rode horses, preferring the rural life at his country villa and farm. He managed money wisely. He was always interested in Sufism and studied it with various masters. Artistic by nature, he became an accomplished calligrapher, and an extremely accomplished master carpenter and cabinetmaker; his cabinetry creations still adorn various sites around Istanbul. He loved European music, as for him traditional Turkish music was, in his words, too sad. He was good at the piano and tried his hand at composing, and as monarch he built the private theater at Yıldız Palace where troupes from Europe performed the operas and operettas he adored.

Through ten of his thirteen harem ladies, Abdülhamid fathered seventeen children, the first when he was 18, the last when he was 63. Thirteen survived into adulthood. The number seems large today (if not particularly so for nineteenth-century royalty), but attests to changing ways at the Ottoman Court: by contrast his father had sired forty-three children.

Prince Abdülhamid seemed far from the throne until the summer of 1876, when the coup that overthrew his uncle Abdülaziz made his brother Murad the monarch, so that suddenly Abdülhamid became the Veliahd. When after only ninety-three days Murad's alcohol-induced mental collapse resulted in his deposition, Abdülhamid became sultan, 31 August 1876.

The British ambassador in these early years left a frank description of the new ruler, whom he came to know well:

> It was impossible not to be taken by the charm of his manners and bearing, which were simple and unaffected yet exceedingly dignified. They were those of a high-bred gentleman. . . . He was fond of general conversation and quite able to hold his own in it—being very ready in reply. He had much humour, told a good story well, and enjoyed one in return. . . . He rarely forgot anything that had been said to him and he was in the habit of noting in a journal . . . any observations or statements made to him which he considered worthy of remembrance. . . . I always found him ready to listen to anything I might have to say to him, however unpleasant or painful it might have been to hear it. . . . He was an early riser . . . very frugal, abstemious and economical in his habits, and given neither to wine nor women or to any

other vices, eating very moderately, fond of his garden, his flowers and his birds which furnished his principal amusement. . . .
In his treatment of those about him he was kind and considered
except when exaggerated fears of assassination clouded and dis-
torted his judgment. . . . The greatest blot upon his character was
the manner in which he treated some of his most loyal and faithful servants whom he removed or banished to the provinces on
the suspicion—the offspring of his disordered brain and encour-
aged by designing intriguers—that they were conspiring against
his throne and life.[9]

Abdülhamid had promised the government ministers to reign as a constitutional monarch, and duly proclaimed a Constitution and summoned a
Parliament, both firsts in Ottoman history. But the war that Russia launched
the following year, which turned out badly for the Ottomans, served as his
pretext to suspend the Constitution and Parliament in 1878. The unstable
times, the challenges to his authority by government ministers, the daring
blows against his uncle and brother by government ringleaders, and especially the armed attempt to reinstate his brother on the throne, had alarmed
him deeply. He would rule as autocrat for thirty years, until forced to reinstate constitutional government in 1908.

Deciding the seaside Dolmabahçe Palace lay too vulnerable to attack,
Sultan Hamid (as he was usually known in Turkish) moved himself and
his family uphill to the more defensible Yıldız Palace. Amid its vast gardens
behind great walls he built villas, offices, kitchens, and barracks, a fortified
compound he never left for the remainder of his reign, except for the twice-
annual ceremonies he could not avoid at Topkapı and Dolmabahçe Palaces
during Ramadan. At Yıldız he welcomed foreign heads of state during their
visits, most notably the German emperor Wilhelm II in 1889 and 1898.

During the years of Abdülhamid's autocratic reign, dissent and criticism,
especially of the monarch, were not allowed. Newspapers, books, and plays
had to avoid forbidden topics such as rebellion and assassination, and forbidden words such as "Constitution," "liberty," "anarchy," "bomb," even
"nose," since Abdülhamid's was rather large. The Sultan instituted a vast
spy network across the empire using the new invention of the telegraph,
so that enormous quantities of informer reports poured into the palace. Po-

litical enemies found themselves exiled to remote posts in the empire, if they hadn't managed to escape to Europe instead, where his opponents began to gather.

Nonetheless Abdülhamid II continued the reforms of his father and grandfather. Extensive new roads and railways opened. Education flourished, with vast numbers of new schools opening throughout the empire. Industry and agriculture expanded.

Realizing the weakness of his military, Abdülhamid kept the Ottoman Empire out of wars, except when Greece attacked in 1897. He accepted the independence of Romania and Serbia, the Austrian occupation of Bosnia, and the loss of northeastern Anatolia to Russia, Tunisia to France, and Cyprus and Egypt to British control. Master at divide and rule, Abdülhamid dusted off a bargaining chip against the "Great Powers" by reminding them of his position as not only Sultan but also Caliph, the spiritual head of Sunni Muslims throughout the world. A word from him, he intimated, could cause untold trouble among the Muslim subjects of these powers.

Abdülhamid managed finances well, but the vast debt inherited from his predecessors tied his hands. Thanks to his prudent management the Ottoman Empire never defaulted, but nor did it escape from the burden of huge debt to foreign banks.

At last, in July 1908, the pent-up demand by the educated classes for a voice in running the country erupted into rebellion, triggered by restless army officers. Abdülhamid backed down, reinstating the Constitution and calling for elections to Parliament, to great rejoicing throughout the empire. For months he played the role of constitutional monarch well, but when the Counter-revolution of April 1909 broke out, the new government leaders used the opportunity to rid themselves of their former adversary. Surrounded at Yıldız by hostile army troops, abandoned by his guard, Abdülhamid accepted his deposition. He and a few members of his family were sent into exile at Salonica. Before Greek troops took the city during the Balkan War of 1912, however, the ex-Sultan was brought back to Istanbul aboard the German Embassy yacht *Lorelei* and confined to Beylerbeyi Palace on the Asian shore of the Bosphorus.

Abdülhamid died in Beylerbeyi Palace on 10 February 1918, aged 75, in the closing months of World War One. His family wished him laid to rest at the tomb of Sultan Mehmed the Conqueror, but this the all-powerful

Minister of War Enver Pasha refused (for unclear reasons; perhaps he con-
templated his own burial there one day?), so that Sultan Mehmed V ordered
his burial here.

With melancholy prayers and cries, huge crowds accompanied the coffin
along Divan Yolu Boulevard to the tomb. Mehmed V's Senior Secretary
numbered among them:

> That day the remains were transported by steamer to Topkapı
> Palace, to the Chamber of the Noble Mantle, where the body
> was prepared for burial, after which the Şeyhülislâm Musa
> Kâzım Efendi conducted the prayer service for the distinguished
> congregation in attendance. Sultan Reşad having appointed me
> to represent him, I attended both the prayer service and the fu-
> neral. The funeral was quite splendid—all the Imperial princes
> and sons-in-law were in attendance, as were the foreign ambas-
> sadors and military attachés, cabinet ministers, and leading re-
> ligious dignitaries, government officials, and military officers.
> They all wore uniform, with the exception of the Imperial sons-
> in-law, who had taken the decision amongst themselves to attend
> in mufti. As he followed the cortege, the Imperial Son-in-law
> Şerif Pasha recited the couplet from [the poet] Bâki's elegy to
> Sultan Süleyman:
>
> > The unruly beast of quarrelsome fortune
> > rose in rebelliousness,
> > The shadow of God's kindnesses covered the earth.[10]

The historian and poet Ahmed Refik witnessed the procession that day
with a bit more emotion:

> Some looked on with indifference, but those of sensitive heart
> felt their eyes brim with tears at this mournful pageantry, these
> sorrowful cries, this religious magnificence. The final ceremony
> for the Ottoman monarch who reigned as caliph for thirty-four
> years was playing out with dignity.[11]

Though Abdülhamid's funeral ended on an unexpected note inside the mausoleum:

> At the head of the open grave the Senior Imam Sûzi Efendi uttered the prayer, but seeing as he was so used to invoking the name of Sultan Reşad, didn't a slip of the tongue trip him up and make him say, "for the noble soul of His Late Majesty Sultan Mehmed Reşad Han"! This faux pas made quite the negative impression on those present, and when the Şeyhülislâm Musa Kâzım Efendi, standing next to me, heard it and let out a guffaw, putting his hands on my shoulders, this elicited yet a further reaction. However, it seems to have been a divinely ordained pronouncement, for indeed only four months later fate decreed the Fatiha to be recited for the soul of Sultan Reşad.[12]

In its obituary at Abdülhamid's death, the *New York Times* aptly summarized the coup d'état that ended the Sultan's reign in 1909:

> At the time, this change of rulers was hailed as the success of liberal and constitutional ideals against the tyranny of a reactionary despot; but subsequent experience has shown that the cabal of Generals and politicians who have ruled Turkey for the last nine years under the nominal authority of Mehmed V, Abdul's brother, who succeeded him, seems to be neither more enlightened nor more successful than Abdul himself.[13]

PALL

The Ghazi Sultan Abdülhamid Khan II, whose abode is Paradise; son of His Majesty the Ghazi Sultan Abdülmecid Khan. Date of birth, 16 Şaban the Esteemed 1258 / 9 Eylül 1258 [22 September 1842]. Imperial accession, 11 Şaban the Esteemed 1293 [31 August 1876]. Died 28 R.ahir [Rebiülahir] 1336 / 10 Şubat 1334 [10 February 1918]. Reigned 33 years, 7 months, 26 days.

Princess Atiye (1). M13

The older of two princesses by this name interred here; for the younger, see Chapter 5.

Daughter of Mahmud II by the lady Pervizfelek, Princess Atiye was born most likely 2 January 1824 (there is confusion as to the day). Only some nine months younger than her half-brother, the future Sultan Abdülmecid, the two largely grew up together and remained close. In August 1840 Abdülmecid, who had ascended the throne one year earlier, arranged her marriage to Field Marshal Ahmed Fethi Pasha as a mark of esteem for the Pasha's many loyal services to the Imperial House. At the time Atiye was aged 16 while her bridegroom was 39 and already married with grown children. Ordinarily the man selected for marriage to an Imperial princess had to divorce any previous wife or wives, but there is some doubt in this case whether the much-favored Fethi Pasha did so. Regardless, the nuptial ceremony took place within the Chamber of the Noble Mantle at Topkapı Palace, followed by splendid wedding celebrations that lasted one week and included foreign ambassadors among the guests.

According at least to the verse composed later by her younger sister, the poetess Princess Âdile, the marriage was not a happy one:

> My brother Abdülmecid ascended the throne
> And made of Princess Atiye a new bride.
> As compliment he gave her to Fethi Pasha,
> For them he expended grace and favor.
> Joy with her husband she knew not,
> Incomplete for her were the pleasures of the world.[14]

Perhaps the allusion to marital discord refers to the Pasha's continued closeness to his first wife. At any rate, if marital discord were indeed the Princess's lot, it did not enter the public discourse and the Pasha's cordial relations with the Sultan continued, as evidenced frequently in the capital's French-language newspaper, for example:

> The Sultan has just made a present of his portrait, enriched with
> diamonds, to his august sisters the princess Athiè-Sultane, wife

of H.H. Ahmed-Féthi Pasha, Grand Master of Artillery, and the princess Adilé Sultane, wife of H.H. Méhémet-Ali Pasha, Minister of the Marine. Sunday last, Ahmed-Féthi Pasha and Méhémet-Ali Pasha received these portraits from H.M., in order to convey them to the princesses.[15]

Two daughters were born to the couple, Princess Seniye in 1843 (interred in the Lady Nevfidan Chamber) and Princess Feride in 1847, both of whom reached adulthood. Afflicted with tuberculosis, after only ten years of marriage Atiye died in 1850, aged 26, her daughters still quite young. The same newspaper recorded her sad demise, mentioning her children with the title *Hanımsultan* that daughters of princesses bore:

Saturday last, the second day of the Bairam, toward eight o'clock of the morning, Her Imperial Highness Atié-Sultan, wife of His Highness Ahmet-Féthi Pasha, Grand Master of Artillery, died in her palace at Arnaout-Keuy, at the age of 27 years, following a long illness.

The funeral of the Princess took place yesterday with considerable pomp. Her Imperial Majesty the Validé-Sultan [the Sultan's mother] ordered the distribution, upon this occasion, of large sums of money to the poor.

The mortal remains of Atié-Sultan were placed within the magnificent mausoleum known as the Sultan-Mahmoud-Turbécé [türbesi, "tomb"], constructed in the Constantinople quarter of Fazli Pasha by His Imperial Majesty Abdul-Medjid, and where the remains of his illustrious father, Sultan Mahmoud II, are at rest.

The Princess Atié carries with her the justly merited regrets of the Imperial Family, of the residents of the capital, and especially of the villages adjoining her country home along the Bosphorus; under the auspices of her august Sovereign and brother, she was able to do much good and to come to the aid of the unfortunate.

It was a most heartbreaking scene presented by the dense crowd that covered the banks of Arnaout-Keuy and Bebek, joining their tears and lamentations with those of the palace people, especially at the moment when the boat carrying the casket set off from the pier at Sultan-Saraï!

The Princess Atié-Sultan leaves, with her death, two young and interesting children: Sénié-Hanoum-Sultan and Féridé-Hanoum-Sultan.[16]

Along with her father and full sister Hadice in this chamber, and her mother in the Lady Nevfidan Chamber, Atiye's widower and both her future sons-in-law Hüseyin Hüsnü and Mahmud Nedim also lie at rest here, the latter three in the graveyard outside the mausoleum, since they were not of the blood-royal.

PALL

The late and laudable Princess Atiye, *may Almighty God settle her in the chambers of the Heavens*, esteemed daughter of His Majesty the Ghazi Mahmud Khan, whose abode is Sublime Paradise, who dwells in Eternal Heaven, *may pails of mercy be poured over his tomb.* 2 Şevval 1266 [11 August 1850].

Empress Mother Bezmiâlem. M10

The only concubine buried here to be considered royalty, because her son ascended the throne during her lifetime, this future consort of Mahmud II was born probably around 1805 to Georgian or Circassian parents and sold into slavery. She entered the Imperial Harem as a purchase or gift probably in the later 1810s, when she received her name, Bezmiâlem ("Feast of the World"). She had been chosen as a concubine of the young Sultan by 1822 at the latest, for the following year, probably still in her teens, she gave birth to her only child, the future sultan Abdülmecid. When her son ascended the throne in 1839 at the tender age of 16, Bezmiâlem became *Valide Sultan*, Empress Mother, or by her other formal Ottoman title, Sublime Cradle of the Sultanate.

A series of engraved seals in the palace collections reflects the upturn in her status. The first seal, made while Mahmud II still reigned, bears the simple inscription "Bezmiâlem." The second dates to the year her son ascended the throne and reads "Her Highness the Illustrious Empress Mother, the Excellent, the Virtuous." The third seal bears the following verse that rhymes in the original:

> Muhammad [the Prophet] came into being from love
> What a fitting bearer of love is Muhammad
> At his appearance Bezmiâlem joined her beloved[17]

The Empress Mother devoted herself to assisting her young son in the momentous reforms he launched, mostly by keeping him well informed of events in the palace. She wrote him letters when he was away from the capital, simple missives with poor penmanship and spelling errors. For all her simplicity, though, she remains the most authoritative Empress Mother of the last era of the Ottoman Court, in her own way influential over both her son and her four grandsons who ascended the throne after her death.

We have one foreigner's description of Bezmiâlem, penned in the 1840s by Dr. Spitzer, the German physician called in to examine her when she had fallen ill. Across her face she wore a veil of thin gauze and appeared to be around the age of 36, the doctor tells us, having kept herself in good condition. Her hands were pure white and delicate, "in the Georgian fashion," as he describes them. She addressed some kind words to the physician and pulled a purse of gold coins from the pocket of her cloak, which she had the eunuch in attendance present to him.[18]

In the course of Bezmiâlem's fourteen years as Empress Mother, the Ottoman monarchy modernized itself by increasingly adopting ceremonial that European Courts used for royal consorts and dowager queens. And so the state apartments designed for Bezmiâlem at the new Dolmabahçe Palace her son was building represented quite a shift from the traditional harem layout at centuries-old Topkapı Palace. As Bezmiâlem died shortly before Dolmabahçe was completed, however, she never occupied the apartments intended for her.

During her son's reign, the people of Istanbul regarded Bezmiâlem with affection and respect, deservedly holding her as a kind of mother who acted with honor and goodwill, assisting especially the poor of the city. Her death from tuberculosis in 1853, around age 48, plunged the city into mourning led by her son, who ordered a lavish funeral along with generous alms distributed to the poor. She left behind a plethora of good works for which she served as benefactress, including the first modern hospital in Istanbul for the poor (still functioning today), the Dolmabahçe Mosque, a bridge across the Golden Horn, a hospital for impoverished Muslims in Mecca, and numerous public water fountains in Istanbul as well as in the Ottoman provinces of Iraq and Arabia. She also built several schools, including (as we shall note below) the Empress Mother School on the heights immediately behind this, her husband's mausoleum.

Students at the school took part in Bezmiâlem's funeral. In his book on the Crimean War, the British admiral Adolphus Slade (also an admiral in Ottoman service at the time) described her sad obsequies, which took place as her son faced that looming military crisis:

In the midst of these troubles the Sultan sustained the affliction deepest felt by a Mussulman, in the death of the Valideh Sultana, his mother. . . . Female screams at dawn in the palace of Beshik-tash, one morning early in May, announced his bereavement to the guard-boats and passing caiks [oared boats], and bade farewell to the body which at that early hour was conveyed in the imperial caik, followed by other caiks with the deceased lady's suite, to the old seraglio [Topkapı Palace]. It was there washed and perfumed according to usage, and laid on a bier covered with cloths of gold and silver. Preceded by incense-bearers and choristers, it was then brought forth from the interior of the palace and deposed under the shade of trees in the centre court for a few minutes, while the court imam recited a prayer for the soul of the departed. . . .

The procession was then formed. Military pashas on horseback, in single file, flanked by their grooms and tchiaushes [guards], led the way, followed by a compact body of Arabian dervishes chanting lustily. Then rode three legal dignitaries, also in single file, the cazi-askers [chief military judges] of Europe and Asia with the evcaf nazir [Minister of Pious Foundations]. A body of royal domestics marched next in order. Then the ministers of state rode in single file . . . after them rode a body of the Sultan's eunuchs, the chief of whom, the kislar agasi [Constable of the Maidens], an aged melancholy-looking Nubian, immediately preceded the corpse. The eunuchs of the deceased lady, scattering new-coined silver money among the crowd, closed the procession.

As the procession passed along the streets, lined at intervals with troops, numerous female spectators in open spaces sobbed audibly; and although Eastern women have ever tears as well as smiles at command, those shed on this occasion were sincere, for the sex had lost that day an advocate, the poor a friend. The procession halted in front of the garden of the Mahmoudieh mausoleum, where, on an elevated slope, the boys of adjoining schools, chanting hymns, were drawn up, and being reformed on foot moved on through gilded gates and rose-beds, slowly to the tomb. As its portals swung open, screams from the valideh's women gathered in the interior of the edifice to pay the last tribute of respect to their kind mistress issued forth, sad and plaintive; to mingle, strangely harmonious, with the chants of dervishes and the neighing of led horses. The body was buried beside that of Sultan Mahmoud II.[19]

When Bezmiâlem died, *The Times* of London wrote rather speculatively of her death:

The mother of the Sultan died last night of suppuration of the knee joint following an attack of acute rheumatism; her age was about 50. She has always been known as a most amiable woman, and was greatly beloved by her son. She was originally a Circassian slave.[20]

adding, the next month, in tribute to her compassion:

The news of her death was a terrible shock for the Turks, and out of the 60,000 persons who accompanied her corpse to the grave, there was hardly one who did not shed tears for the "friend to the poor". . . . The Sultan and his brother are inconsolable, and the former hardly quitted his mother during the last few days of her life. The deceased was buried with great pomp by the side of the late Sultan Mahmoud.[21]

PALL

The journey to be enfolded in mercy, of Her Majesty the Empress Mother Bezmiâlem, *glory upon her, may her grave be illumined and Paradise made her dwelling*, esteemed mother of Sultan Abdülmecid Khan, the Adorner of the Throne of the Exalted Sultanate, *may his dominions and his reign endure until the end of time*, took place 23 Receb 1269 [2 May 1853].

Princess Emine (1). N9

Daughter of Sultan Abdülaziz by the lady Edâdil, this baby was born in 1866 but died only months later.

PALL

Her Highness the late and divinely pardoned Princess Emine, honored daughter of the Shahanshah of the World. Date of birth 22 B. [Receb] 1283, Thursday [30 November 1866], Date of death 15 Z. [Zilhicce] 1283, Saturday [20 April 1867].

Princess Emine (2). M12

Youngest daughter of Sultan Abdülaziz to survive into adulthood, Princess Emine was born in Dolmabahçe Palace on 24 August 1874 to the Sultan's Fourth Consort, the lady Nesrin. Her full brother Prince Şevket had been born two years earlier. She was the second daughter of Abdülaziz to bear this name, the first having lived but a few months (see preceding entry).

With the suicide of her deposed father on 4 June 1876, followed only eight days later by her mother's death from (probably) tuberculosis, the child was orphaned before the age of two. Her half-brother Prince Yusuf İzzeddin took her in (and probably her brother too) and raised her. In 1901 Emine married Şerif Pasha, the distinguished litterateur, poet, and translator who later served as governor of Istanbul, Minister of Education, and Minister of the Interior. The couple took up married life in the villa in Üsküdar presented them by her cousin Abdülhamid II, their happy union saddened by the death of their only child as a baby.

Emine died in 1920, at age 45, a victim of the worldwide influenza epidemic that followed World War One. In the flowery words of the official report of her death, required by the regulations of the dynasty and signed by the Grand Vizier as well as two senators, "Princess Emine, the daughter, beauteous in virtue, of His Majesty Sultan Abdülaziz, whose abode is Heaven, passed away on Friday night, 29 January. In accordance with the Imperial pronouncement, her remains were laid to rest in the noble mausoleum of His Majesty the Paradise-dwelling Sultan Mahmud II, where her father is interred. The deceased had begun to be afflicted with influenza, and on the aforementioned night she took a sudden turn for the worse, and departed this life."[22] The Princess was laid to rest in this chamber near her brother Şevket, who had died in 1899.

At her untimely death, Emine's grieving widower composed a poignant elegy of rhyming couplets in her honor, commissioned the famed calligrapher Hulûsi to render it elegantly, and set out the resulting work of art at her catafalque. Today this superb gem of calligraphy is preserved in museum storage. The loving sentiments that Şerif Pasha expressed in it reach out to us across the decades:

Pearl of the crown of the firmament, pride of the House
   of Osman,
Joy to the eye of angels, the Princess Emine.
Born in the year Ninety-one,
Modestly the Cradle of the Age ushered in glory.
Her illustrious father, the sultan Aziz, rare of essence,
Fate hid from the eye of the world when she was but an infant.
Seven days later the Messenger of Death arrived
And concealed her chaste mother among the dust.
Losing her father and mother thus
Left her weeping from pain of separation and longing.
Raised at her brother's Court of mannerly training,
Her good character won fame and honor.
Judging me worthy of wedlock, the Shah of the World
Kindly granted me that unique jewel.

Nineteen years blessed together,
The days we lived worthily, happily.
On this earth my true friend,
The light of her perception shown in every instance.
Her kindly person combined
Virtue and faith and modesty, intelligence and discernment
   and insight.
Not once causing me grief,
If I were sad she cured my troubles.
The predicaments of the government and country
Left her not one moment free of thought and worry.
Thus encumbered, the bird of her soul
Took sudden wing to the heights of the heavens.
At her passing her age numbered but forty-five;
So young, she walked the meadows of Paradise.
Those saintly and pure remains of noble line,
In burial near her father, disappeared from view.
Friend or stranger, all took to mourning,
The eyes of all shed pearls of tears.
To His servant He gave that Princess most illustrious,
Then took her back to Him, God the All-Bounteous.
The fire of separation burned heart and body and soul;
Ah, how can one deflect the blows of misfortune.
I asked the Creator not to show me her death;
This my prayer, alas, He deemed unworthy.
May my moist tears never cease, my eyes turn to blood,
My woebegone heart grieve until Judgment Day.
I hope from God in His kindness that forgiveness and mercy
Will honor that Princess in the world to come.
With sadness, wretched Şerif has spoken this date:
"Princess Emine sought refuge in the Garden of Eden."

The year 1338 [1919-1920]. Hulûsi calligraphed this, with
God's forgiveness.

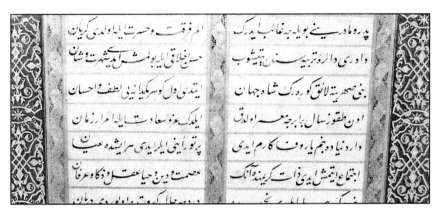

The exquisite intricacy of the framed elegy to Princess Emine.

In the second couplet of his verse, the widowed Şerif Pasha mentions "Ninety-one" as his late wife's year of birth—meaning 1291 of the Muslim calendar, corresponding to 1874-75 of the Western calendar. The chronogram in the last couplet totals 1,273; since the Princess died in the Muslim year 1338, we must look to the preceding line for a clue to achieve the correct total, and find it in the phrase "with sadness." By adding in the value of the letters in the Ottoman word for "sadness" (*hüzn*), or 65, we arrive at 1,273 + 65 = 1,338.

CAST IRON PLAQUE

Her Imperial Highness Princess Emine, who dwells in Paradise, *compassion and pardon be upon her*, esteemed daughter of His Majesty Sultan Abdülaziz Khan, whose abode is Heaven, and esteemed wife of the Minister of the Interior, Mehmed Şerif Pasha. Born Sunday, 11 Receb the Peerless 1291 / 11 Ağustos 1290 [24 August 1874]. Died Friday eve, 8 Cemaziyül'ula 1338 / 10 Kanun-ı Sani 1336 [29 January 1920].

Princess Esma. M16

The mausoleum stands in the former garden of this princess, Sultan Mahmud's half-sister. Esma the Younger, as she was known to distinguish her

from her aunt by the same name, was born probably 17 July 1778 (there is
some confusion as to the date), daughter of Sultan Abdülhamid I by the
lady Ayşe Sineperver. Sultan Mustafa IV, Mahmud's predecessor on the
throne, was her full brother, one year younger than she.

Esma's father died when she was but 11, and when she reached 14, in
1792, her cousin Sultan Selim III arranged her marriage. Youthful brides
were no rarities in royal circles whether Ottoman or Christian European,
and so for example Queen Victoria arranged *her* eldest daughter's engagement when the latter was 14. In Esma's case the groom was Selim's "milk
brother" (meaning they had shared the same wet nurse in infancy, a mean-
ingful relationship in Ottoman culture), Admiral of the Fleet Hüseyin Pasha,
aged 36, as a token of the Sultan's esteem for the Admiral's work in reforming the Navy. In accordance with Court custom the wedding celebrations took place over several days and included elaborate processions
through the city streets. At the end of it all, the couple took up residence in
their three-story town house atop the ridge along Divan Yolu Boulevard,
in whose gardens this mausoleum would later be built.

Dubbed *Kapudanpaşa Sultanı*, "Admiral Princess," from her husband's
profession, Esma produced no children. Her husband's death in 1803 after
their eleven-year marriage left her a widow at the age of 25, but she never
remarried—unusual for an Ottoman princess of her era but reflective of her
independent spirit. In the turbulent years of 1807 and 1808 she and her
mother involved themselves in political efforts to retain her full brother
Mustafa IV on the throne, efforts that involved Mustafa's ordering the murder of his deposed uncle Selim III and his half-brother Mahmud, although
the latter managed to escape.

After Mustafa's deposition and murder in 1808, Esma reconciled with
her younger half-brother, the new sultan Mahmud II. Her sharp mind, col-
orful personality, and interest in music mirrored the monarch's own, and
the two became quite fond of one another, visiting each other frequently.
Mahmud's son, the future sultan Abdülaziz, was born in her villa along the
Golden Horn at Eyüp in 1830. Referring to their days as antagonists, Mahmud was reputed to have told her later, in admiration of her strong character,
"Oh Sister, if you had been born a man, what would have become of me?"[23]

Mahmud afforded his sister a freedom of action beyond the reach of any
Ottoman woman other than a princess. Esma also benefitted from the lu-

crative tax revenues assigned her, amassing one of the great fortunes in Istanbul that made possible a luxurious life in her villas in and around town. Her expensive clothes set fashion, her outings into the countryside accompanied by female slaves sparked legends, her excellent musical ensembles brought her renown. Of course her extravagant and public life also brought criticism and gossip, which she ignored.

In 1839 her brother Mahmud II passed away in her country house atop the hill at Çamlıca, across the Bosphorus. When she herself died nine years later, in 1848, at the age of 70, having witnessed the reigns of five sultans, the passing of the celebrated society maven merited mention in the capital's French-language newspaper, which gave her age according to the Muslim calendar:

> Her Highness Esma-Sultane, sister of Mahmoud II, and aunt of the present sovereign, Abdul-Medjid, died Saturday last in her palace at Eyoub, at the age of 73 years.
>
> During the reign of Selim III, Esma-Sultane was married to the celebrated Grand Admiral Hussein Pasha, the favorite of that monarch.
>
> On Sunday, the day before yesterday, the Grand Vizier, the Şeyhülislâm, all the ministers and the functionaries of the various departments, proceeded to the pier at Bagtché-Capoussou in order to receive the mortal remains of Esma-Sultane and to accompany her, with the traditional ceremonial, to her last resting place. The remains of this Princess have been inhumed within the monument known under the name of the Tomb of Sultan Mahmoud.[24]

PALL

The journey to be enfolded in mercy of Her Highness Princess Esma, whose abode is Paradise and who has attained mercy, *may her grave be illumined and Paradise made her dwelling*, esteemed sister of His Majesty the Ghazi Sultan Mahmud Khan the Just, whose abode is the Illiyin, who dwells in Paradise, *may Almighty God settle him in the chambers of the Heavens*, took place Sunday, 2 Receb 1264 [4 June 1848].

Princess Hadice. M17

Daughter of Mahmud II by the lady Pervizfelek (alternate name Fürsifelek, and interred in the Lady Nevfidan Chamber), Princess Hadice was born 6 September 1825 but died of smallpox in the palace at Beşiktaş in 1842, aged 17 (16 by the Muslim calendar), unmarried. The unfortunate young woman thus became the third person interred in this chamber, after her father and her aunt Hibetullah. Her full older sister Atiye also lies in this chamber.

Hadice and Atiye had been quite close to their younger half-sister Princess Âdile, the poetess of the House of Osman. Following the loss of both siblings, Âdile penned these lines in loving tribute to them:

> Princess Atiye, my third sister
> My beloved, rose-faced lucky star,
> And Princess Hadice, fourth sister,
> Another daughter of Mahmud Khan,
> Born of one mother they were, of moon-like beauty,
> The two, moon and sun to the earth.
> Their mother's name, Fürsifelek;
> My late father's cherished angel.
>
> Princess Hadice by command God surrendered
> To the Angel of Death.
> Our maiden sister perished,
> And all Creation shed tears.
> Aged sixteen the young girl departed—Ah—
> Giving her soul back to God.[25]

PALL

The late and laudable Princess Hadice, *may Almighty God settle her in the chambers of the Heavens*, esteemed daughter of His Majesty the Ghazi Mahmud Khan, whose abode is Sublime Paradise, who dwells in Eternal Heaven, *may pails of mercy be poured over his tomb.* 16 Zilkade 1258 [19 December 1842], Monday.

Princess Hibetullah. M14

Daughter of Sultan Abdülhamid I by his consort the lady Şebisefa, Princess Hibetullah was born in March 1789, only three weeks before the death of her father and accession to the throne of her cousin Selim III. At age 12 she was betrothed to her cousin Alâeddin Pasha, the grandson through his mother of Sultan Mustafa III, and some fifteen years her senior. For this Imperial marriage the Pasha was obliged to divorce his first wife, by whom he already had children. The couple married in October 1804, when she was 15, and moved into the extensive villa at Kadırga Limanı ("Galley Harbor") that Hibetullah had inherited from a sister. Constructed by the famed architect Sinan in the sixteenth century, it was the only Ottoman royal villa on the Sea of Marmara, with concentric courtyards as at Topkapı Palace. The venerable villa and its gardens with fountains were extensively renovated in preparation for the young Princess's marriage.

When her mother died in 1805 Hibetullah inherited the latter's extensive landed property and tax farms, making her a wealthy teenager indeed. Three years later, upon the dethronement of her half-brother Mustafa IV, whose cause she had supported, she was placed for some time under house arrest by the new sultan, her half-brother Mahmud II, and forbidden to visit or correspond with anyone, but this was subsequently relaxed. Her husband's death in 1812 left Hibetullah a widow at 23, but like her half-sister Esma (also buried here) she never remarried. Nor did she have children, at least none who survived infancy.

The wealthy widow Hibetullah built other mansions and seaside villas around town, but in all likelihood continued to live primarily at the historic Kadırga Villa. When she died in 1841, aged 52, she became only the second person interred in the two-year-old mausoleum, after her brother Mahmud II himself. *The Times* of London of 16 October 1841 briefly noted her funeral:

> The Sultana Heibetullah, sister of Sultan Mahmoud, died on the 16th inst. [*sic*], and a day or two afterwards she was buried with great solemnity. The funeral procession, which was attended by the assembled dignitaries of the empire, moved from the Scala Bagtshi Kapussi to the new mausoleum of Sultan Mahmoud, where the remains of the deceased Princess were deposited.

Or as famed chronicler Lûtfi Efendi more opulently described it in the florid language of the day, the Princess "with the arrival of the predestined hour of death, journeyed to the palace of eternity."[26]

Hibetullah's sixteenth-century villa at Kadırga burned in the fire that swept through the quarter in 1864; its remains decayed over the ensuing decades and have now disappeared entirely.

PALL

The journey to be enfolded in mercy of Her Highness Princess Hibetullah, whose abode is Paradise and who has attained mercy, *may her grave be illumined and Paradise made her dwelling*, esteemed sister of His Majesty the Ghazi Sultan Mahmud Khan the Just, whose abode is the Illiyin, who dwells in Paradise, *may Almighty God settle him in the chambers of the Heavens*, took place Friday evening, 2 Şaban 1257 [19 September 1841].

Princess Kâmile. M5

Granddaughter of Sultan Abdülaziz through his daughter Saliha (niece of the Princess Saliha buried in this chamber) and her husband Ahmed Zülkifl Pasha, this baby was born and died in 1896. Her parents had no other children. The infant was buried next to her grandmother, the lady Dürrinev.

PALL

Born 5 Cemaziyül'ula 1314 [12 October 1896], died 14 Receb 1314 [19 December 1896]. Princess Kâmile, newly born daughter of Her Imperial Highness Princess Saliha—the daughter of radiant virtue to His Majesty Abdülaziz Khan, whose abode is Paradise, who dwells in Heaven—and of Ahmed Zülkifl.

Sultan Mahmud II. M7

Son of Sultan Abdülhamid I, Mahmud was born 20 July 1785 to the lady Nakşıdil. Popular legends, particularly in Europe, that his mother was French are completely groundless; she was from the Caucasus, possibly Georgian.

As Mahmud was the only living Ottoman prince at the execution of his half-brother and predecessor Mustafa IV in November 1808, all subsequent members of the Ottoman Dynasty descend from him.

His thirty-one-year reign, from 1808 to 1839, saw the revitalization of the Ottoman Empire through the imposition of reform from above.

At his accession, the Ottoman throne was hostage to the recalcitrant Janissary corps, who resisted efforts to reform the army and the state. But Mahmud was a patient man, waiting eighteen years to carefully prepare the coup that annihilated the Janissaries in 1826, at last freeing his hand to initiate reforms. Mahmud reigned only thirteen more years after this event, but during those years he introduced a new army corps trained along European lines, as well as schools for military officers and for the population at large in order to produce trained government officials who could speak foreign languages. Thanks to Mahmud, these thirteen years also saw the first Ottoman census, a revamped tax system, the first newspaper, creation of the post office, construction of new roads, composition of a march that served as the first national anthem, evolution of the design that would become the national flag, new ministries of state, and most visibly, the introduction by Mahmud of the fez to replace the traditional turban for all males except men of religion. Encouraging and symbolizing the changes himself, the Sultan abandoned traditional Ottoman Court dress in favor of European military uniforms.

Alongside his leadership qualities, Mahmud II possessed talent as a poet in the traditional Ottoman style, and as a composer and performer of traditional Ottoman Court music, setting many of his own verses to music. He was also a trained calligrapher of significant merit.

In 1810 Mahmud received the British ambassador accompanied by the traveler J. C. Hobhouse, who left this description of the young monarch before he had abandoned traditional Court dress:

> Sultan Mahmoud was placed in the middle of the throne, with his feet upon the ground. . . . He was dressed in a robe of yellow satin, with a broad border of the darkest sable: his dagger, and an ornament on his breast, were covered with diamonds: the front of his white and blue turban shone with a large treble sprig of diamonds, which served as a buckle to a high straight plume

of bird-of-paradise feathers. He for the most part kept a hand on each knee, and neither moved his body nor head, but rolled his eyes from side to side, without fixing them for an instant upon the Ambassador or any other person present. Occasionally he stroked and turned up his beard, displaying a milk-white hand glittering with diamond rings. His eye-brows, eyes, and beard, being of a glossy jet black, did not appear natural, but added to that indescribable majesty which it would be difficult for any but an Oriental sovereign to assume: his face was pale, and regularly formed, except that his nose (contrary to the usual form of that feature in the Ottoman prince) was slightly turned up and pointed: his whole physiognomy was mild and benevolent, but expressive and full of dignity. He appeared of a short and small stature, and about 30 years old, which is somewhat more than his actual age.[27]

Alas for Mahmud, his reign was beset with troubles quite apart from the rebellious Janissaries. The Serbs revolted, forcing Mahmud, under Russian threats, to grant autonomy to Serbia and the two Romanian provinces. The Wahhabis rebelled in Arabia, compelling Mahmud to send his Egyptian governor to put down the revolt. Inspired by the French Revolution, the Greeks rebelled in 1821, leading to European intervention, the destruction of the Ottoman fleet, and Greek independence in 1830. Russia invaded in 1828, part of the Russian dream to annex the Bosphorus and secure Russian access to the Mediterranean, leading to increased demands by Ottoman Christian subjects in the Balkans and to huge influxes of Muslim refugees from the Caucasus. The French seized the province of Algeria in 1830 on a trumped-up pretext. Mahmud's vassal governor of Egypt, Muhammad Ali—originally an Ottoman general—then attacked Mahmud himself in 1832, pushing the Sultan's new army back as far as Bursa. At this point, in 1833, the English traveler and writer Julia Pardoe recorded this optimistic description of Mahmud, who was currently bearing the humiliation of having to call in the Russians for help against his Egyptian vassals:

It is this imposing, lofty air, accompanied by extreme energy of will, which has given to the Sultan the wonderful ascendant he possesses over the minds of all who surround him. Those who have been accustomed to intercourse with royalty, and contact with the most distinguished statesmen and geniuses of their time, speak of the Moslem monarch as the most remarkable person they have ever seen, beside whom every other individual sinks into insignificance. A stranger meeting him incognito, would be struck by his appearance, as if denoting a more than common dignity; and at times, the expression of his countenance will cause an impression which none other could excite. His features are manly, though not regular, his cheeks being angular and prominent, and his complexion is flushed, when he is in exercise, as if from vigorous health. His person is a little above the middle size, neither spare nor corpulent, well-proportioned except in the legs, which are bent slightly inwards from the knee; and his whole appearance much enhanced by a handsome jet beard, arranged and preserved with special care. In minute attention to his person and dress he resembles George IV.; but he is, both physically and mentally, more active than that monarch. While flattered by the deference he inspires, and the observance of the forms of devotedness paid to absolute sovereignty in the East, he assumes no studious gestures, or affectation of majesty. Regality is stamped by nature on his brow, animating every feature and every movement; and even on that day, when surrounded by Russian bayonets, and his armies scattered in the field by a vassal—his spirit remained unquenched—he was "every inch a king!"[28]

From among the eighteen ladies whom Mahmud took as concubines throughout his reign, he produced some thirty-three children of whom only six survived into adulthood, two sons and four daughters. One of these daughters, the poetess Princess Âdile, later put her father's poignant family situation into verse that rhymes in the original:

As that King of kings of lofty station
Contentment knew with many children,
Sown of a garden, roses they were,

Tulips and basil and hyacinths.
Some innocent, some wise, some young;
Some departed, some remained and suffered.
Most of them he mourned, that Padishah;
The others at their father's death sighed *Ah*.[29]

Mahmud II's portrait on the first-ever Ottoman decoration constituted just one
of the groundbreaking changes he introduced into Ottoman culture.

Muhammad Ali invaded again in 1839, carrying all before him. Having just received news of his army's rout during this conflict, Mahmud died 1 July 1839, of tuberculosis, the scourge of the Ottoman palace of the nineteenth century.

British pressure saved the Ottoman throne by forcing Muhammad Ali to back down, but the future seemed dark for the Ottomans at Mahmud's death in 1839. All was not lost, however. The Sultan had solidly set the empire on the path to reform, a legacy his 16-year-old son and heir Abdülmecid carried on with intelligence and compassion.

When Mahmud died, his death notice in *The Times* of London reflected his positive image in Western Europe:

> The Sultan had seen some of the largest and fairest provinces of his immense empire wrested from him by conquest, or partly alienated by treaty and usurpation of his sovereign rights. . . . He was one of the greatest reformers of his age, had freed the Porte from the military domination of the Janissaries, and had gone far towards effecting a social re-organization of the Turkish nation. His Highness was greatly esteemed and respected by all who had been diplomatically, or otherwise, introduced to his notice ; he was warmly beloved by his family and his subjects ; and he may be justly styled to have been a great and a good man.[30]

PALL

Bequeather of the foundation of order to the State, Sovereign of the high station of the Illiyin, the Ghazi Sultan Mahmud Khan the Just, son of His Majesty the Ghazi Sultan Abdülhamid Khan, *may God settle him in the Paradises of the Heavens.* Felicitous birth, 14 N. [Ramazan] 1199 [20 July 1785]. Imperial accession, 4 C.ahir [Cemaziyül'ahir] 1223 [28 July 1808]. Died 19 R.ahir [Rebiülahir] 1255 [1 July 1839]. Reigned 14 days, 10 months, 31 years.

Prince Mahmud Namık and Prince Ömer Faruk. M9

These two cousins are interred in the same grave. Both eventually settled in Egypt after the 1924 exile of the Imperial Family, dying there in the 1960s and buried in Cairo. But in 1977 their remains were repatriated to Istanbul for interment here, in the mausoleum of their mutual ancestor, Mahmud II.

1. Prince Mahmud Namık. Son of Prince Ömer Hilmi by the lady Gülnev, Namık was born 23 December 1913 in Dolmabahçe Palace during the reign of his grandfather Mehmed V Reşad. He married Sheherazade Ratib, whose mother was a member of the Egyptian Royal Family, and had one son, Ömer Abdülmecid, born in 1941 in Alexandria. Later divorced, Namık worked for many years as the popular director of Alexandria Tramways, dying of a stroke in Cairo on 13 November 1963 at the age of 49.

Prince Mahmud Namık wearing the Order of the Ottoman Dynasty, presented to members of the Imperial House.

2. Prince Ömer Faruk. Only son of the future Caliph Abdülmecid II, by the lady Şehsuvar, and so grandson of Sultan Abdülaziz, Faruk was born in his father's villa at Ortaköy, Istanbul, 28 February 1898. He attended the military academy at Potsdam, Germany, during World War I and participated in the battle at Verdun. Returning home after the war, on 29 April 1920 in a grand ceremony at Yıldız Palace he married his first cousin, Princess Sabiha, daughter of the reigning monarch Mehmed VI Vahideddin. It was the first marriage in Ottoman history between members of the Imperial Family, heralding the fast-approaching end to the harem system. Alongside his official duties, Faruk was elected president of the city's renowned Fenerbahçe Foot-

ball Club from 1920 to 1923. In 1921 his father-in-law the Sultan dispatched Faruk to Anatolia to meet with the nationalist government in Ankara, but he did not succeed in this attempt. In 1925 he was considered for selection as king of Albania.

The couple had three daughters—the youngest born in Nice, where the Prince settled his family after the 1924 exile, near his father—but divorced in 1948. That year, in Alexandria, where he settled after leaving France, Faruk married another relative, his first cousin Princess Mihrişah, posthumous daughter of his late uncle Yusuf İzzeddin. There were no children from this second marriage, and they later divorced.

Prince Ömer Faruk's promising service to the state ended abruptly with the Imperial Family's exile in 1924.

Faruk's three daughters all married into the Egyptian Royal Family, and his granddaughter Fazile was engaged to King Faisal II of Iraq (whose great-great-grandfather Sherif Ali Pasha is buried in the garden graveyard) when the young King was murdered in the Iraqi coup of 1958. Prince Faruk died in Alexandria 28 March 1969, aged 71.

There is no inscription on the pall.

Princess Rebia. M18

Granddaughter of Abdülhamid II through his daughter Princess Refia and the latter's husband Ali Fuad Bey (whose father Ahmed Eyyûb Pasha is buried in the garden graveyard), Princess Rebia was born 13 July 1911 in her parents' villa in Istanbul and accompanied them into exile at Beirut in 1924. Her younger sister Ayşe Hamide died of an accident in Nice in 1934 and was buried in Damascus, as was her mother when she died in 1938. Rebia, who never married, continued to live with her father in Beirut but returned to Turkey after his death in 1953, since the exile of princesses had been rescinded the previous year.

Princess Rebia lived in Istanbul until her death 19 June 1988 at age 76. She was the last person interred in the mausoleum.

There is no inscription on the pall.

Princess Şadiye. M6

Daughter of Abdülhamid II by the lady Emsalinur, Princess Şadiye was born in Yıldız Palace 30 November 1886. Engaged in 1909, her wedding was postponed when her father was deposed that year and Şadiye accompanied him into exile at Salonica. Returning to Istanbul the next year, she married Fahir Bey, who had been posted to the Ottoman Embassy in Bucharest, and in 1918 Şadiye gave birth to a daughter, Princess Samiye. Her husband died young, in 1922, and is buried in the garden graveyard.

At the exile of the Imperial Family eighteen months later, Şadiye and her young daughter made their way to France. In a rented flat she raised her daughter, continuing her hobbies of playing piano and reading poetry, and generally recovering her balance. As she wrote much later, "To live in this world, one must not be sensitive, one must not feel, one must not love . . . but how hard it is to put this sort of thing into practice!"[31]

In 1931 in Paris the widowed Princess married former Turkish diplomat Reşad Halis, who had been secretary in her father's embassy in Paris, then ambassador to Switzerland in 1920, and had lived decades in Europe. The marriage between the two Turkish expatriates was happy, and Reşad's death in 1944 left the Princess a grieving widow for the second time. At war's end she emigrated to Venezuela, then on to New York, where she lived six years with her daughter and American son-in-law. At the 1952 revocation of the exile of princesses, Şadiye returned to Istanbul after an absence of nearly thirty years. In 1966 she published her memoirs in Turkish, *The Pleasant and Painful Days of My Life.*

Princess Şadiye died in Istanbul 20 November 1977, aged nearly 91, the last surviving child of Abdülhamid II.

There is no inscription on the pall.

Princess Saliha. M15

Daughter of Mahmud II, Princess Saliha was born to the lady Aşubcan 17 June 1811 and proved to be one of the five of Mahmud's nineteen daughters—and eldest child—to survive into adulthood (two of the other daughters, Atiye and Hadice, are also buried here). The palace archives record the celebrations ordered at her birth, including the firing of cannon. Her father arranged her marriage when she was 22 to Halil Rifat Pasha, aged about 38 (and already married with a family but required to divorce his wife), Commandant of the Imperial Gun Foundry at Tophane and later Admiral of the Fleet and Minister of War. Per custom, the monarch informed his government of the impending marriage by Imperial decree and commanded the necessary arrangements, including assembling his daughter's dowry.

The elaborate wedding—the first state marriage of Mahmud's reign—took place 24 May 1834 at the Imperial palace where Dolmabahçe Palace stands today, with Saliha proceeding in state from that now-gone palace to the seaside villa presented to her as a married lady, in the Fındıklı District, just south of it. Her son Abdülhamid was born in 1835 but died at age 2, and her son Cavid was born most likely in 1837 but died an infant. When Saliha herself died aged 31, in 1843, probably of tuberculosis, the Ottoman press reported her passing in the dignified tones of the day:

> Following the death on Monday of Princess Saliha, honored sister of His Majesty, her remains were brought to Bahçekapı [locale beside the entrance to the Golden Horn], then conveyed by eminent procession organized in accordance with observed custom, and buried at the pleasant tomb of her father, His Majesty Sultan Mahmud Khan, whose abode is Paradise.[32]

Her widower soon returned to his first wife, fathering a daughter, Ayşe Sıdıka, later wife of Server Pasha (who is buried in the garden), and a son, Mahmud Celâleddin Pasha, who tied the line again to the Imperial Family by marrying Princess Seniha, daughter of Sultan Abdülmecid.

After Saliha's demise, her poetess sister Princess Âdile penned two loving verses in her memory, the second relating that Saliha (whose name, as the verse mentions, means "pious") foresaw her own approaching death:

Princess Saliha, of my sisters one,
The moon-faced figure of the heavens of the dynasty;
Her loving mother Aşubcan
Is separated, mercilessly, from a source of her life.
Our Imperial father graciously saw fit
To give her in marriage to Halil Pasha.
Torn by separation, she suffered deeply,
The cruelty pierced her wounded heart.
Good of character she was, pretty, innocent,
Merciful, peerless, of God's mercy recipient.

Pious like her name, Saliha, the devoted servant,
Reciting God's praises, thankful, temperate.
Forty days lay yet before her death
When God disclosed to her the mystery.
With divine permission she revealed many secrets
And announced the hour of her passing.
Abundant miracles worked, she fairly
Took wing to the garden of Paradise.[33]

At her own death some twenty-seven years later, Saliha's mother Aşubcan
was interred in the adjoining chamber.

PALL

The late and laudable Princess Saliha, *may Almighty God settle
her in the chambers of the Heavens*, esteemed daughter of His
Majesty the Ghazi Mahmud Khan, whose abode is Sublime Paradise, who dwells in Eternal Heaven, *may pails of mercy be
poured over his tomb*. 5 Muharrem 1259 [5 February 1843].

Prince Selim. N7

Infant son of Sultan Abdülaziz, this prince was born in 1866 but died the
next year. Which of Abdülaziz's concubines was his mother remains un-
certain.

PALL

His Highness the late and divinely pardoned Mehmed Selim Efendi, princely son to the Shahanshah of the World. Date of birth Friday, 18 C.a. [Cemaziyül'evvel] of the year 283 [28 September 1866], date of death Tuesday, 26 C. [Cemaziyül'ahir] of the year 284 [25 October 1867, which actually was a Friday].

Princess Seniye. N5

Granddaughter of Mahmud II through his daughter Princess Atiye and her husband Ahmed Fethi Pasha, Princess Seniye was born in 1843. In 1860 she married Hüseyin Hüsnü Pasha, but the couple had no children. A widow since 1898, Seniye died 29 December 1911 at her villa in the Istanbul district of Nişantaşı. As the Palace Chancery records of that day tell us, the Princess's "remains, pardoned of sin, and dwelling in Paradise, will be taken from her residence to the pier at Beşiktaş, conveyed from there by steamboat to the pier at Sirkeci, thence to the noble New Mosque for the funeral services following the afternoon prayer, after which the remains will be delivered to the private chamber which adjoins the noble mausoleum of His Majesty Sultan Mahmud."[34] Her mother lies in the main chamber of the mausoleum, while her father and husband are at rest in the garden graveyard.

When Seniye reached the age to begin school lessons from a *hoca* or teaching master, her mother arranged the elaborate ceremonial that traditionally marked the occasion for youngsters of the Imperial House, and served as one of the means by which the dynasty discharged its duty of benevolence toward the less fortunate. The capital's French-language newspaper described the scene in Seniye's case, in 1848 when she was about 5 years of age, mentioning her title of *Hanımsultan* that daughters of Ottoman princesses bore:

> Last Thursday, conforming to the ancient custom, H.I.H. Atiè-Sultane, the wife of H.H. Ahmed-Fèthi Pasha, Grand Master of the Artillery, gave a hodja to her daughter Seniè Hanoum-Sultane, with the utmost solemnity, in her beautiful country home at Arnaout-Keuy.

His Majesty the Sultan, accompanied by his usual suite, deigned to arrive at an early hour to the invitation of the Princess, and attended the first reading lesson given the child by Shahri-Hafouz efendi, the distinguished member of the corps of oulemas and mufti to the Council of the Minister of War. Their Imperial Highnesses the princes Mohamed Murad and Abdul Hamid [the later sultans Murad V and Abdülhamid II], and H.I.H. Adilè-Sultane were present at this ceremony.

The Princess Atiè neglected nothing in bestowing the greatest possible splendour to this solemnity, which was for her an occasion to carry out a pious duty. After the lesson, the young and pretty Seniè, clothed in a most rich and elegant costume, her head covered in brilliants and her shoes decorated with jewels, entered a luxurious equipage awaiting her at the gate, and made a promenade along the quay, to the square of the barracks adjoining the village mosque, escorted by gentlemen of the palace in full dress uniform. The carriage was followed by a large cortege of children, numbering some five thousand, whose voices rose into the air, at short intervals, calling the benedictions of heaven upon the Hanoum-Sultane.

Upon her return began the celebrations that lasted for three days. Numerous tents were erected in the courtyard of the palace where, before engaging in games, one thousand children of both sexes, belonging to poor families, and dressed in new clothes at the expense of the Princess Atiè, also took their first lesson under the direction of several hodjas; an excellent dinner was subsequently served them by palace servants.

A considerable sum of money was distributed to the hodjas and to the children who formed the cortege.

H.M. the Sultan took his evening meal at the home of his sister Atiè-Sultane, and then returned to his palace of Tchèragan at a very late hour of the night.[35]

There is no inscription on the pall.

Prince Şevket. M8

Son of Sultan Abdülazız by his Fourth Consort, the lady Nesrin, Şevket was born at Dolmabahçe Palace on 5 June 1872. His full younger sister Emine was born two years later. With the deaths of his deposed father and his mother in June 1876, the boy was orphaned at the age of four. Most likely he was raised in the household of his older half-brother, Yusuf İzzeddin (his sister certainly was). Once he had reached his later teens, he was allowed to take a concubine, the lady Fatma Ruyınaz, and their son Cemaleddin was born in 1890.

Before he could make a mark on life besides beginning his family, however, at the age of 27 Şevket died at his villa in Çamlıca on the Asian shore of the Bosphorus, in 1899. The next day, the florid memorandum informing government ministries of his death tells us "His Highness Prince Şevket, son of His Majesty Sultan Abdülaziz (whose dwelling place is Heaven), having journeyed to the Abode of Perpetuity, his remains, traced with God's pardon, will be interred this day in the noble mausoleum of Sultan Mahmud."[36] The death notice in the capital's English-language newspaper was more matter-of-fact:

> An attack of typhoid complicated with pneumonia, which began last week, yesterday ended the life of H.I.H. Prince Shevket Effendi, one of the sons of the late Sultan Abdul Aziz, who died in his residence at Tchamlidja. The funeral takes place to-day, and the mausoleum of the Mosque of Sultan Ahmed [*sic*] is appointed for the place of burial.[37]

The following day's edition described the Prince's funeral:

> The funeral of his Imperial Highness Prince Shefket Effendi, who died on Sunday in his residence at Tchamlidja, was solemnised yesterday. A numerous gathering of Court and State officials awaited at Sirkedji the mortal remains, which were ferried across from Scutari in a ten-oared caique. Headed by Sheikhs, Dervishes, and Muezzins, and escorted by constabulary and gendarmery, the funeral procession wended its way to the Mau-

soleum of the Mosque of Sultan Ahmed [sic], in Stambul, and here, at the close of the funeral service, the remains of the late Prince were laid to rest near the tomb of his father, the late Sultan Abdul Aziz Khan.

Of the large congregation we may mention his Highness Gani Agha, Dar-us-Saadet-ul-Sherife Aghassi [Constable of the Noble Abode of Felicity, or Chief Eunuch at the Palace]; Redvan Pasha, Prefect of the City; Saadeddin Pasha, commanding the garrison of Constantinople; . . . Abdullah Hadji Ali Bey, Court Chamberlain; Khalid and Kemaleddin Pashas, sons-in-law of his Majesty; Shefik Bey, Minister of Police, Enver Bey, Governor of Pera; Nussuhi Bey, formerly Turkish Commissioner at Sofia; Hussein Hassib Bey, Director of Posts and Telegraphs, and many others.

Yesterday the Ministers went to Yildiz Kiosk, and offered their sympathy to the Sultan on the occasion of the death of Prince Shefket Effendi.

On the occasion of the Prince's death, alms were distributed to the poor.[38]

Although Şevket died young, as fate would have it all descendants of Sultan Abdülaziz in the male line today descend from him. His full sister Emine is also buried in this chamber.

PALL

A Fatiha for the soul of His Imperial Highness Prince Şevket, esteemed son of His Majesty Sultan Abdülaziz Khan, whose abode is Paradise. Born in the year 1286 of the Hegira [1869-70; in error for 1289]. Died 16 Cemaziyül'evvel 1317 [in error for Cemaziyül'ahir] / 10 Teşrin-i evvel 1315 [22 October 1899].

Prince Yusuf İzzeddin. M11

Eldest son of the future sultan Abdülaziz by the lady Dürrinev, both of whom are buried in this chamber, Yusuf İzzeddin was born when his father was still a prince. Due to the centuries-old Court tradition that only the ruling monarch may father children, his birth was kept secret until his father ascended the throne in 1861. As a result, details of his birth remain enshrouded in mystery. His date of birth was 11 October 1857 according to the later list of princes in the official Imperial almanacs, but 25 October 1855 according to the embroidered pall over his tomb here; still other state almanacs show 1859. And sources disagree on whether he was born in Dolmabahçe Palace or in the town house of a Court functionary. He does appear to have been raised secretly outside the palace, in the villa at Eyüp of the trusted Court functionary Kadri Bey. No doubt the distress over separation from his son, along with the continued evolution of the Ottoman monarchy over the nineteenth century, is what led Abdülaziz to decree, once he came to the throne, that henceforth Imperial princes could father children.

As oldest son of the reigning monarch, Yusuf İzzeddin was much in the public eye, accompanying Abdülaziz on his state visit to Europe in 1867, for example. At one point the Sultan considered altering the rules of succession to make his son his heir (as his vassal, the Egyptian viceroy, had done) but in the end he was compelled to abandon the idea.

Over the decades following his father's deposition and death in 1876, Yusuf İzzeddin led a rather secluded life as three of his older cousins occupied the throne. Testament to the changes in Court custom since his own birth, the relaxation in the regulations of the Imperial House allowed him to sire children from his Court ladies. Although Yusuf İzzeddin took apparently five ladies as concubines, he had children only from the last, the lady Leman: two sons and two daughters, the last daughter born six months after his death.

Yusuf İzzeddin reentered public life when, as the dynasty's eldest prince, he became Veliahd upon the accession of his cousin Mehmed V Reşad in 1909. Among other duties as Heir, such as chairing the Naval League and the Red Crescent Society, he represented the Ottoman Empire in London at the funeral of King Edward VII in 1910 and the coronation of King George V in 1911.

As the years went on, however, Yusuf İzzeddin came increasingly to exhibit symptoms of depression and anxiety that most who came in contact with him readily noticed, centering upon whether the ruling C.U.P. party (whose policies he vehemently opposed) or the Sultan might depose him

Prince Yusuf İzzeddin, flanked by his A.D.C.s circa 1912
when he was Heir to the Throne.

as Heir. Matters came to a head on 1 February 1916, when he took his own
life in his villa at Zincirlikuyu, Istanbul, at age 58, having called at this
mausoleum the previous day for prayers at his father's tomb. Conspiracy
theories abounded both at home and abroad that he had been murdered by
the C.U.P., who foresaw only difficulties should he come to the throne, but
no credible evidence of foul play has ever surfaced. Had he lived he would

have become sultan some seventeen months later, on the death of his cousin Mehmed V in 1918.

To add to the confusion about Yusuf İzzeddin's vital statistics, inexplicably the year of death embroidered onto the Prince's pall is in error.

PALL

A Fatiha for the soul of His Imperial Highness Prince Yusuf İzzeddin, Veliahd of the Exalted Sultanate, esteemed son of His Majesty Sultan Abdülaziz Khan, whose abode is Paradise. Born 13 Safer the Auspicious 1272 [incorrectly, 25 October 1855; probably the date should be 21 Safer 1274, 11 October 1857], Died 26 Rebiülevvel 1333 [in error for 1334, to equal 1 February 1916].

Imperial Concubines

The lady Aşubcan. N6

Third Consort to Mahmud II, the lady Aşubcan was born around 1793 in, most likely, the Caucasus. She entered palace service as a slave girl probably around 1800, at which point she received her permanent name ("Tumult of the Soul"). Selected as concubine to the newly enthroned Mahmud in 1808, in August 1809 she gave birth to Princess Ayşe, the monarch's second child. Aşubcan's baby died, however, around the age of seven months. In June 1811 she gave birth again, to Princess Saliha, who lived to adulthood.

During Mahmud's lifetime as well as after, rather unusually the lady Aşubcan resided not in the palace harem but in her villas in the Maçka district of the city, along the sea at Beşiktaş, and atop the hill at Çamlıca on the Asian side of the Bosphorus. She was delighted to receive Mahmud and his two sons whenever they called on her. The thank-you letter she sent in return for one such visit (probably dictated to the female secretary in her household, since in all likelihood Aşubcan was illiterate) still exists in the palace archives, in awkward penmanship with spelling and grammatical errors yet touching in its simplicity nonetheless:

My lord, our most excellent lord, I took such a measure of
delight in the honor of your Imperial visit of yesterday. . . . May
Almighty God bless the two noble princely youths.[39]

The lady Aşubcan outlived her husband by some 31 years and her daughter Saliha by 27 years, passing away 10 June 1870 at the age of approximately 77. As an adjunct of the Imperial House rather than a member of it,
she was buried in the side chamber of the mausoleum, whereas her daughter
Saliha, as a princess of the blood-royal, lies in the main chamber.

There is no inscription on the pall.

Senior Consort Dürrinev. M4

Of probably Circassian origin and born in Batum 15 March 1835, as a
young girl the future Imperial Consort entered service at Court probably
around 1850 as either a purchase or a gift, and received her new name
("New Pearl"). Assigned to the entourage of then-Prince Abdülaziz, five
years her elder, she became his concubine, giving birth to his first child,
Prince Yusuf İzzeddin, in 1857. As we have noted, longstanding palace tradition forbade a prince to sire children before he came to the throne, but
by the mid-nineteenth century customs were changing and Sultan Abdülmecid turned a blind eye to Dürrinev's son with the condition that his
existence be kept secret.

When Abdülaziz ascended the throne four years later, in 1861, he named
Dürrinev his Senior Consort, which placed her second only to his mother
in the harem hierarchy. Their daughter Saliha was born in August the following year. The new sultan also now took other ladies as his concubines,
alongside Dürrinev.

After the death of her husband in 1876, Dürrinev resided with her son.
When she died in 1895 at the age of 60, in the Fer'iye Palace along the
Bosphorus, she became the first consort buried in the main chamber of the
mausoleum who had not held the rank of Empress Mother. Her rank as
Senior Consort to Sultan Abdülaziz probably ensured her interment in the
main chamber, since her harem "sister" the lady Hayranıdil, who predeceased her by just one week, had been buried in the adjoining Lady Nevfidan Chamber probably because she "only" held the rank of Second

Consort. Dürrinev's son, and her granddaughter Princess Kâmile, are also interred in this chamber.

PALL

> Her Highness Dürrinev Kadınefendi, Senior Consort to His Majesty Sultan Abdülaziz Khan, whose abode is Paradise. 16 Cemaziyül'ahir 1313 [4 December 1895], Tuesday.

The lady Edâdil. N4

The future consort to Sultan Abdülaziz was born around 1845, probably in the Caucasus, sold into slavery as a young girl, and eventually sold or presented to the palace as a gift, and given her Court name ("Coquetry-heart"). She began service in the entourage of then-Prince Abdülaziz most likely by around 1860. After Abdülaziz acceded to the throne in 1861 he appointed concubines in addition to his Senior Consort Dürrinev, naming Edâdil as Third Consort, when she was around age 16. In November 1862, Edâdil gave birth to Prince Celâleddin (who lived to the age of 25), and in 1866 she gave birth to Princess Emine, who died as an infant and is also buried in this chamber.

Edâdil died in Dolmabahçe Palace aged around 30, probably of tuberculosis, in 1875, during the last full year of her husband's reign.

There is no inscription on the pall.

The lady Hayranıdil. N1

Of Circassian origin, the lady Hayranıdil was born 2 November 1846 at Kars and entered palace service probably around 1860, when she would have received her name ("Adoring of Heart"). Chosen as a concubine by Sultan Abdülaziz probably around 1864, she gave birth to Princess Nâzıme in February 1866 at Dolmabahçe Palace, followed two years later, in May 1868, by her delivery at the same palace of Prince Abdülmecid. As Second Consort at the Court of Abdülaziz after 1875, the lady Hayranıdil ranked immediately below the lady Dürrinev in this Sultan's harem hierarchy.

After her husband's deposition in 1876, the lady Hayranıdil and her two children were settled in the Fer'iye Palace, part of the Çırağan Palace complex along the Bosphorus. Known for her beauty and gentle manners, here she quietly lived out the remaining nineteen years of her life until her death in 1895 at age 49.

Both her children lived to advanced ages. The lady Hayranıdil would have participated in the celebrations of her daughter's marriage in 1889 to Halid Pasha, whose father, the renowned Derviş Pasha, is buried in the garden graveyard. Her son reigned as Caliph Abdülmecid II from 1922 until the Imperial Family's exile in 1924; he was the last Caliph of Islam (to date) and is equally known today as an artist of considerable talent, as was his father.

PALL

A Fatiha for the soul of Hayranıdil Kadınefendi, Second Consort of His Majesty Sultan Abdülaziz Khan, whose abode is Paradise. 8 Cemaziyül'ahir 1313 [26 November 1895].

The lady Hüsnümelek. N3

Senior İkbal to Mahmud II, and so one step below the monarch's four consorts on the harem hierarchical ladder, the lady Hüsnümelek was born around 1807. Possibly she was Armenian, but nothing of her life before palace service is certain.[40] Sold into slavery as a young girl, she was known by her new name ("Angel Beauty") in the entourage of Princess Esma, Mahmud's sister in whose garden this tomb lies.

Hüsnümelek mastered the traditional Turkish dances performed at Court and exhibited talent for choreography. When Mahmud saw her while visiting his sister and fancied her, Princess Esma presented Hüsnümelek to him as a gift. In her honor Mahmud composed a song with the verse beginning:

Hüsnümelek is a fairy,
The beauty of them all.[41]

Hüsnümelek had no children. From her letters we know that even during Mahmud's lifetime she lived outside the palace in a seaside villa of her own on the Asian shore of the Bosphorus at Beylerbeyi, where she received visits from members of the Imperial Family and Imperial consorts. As a widow, and though no longer dancing herself, she taught intricate dance movements to her slave girls, who performed them, for example, at the wedding of Princess Münire in 1858.[42] Hüsnümelek died in October 1886, around the age of 79, having survived her husband some forty-seven years.

There is no inscription on the pall.

The lady Lebriz. N10

Fourth İkbal to Mahmud II, Lebriz ("Brimming," the name given her at Court) was born around 1810, probably in the Caucasus. Apparently childless, she resided in her seaside mansion at Ortaköy, passing away on 9 February 1865 at the age of approximately 55.

There is no inscription on the pall.

Senior Consort Nevfidan ("the Pilgrim"). N11

Born around 1793, this future consort to Mahmud II was most likely Circassian by birth, sold into slavery while a young girl, and either purchased or presented as a gift for palace service probably around 1800, when she would have been given her new name ("New Sapling"); she was also known as Pertev Piyale ("Eye of Light") Nevfidan. Since Court tradition allowed only the reigning monarch to beget children, Nevfidan would have been taken as a concubine to the new monarch once he ascended the throne in July 1808, when she was around 15 and he 23. At this point Mahmud named her one of the four Imperial Consorts at his newly formed Court. At the death of Mahmud's Senior Consort Alicenab (whose date of death is unknown), Nevfidan was raised to that lofty rank.

Due to the extreme privacy that enshrouded the Imperial Harem, confusion reigns today when attempting to establish the birth order of Mahmud's children and identify their mothers. The following February (1809) Nevfidan gave birth (or possibly, was named adoptive mother) to the new monarch's first child, Princess Fatma, who was thus apparently born two months prematurely, to judge from Mahmud's date of accession of the preceding August. As this baby was the first to be born in the palace for some twenty years, her birth was roundly celebrated; unfortunately, the infant contracted smallpox and lived only six months. Nevfidan produced four more children: the second Princess Fatma, born in 1810 but dying of smallpox in 1825 at age 15, twins Prince Osman and Princess Emine, born in June 1813 but dying within months, as well as the second Princess Emine, born in December 1815 but dying in a fire when not yet two years old.

As all of Nevfidan's children had died, Sultan Mahmud gave her the four-year-old Princess Âdile to raise when that child's mother, the lady Zernigâr, died in 1830. The youngster, whom Nevfidan raised as her own daughter, grew up to become the most prolific poetess of the House of Osman, as well as the longest-lived of Sultan Mahmud's daughters when she died in 1899.

The death of Mahmud II in 1839 left Nevfidan a widow at about age 46, still in good health and interested in the world. In September 1842 she undertook the pilgrimage to Mecca—the first Ottoman Imperial Consort known to have done so. Indeed only one other Imperial Consort in Ottoman history, the lady Hoşyar, also a lady of Mahmud's, is recorded as having performed the pilgrimage. The lady Nevfidan traveled to Mecca in the entourage of the Caravan of the Purse, the annual dispatch of Imperial gifts from Istanbul to Mecca, her presence constituting an event so unusual that it made the columns of the capital's English-language newspaper:

> The "Pious embassy" departed for the holy cities of Mecca and Medina on the 23d, with the usual solemnity. . . . The cortege, composed of a large number of pilgrims of all classes, set out, preceded by the bands of several regiments of the guard. The first wife of Sultan Mahmoud . . . accompanied the caravan. This is the first time a Sultana ever proceeded on a pilgrimage to Mecca.[43]

When Nevfidan returned from the pilgrimage she took the title *Haciye*, "Pilgrim," and thereafter used a seal engraved, "Her Highness the Illustrious Pilgrim Nevfidan, Senior Consort to the late Sultan Mahmud."[44]

For his part, Sultan Abdülmecid was devoted to his late father's consort. She was a most pious lady who generously donated funds for benevolent causes, including, among others, constructing a mosque in the Ahi Çelebi district and a water cistern at the Mesnevihane Mosque in Stambul, erecting a primary school in Üsküdar named for her, and establishing charitable foundations to assist the poor of Mecca and Medina. After her death on 25 December 1855, aged about 62, her adoptive daughter Princess Âdile penned the following verse in warm tribute to her foster mother:

> Then the lady Nevfidan became to me
> A devoted mother, as to her own child.
> No one else could dry my eyes,
> Never did she imply she was not my mother.
> To her bosom she pressed me, and arranged my marriage,
> May God make Paradise her station.[45]

Expressing the attachment he felt for this lady of his father's even years after her death, Sultan Abdülaziz invoked her alternate name when he christened his new Imperial yacht *Pertev Piyale* after her, sailing aboard this vessel to Toulon in 1867 for his state visit to France and England.

There is no inscription on the pall.

The lady Nuritâb. N2

Rising to the rank of Fourth Consort to Mahmud II, Nuritâb ("Light of Ardor") was born around 1810 and probably entered the Sultan's entourage in the 1820s. She apparently had no children, certainly none who survived infancy. Nuritâb died 2 January 1886, aged around 76. At her death she was the last surviving lady of Mahmud II, having outlived her husband nearly forty-seven years.

There is no inscription on the pall.

The lady Pervizfelek. N8

Born probably around 1805, Pervizfelek (or Piruzfelek, "Fortunate Fate") entered palace service by around 1820, after which she was named an Imperial Consort to Mahmud II. In 1824 she gave birth to Princess Atiye, followed in 1825 by Princess Hadice. Both her daughters were interred in the Mahmud II Chamber at their deaths in 1850 and 1842 respectively. Her third daughter, Fatma, was born in 1828 but died two years later and so is buried elsewhere since this mausoleum had not yet been built.

The lady Pervizfelek died 21 September 1863, aged around 60, having outlived her husband and daughters by many years. Some fifty years later, her granddaughter Princess Seniye was also buried in the Lady Nevfidan Chamber at her death in 1911.

There is no inscription on the pall.

The lady Saliha Naciye. M2

İkbal to Abdülhamid II, this Circassian lady was born around 1887 in Bartın on the Black Sea, came to palace service probably around 1900, and entered the ranks of the Sultan's concubines in 1904, when she was 17 and he 62. Abdülhamid II was particularly fond of her, the youngest and last of his harem ladies, of whom she was the eleventh when she was created an ikbal some forty-one years after he had taken his first concubine. In September 1905 she gave birth at Yıldız Palace to Prince Âbid, followed in January 1908 by Princess Samiye, as fate had it the last births to a reigning sultan in Ottoman history.

The lady Saliha Naciye lost her baby Samiye to pneumonia in January 1909, just three months before the overthrow of Abdülhamid. She remained with her husband after his deposition, as she and their four-year-old son accompanied him and others of his family into exile at Salonica, undergoing the privations of house arrest there and at Beylerbeyi Palace, where the ex-Sultan was moved in 1912. She was with him still when he died in 1918.

With the death of the ex-monarch, the lady Saliha Naciye and her son settled in a villa in the Erenköy district of Istanbul, where she died only six years later, aged about 37, one month before the exile of the Imperial Family. As such she was the last member or adjunct of the Imperial House to be buried in this mausoleum until 1977, when interments resumed.

The lady Saliha Naciye is the only harem lady interred in the mausoleum's main chamber who did not hold the rank of either Senior Consort or Empress Mother—an indication of relaxation, at the very end of the monarchy, in the protocol of who might and might not be buried here. Her son Prince Âbid went on to marry a sister of King Zog of Albania in 1936 and served as Albanian ambassador at Paris until 1939; he died in Beirut in 1973 and was buried in Damascus.

PALL

Saliha Naciye Hanım, exalted lady to His Majesty Sultan Abdülhamid II, whose abode is Heaven, who dwells in Paradise.
Died 28 Cemaziyül'ahir 1342 / 4 Şubat 1340 [4 February 1924].

The funeral cortege of Abdülhamid II proceeds to the ex-monarch's final resting place
in the mausoleum, February 1918. In gala uniform, the Palace Household Staff,
sent by Sultan Reşad to honor his deceased brother, escort the casket.

— CHAPTER 5 —

FROM GARDEN TO GRAVEYARD

The new tomb brought in its wake dramatic changes to the old winter residence that Princess Esma formerly enjoyed for herself. Shortly after her death and burial in 1848 within the mausoleum of what used to be her garden, Esma's villa was pulled down by Imperial order, leaving the twin ramps in stone along the back wall of the garden as the only surviving clue to the previous existence of the mansion on the heights above. In the villa's place rose the Empress Mother School, opening in March 1850 and still in operation today, under a different name. The Empress Mother Bezmiâlem financed construction of the school deliberately on this spot overlooking the tomb of her deceased husband Mahmud II in order to underscore his role, and that of the dynasty as a whole, in reforming and encouraging education. Personally tying the dynasty to the school overlooking his father's tomb, once the school opened the Empress Mother's son Sultan Abdülmecid enrolled in it his two eldest children, Murad and Fatma[1]—a bold break with the tradition of educating royal children by tutors in the harem, and an innovation of which Mahmud would have approved.

Meanwhile, fourteen years after the tomb's construction, the flower garden in which the tomb was set began its radical metamorphosis into a burial ground. Such a prestigious "address" at the city's newest Imperial tomb meant that only high-ranking persons in service to the Imperial House— people the Sultan personally wished to honor—would be buried here. Maintaining the social stratum that parted them in life, then, as we have seen, the garden served for burial of these prestigious commoners, while the mausoleum housed the Imperial Family and its concubines.

The garden's use for burials reflected the trend, in the second half of the nineteenth century, of burying important persons at the gardens of the eight Imperial mosques within Stambul. Before then, with few exceptions no burials took place in the gardens of Imperial mosques, or in fact anywhere within Stambul, by law. Instead, grandees and palace personnel went to their eternal rest in the great cemeteries outside Stambul's walls. But as reforms changed the nature of Ottoman governance over the nineteenth century, the palace realized the promotional value in publicly rewarding loyal servants by according them burial at these prestigious sites (Muslim grandees, that is; Christians and Jews were buried in their religion's own graveyards, of course). As the newest Imperial burial site within Stambul, the Mahmud II tomb complex came to serve as the primary such reward, particularly under Mahmud's grandson Abdülhamid II, who as a mark of favor ordered the burial of some eighty dignitaries here (more than half the interments at this site) during his long reign between 1876 and 1909.

The first burial in the garden, in 1854, was that of Dr. Abdülhak Efendi, Court Physician to both Mahmud II and his son Sultan Abdülmecid, the latter wishing to honor the celebrated doctor by ordering his interment beside the Imperial tomb. His was the only burial in the garden for four years, until Field Marshal Ahmed Fethi Pasha, Abdülmecid's brother-in-law, was laid to rest immediately beside the doctor. When the Marshal's wife, Princess Atiye, had died eight years earlier, she was interred within the mausoleum, but preserving the distinction between royalty and commoners, at his own death her widower was buried in the grounds outside the building.

Two years after the Marshal's interment came the third burial in the garden, and the first woman: the lady Şevknihal, a *Hazinedar Usta* or high-ranking female administrator of the Imperial Harem. Like the two male courtiers who preceded her, Şevknihal's tomb stands just inside the western gate into the garden, but across the path from the gentlemen, thus preserving in death a measure of the gender segregation by which Ottoman culture separated them in life. Clearly this prominent lady in palace service held the love and esteem of the Imperial Family, bringing Sultan Abdülmecid to order her interment here at her death in 1860.

During the monarchy only three other females were buried in this graveyard (females buried here due to their own accomplishments, that is, rather than as wives of statesmen). In 1869, 1870, and 1891, respectively, the ladies Revnak, Ferahnüma, and Kiryalfer, each top-ranking managers of the Imperial Harem, all came to rest together in this same corner of the garden. It is not surprising that the only such females in this garden worked in the palace harem, since that was the only venue by which working women could rise to a sufficiently prestigious post to earn their interment here.

Also from the palace, but buried (in 1876 and 1887) across the path and so separated from the Hazinedars in death as in life, lie two top-ranking Court Eunuchs. After 1891, however, Court personnel were buried elsewhere (mostly at the Yahya Efendi Cemetery near Yıldız Palace) as the Mahmud II graveyard was given over solely to interments of leading male dignitaries of the state. It was as though Abdülhamid II realized that given the space restrictions here, if in line with his priorities in securing his reign he were to honor the maximum number of state dignitaries at their deaths, then palace staff (who wouldn't have the same political clout) would have to go somewhere else.

And so, what began as the tomb for one monarch and his family evolved into a National Necropolis of the Noted. As an emerging national symbol,

The first interments in the garden graveyard flanked the western gate (at the end of the path); to the left, the dome of the water kiosk.

though, the garden not surprisingly underwent shifts in burials that paralleled the fluctuations in political power over time. From the first garden burial, in 1854, until the overthrow of Abdülhamid II in 1909, the graveyard functioned as National Pantheon for the Empire's Honored Dead: overwhelmingly governors, ambassadors, field marshals, and admirals, sprinkled with other noted men tied somehow to the Imperial Court; it was a way for the Imperial House to thank these elite subjects and to demonstrate magnanimity by ordering their burial here, usually at state expense. And so, looking back upon that epoch, the magnificent sarcophagi and tombstones in the garden not only commemorate the dead interred beneath them, but become a powerful symbol, cut in stone, of the benevolence of the House of Osman toward its subjects—in this case its highest-ranking subjects—as the monarch himself ordered and paid for their burial here.

Then, in the politically charged months following Abdülhamid's ouster in the 1909 coup, the site assumed two additional if temporary incarnations, as National Graveyard for Martyrs Against Tyranny, and then National Cemetery for Members of the Reconvened Parliament Who Happened to Die in Office. As the leveling hand of fate would have it in those turbulent years, both loyal supporters and ardent opponents of Abdülhamid came to rest together in this garden, near the great monarch himself after his burial in the mausoleum in 1918.

Given that some Ottoman elite families sent more than one son into state service, and that these sons intermarried among other elite families, soon enough the garden quite unintentionally became on occasion a kind of extended family graveyard. As one example over the decades, the influential Sırkâtibizâde family saw its scion Hüsnü Pasha buried here (and saw his wife Princess Seniye buried in the mausoleum), along with his nephew Osman Hâmi Bey (and the latter's wife Princess Atiye), as well as Kâmil Pasha, husband of his niece Ferdâne, whose grandfather Ahmed Fethi Pasha is here as well, as are three of the latter's sons-in-law, one of whom was the Hüsnü Pasha with whom we started this genealogical exercise!

In what must have subsequently seemed a flashy last hurrah for the Mahmud II tomb garden on the national stage, the nascent Turkish republic emulated its Imperial predecessor by interring here its own hero, the nationalist theoretician Ziya Gökalp, in 1924. Burials ended the following year, after the exile of the Imperial Family and transfer of political power to Ankara.

Or perhaps they continued in the ensuing decades, since nine graves are mysteries with unknown occupants, a circumstance unlikely (though not impossible) to have occurred during the monarchy, when the sultans were carefully doling out the graves. We do know that three old remains (seventeenth century) were transferred here in 1957 when the nearby graveyard in which they had lain was demolished, and a set of fifteenth-century remains were brought here in 1961, but these reburials were not state occasions. Nonetheless, long after state burials here had ceased, the graveyard retained its aura as burial ground of the prominent and powerful, so much so that the statesman (and playwright) Ahmed Vefik Pasha is said to have quipped, "I want to be buried at Rumelihisarı—I refuse to be buried at Sultan Mahmud's tomb, and have to tussle for all eternity with the same men I battled in life!"[2]

After forty years of quiet, burials resumed in 1965, quite sporadically, as the garden entered upon its final incarnation, Repository of Royals Returned from Exile (not the only such site, but the most prestigious because of its central location in the historic heart of the city). This use of the garden was new since, as we have seen, during the monarchy Imperial Family members would have been buried inside the tomb. But space inside the tomb was running out. And so this new role for the Mahmud II tomb garden brings new fame to the old site, as it shares in today's increasing fascination with Tur-

The superb marble panel, carved in arabesque pattern, adorning the sepulchre of Said Halim Pasha.

Modified with rococo flourishes, the Ottoman coat of arms graces the tomb
of General Eyyûb Halid Pasha.

key's royalty. The last such interment to date, in 2009, to vast international
media coverage, of Prince Osman Ertuğrul, Head of the Imperial House,
marked the 147th burial in this garden—and nearly the last, as precious
little unused ground remains.

All told, then, in the seventy years between 1854 and 1924 some 138
sarcophagi and tombstones came to adorn the garden. Their intricate design
and superb workmanship testify to the high artistry attained by Ottoman
stone carving in the period, and combine with the inscriptions to lend the
graveyard the appearance of an open-air museum of late Ottoman
stonework and calligraphy, which indeed it is.

Meet the Ottomans

Bright names at rest in the garden—to pick just a few examples—include
Abdülfettah Efendi (master calligrapher), Agâh Efendi (cofounder of the
first private Ottoman newspaper), Fethi Pasha (founder of the Imperial Ottoman Museum), Sherif Ali Pasha (grandfather of the first kings of Jordan
and Iraq), Hasan Fehmi (journalist whose murder helped trigger the 1909
Counter-revolution), İsmail Pasha (Chief Physician to Sultan Abdülmecid),

Muallim Naci (poet, author, teacher, dictionary compiler), Münir Pasha (Grand Master of Ceremonies at the Imperial Palace), Necib Pasha (composer of the national anthem under Abdülhamid II), Osman Zeki Bey (founder of the great publishing house, Osmaniye Press), Sadullah Pasha (ambassador to Austria-Hungary, poet), Said Halim Pasha (Egyptian prince, Grand Vizier during World War One, author, intellectual), Süreyya Pasha (Private Secretary to Abdülhamid II), Talha Ağa (Chief Eunuch at the Court of Sultan Abdülaziz), and Ziya Gökalp (sociologist, "Father of Turkish Nationalism").

Of the 147 persons buried in the garden, biographies of 94—those with more intriguing life stories or epitaphs—are given below within the categories that best describe the profession or calling of the deceased in life:

> Ambassadors
> Artists and Artisans
> Cabinet Ministers and Grand Viziers
> Generals, Admirals, and Governors
> National Heroes
> Palace Staff
> Parliamentary Deputies and Senators
> Physicians
> Royalty and Nobles
> Scholars and Religious Figures

Within each category, entries are alphabetical by given name (surnames not being in use for Muslims during Ottoman times). Since males typically had at least two given names, listings come under the name by which the man was known more commonly in life. Thus, for example, Mahmud Server Pasha is listed under "Server Pasha."

Following the deceased's name and profession is the location of the grave on the accompanying map. For example, "E106" indicates Section E, lot 106.

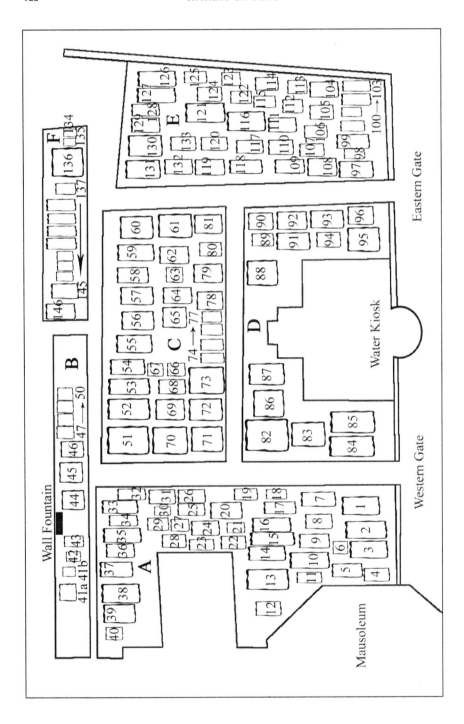

Ambassadors

Agâh Efendi. Journalist, Ambassador. E106

Born in 1832 to a prominent family in Yozgat (central Anatolia), son of Çapanzâde Ömer Hulûsi Efendi, the young Agâh attended the Imperial medical school in Istanbul for a period before accepting work, thanks to his knowledge of French, in the Translation Bureau of the Sublime Porte. In 1852 he served as secretary to the Ottoman ambassador in Paris, after which he embarked upon a series of government posts: Assistant Director of the Quarantine Office, Chief Translator for the army in the Balkan provinces, Chief Administrator in Mostar (Herzegovina) and on the islands of Rhodes and Lesbos. As Director of the newly formed Imperial Post Office in the early 1860s, he oversaw the introduction of the empire's first postage stamps.

Perhaps Agâh Efendi's greatest service to society, however, lay in his co-founding the first private Ottoman newspaper, the influential *Tercüman-ı Ahval* ("Translator of Events"), in 1860. As member of the Young Ottomans

Society, Agâh Efendi's ideas clashed with those of government leaders, and he fled to Europe in 1867. Still his skirmishes with authority did not prevent his return to grace in 1871, following the deaths of his adversaries. Subsequent promotions brought him to the civil rank of *Bâlâ*, one step shy of the rank that would have brought him the title *Pasha*.

His career was crowned by appointment as ambassador to Greece in November 1885. But before his diplomatic career could blossom, only shortly after taking up his post Agâh died unexpectedly in Athens in 1885, aged 53, with his remains returned to the Imperial capital for burial here.

Agâh Efendi in his younger days, when he founded the first private Ottoman newspaper.

TOMBSTONE
A Fatiha for the soul of the late, divinely pardoned Agâh Efendi
Holder of the civil rank of *Bâlâ*
Who journeyed to the Abode of Eternity while Ambassador at Athens
15 Rebiülevvel 1303 [22 December 1885]
Calligrapher [name badly worn, possibly Sami]

Es'ad Pasha. Ambassador. C69

Born around 1836 to a prominent family in Izmir, Es'ad launched his career at a tender age as apprentice in the offices of the Imperial Council in 1850, continuing in the government's Translation Bureau. Sent by the government to Paris in 1855 at age 19 to further his command of French, the rising statesman remained three years in the French capital before transferring to a secretarial post at the St. Petersburg embassy. By 1860 he was back in the Ottoman capital at the Translation Bureau, rising slowly through the ranks of the civil service, returning to Paris in 1861 as Second Secretary at the embassy, followed six years later by promotion to First Secretary. At his return to Istanbul in 1867 he took up the post of Director at his old office, the Translation Bureau, receiving steady promotions in civil service rank, as well as decorations. In 1870 the capable statesman was sent to Hungary as Ottoman Consul-general at Pest.

Rising to the upper ranks of state service, Es'ad received appointments through the 1870s as ambassador, to Athens, Rome, and Vienna. The end of the decade brought him back to Istanbul as Undersecretary of Foreign Affairs before departing for Paris as ambassador, in 1880—twenty-five years after he first visited the City of Light. The year after his appointment to Paris, Es'ad Pasha was honored by the Sultan with the highest rank in civil service, *vizier*.

Es'ad Pasha retained his prestigious posting to France nearly fourteen years, a long tenure that reflects the deep trust Abdülhamid II placed in him. Suffering health problems, Es'ad Pasha resigned the Paris embassy in 1894 and returned to Istanbul, where he died 7 April 1895, aged about 58, after some 45 years in government service under four monarchs.

At his death the capital's English newspaper ran a lengthy obituary and funeral notice on the well-known statesman, including details of the honors showered upon him:

We are sorry to have to announce the death of his Excellency Essad Pasha, who lately occupied the post of Ottoman Ambassador in Paris. Essad Pasha, who has been ailing for several months past, died yesterday in his yali at Emirghian. The funeral takes place today. . . .

The Sovereign, recognizing his loyal services, promoted him to the rank of bala and conferred upon him the Grand Cordon of the Medjidieh . . . [H]e was appointed Ambassador to Paris, a post which he occupied until a few months ago. The Sultan then conferred upon him the Grand Cordon of the *Osmanieh* and later on the star in brilliants of the same Order, as well as the medal of the *Iftihar* and the gold and silver medals of the *Imtiaz*. While occupying this last post he was promoted to the rank of vizier which carried with it the title of Pasha, and was entrusted with a special mission to the Court of Madrid. Deceased possessed several foreign orders, among them the Grand Cordons of Charles III of Spain, of Leopold of Austria, of the Legion of Honour, and the Holy Saviour of Greece.[3]

The funeral of the late Essad Pasha took place on Thursday last from the deceased's residence at Emirghian. At eleven o'-clock the remains were placed on board a tug-boat and conveyed to Sirkedji where the procession was formed. The cortege, which was headed by sheikhs and detachments of gendarmes and police and municipal agents, proceeded to the Mosque of St. Sophia, where the prayers for the dead were said. By order of his Majesty the remains were interred within the precincts of the mausoleum of Sultan Mahmoud. The mourners included their Excellencies Turkhan Pasha, ex-vali [Governor-General] of Crete; Sherif Abdullah Pasha and Reshid Bey, Councillors of State; Nouri Bey, secretary-general of the Foreign Office; Daoud Effendi, first dragoman of the Imperial Divan; Hakki Bey, legal counsellor of the Porte; Baki Bey, chief of the archives office of the Porte; General Abdullah Pasha, aide-de-camp of the Sultan; General Izzet Pasha, Grand Equerry; Mehmed Pasha of Egypt; Zia Bey, president of the technical council of the

Ministry of Agriculture; Ali Ferroukh Bey, Councillor of the Turkish Embassy in St. Petersburg; Hassib Bey, a secretary of the Paris Embassy, etc.[4]

TOMBSTONE
He is The Eternal One, The Creator
The Fatiha for the soul of
The late and divinely pardoned
Es'ad Pasha
Acknowledged vizier of the Exalted Sultanate
And minister of the Sublime State
Ambassador to Paris
11 Şevval the Sacred 1312 [7 April 1895]

Halil Şerif Pasha. Ambassador. A17

One of the best-known Ottoman diplomats on the nineteenth-century international stage, Halil Şerif Pasha was born in Egypt around 1822, son of the Turkish officer Şerif Pasha who served Muhammad Ali, governor of that virtually independent province. The young man's father sent him to Paris in the 1840s to further his education, gaining him complete comfort in French language and culture.

After training in political science Halil returned to Cairo to work in the Egyptian government's translation bureau in the 1850s, but managed to transfer up to the Ottoman diplomatic service, citing eye problems in the stark light of Egypt as bad for his health. His service to the Sublime Porte began with his posting as minister to Athens in 1856, a minor capital that, his colleagues teased him, he would find far less convivial than the Paris he adored. St. Petersburg followed in 1861; he held out in the cold northern post for four years, but in 1865 took up residence as a private citizen in Paris. Thanks to his inheritance upon his father's death, here Halil lived the life of a rich and generous foreigner, frequenting parties and gambling halls and race tracks, entertaining the French literati and belle monde, collecting art for his renowned private art gallery (even commissioning Courbet's famed erotic painting "The Sleepers"), becoming the toast of the town—and saddled with debt.

During his residence in Paris, Halil mixed with the liberal Ottomans who gathered in exile there, seeking to reform the government of Sultan Abdülaziz back home along progressive Western lines. He himself penned a memorandum in 1867, probably in French, outlining what he saw as the grave issues facing the Ottoman Empire, along with his proposal for resolving them, namely by introducing constitutional government. The next year he returned to Istanbul to live, probably because his huge debts meant he could no longer afford Paris. Back in the Imperial capital, working at the Foreign Ministry—and none the worse for the memorandum he had penned—Halil was known for his western ways.

High posts followed for the able diplomat, including ambassador to Vienna from 1870 to 1872 (an enjoyable milieu for the cultured Halil), then foreign minister in 1872, at which *The Times* of London sang his praises:

> This appointment has given great and general satisfaction. The eminent qualities displayed by Khalyl Sherif Pasha in the different offices he has held, and his sound knowledge of all that concerns European and Eastern politics, have pointed him out since Aali Pasha's death as his natural successor at the Foreign Office.[5]

The year he became Foreign Minister, around the age of 50, Halil finally settled down, marrying the Egyptian princess Nazlı, niece of the Khedive and daughter of the rich Prince Mustafa Fazıl Pasha. Scoffers claimed he was just out to cancel the debts he owed his future father-in-law. Thanks to the progressive views of her father, though, Princess Nazlı had been well educated, knew French and English, dressed in Parisian fashions, and played the piano, making her a fitting match for her worldly husband.

At last Halil's dream came true, when in July 1875 Sultan Abdülaziz appointed him ambassador to Paris. Just as quickly did the dream evaporate, when two weeks later the Sultan canceled the appointment. Small wonder that Halil, who must have been crushed by this fickle treatment, lent his support to the movement that overthrew Abdülaziz the following year. His brief appointment in 1876 as Minister of Justice ended due to health problems more serious than reported:

We hear with much regret that Khalil Sheriff Pasha, Minister of Justice, is suffering from the effects of sun-stroke. His excellency was at the palace of Dolmabaghtché on Friday, and while there, was taken ill somewhat suddenly and was obliged to go home—a partial, and it is hoped temporary, paralysis of the face affecting his speech. The physicians in attendance pronounce his excellency to be somewhat better today.[6]

Once Halil had recovered to a degree, the new monarch, Abdülhamid II, capped the Pasha's long career with the coveted ambassadorial post at Paris, in March 1877. We lack details on his final residence in the City of Light, but given the Ottoman entanglement in war with Russia then, his stay would have been far more sober than his exhilarating experience of ten years earlier. For unclear reasons—quite likely another stroke—Halil was replaced as ambassador in September that year, after only six months on the job. He returned to Istanbul, where he died a little over a year later, in January 1879, aged around 57.[7]

TOMBSTONE
He is The Eternal One, The Creator
A Fatiha for the soul of Halil Şerif Pasha
Son of the late Mısırlı [Egyptian] Şerif Pasha
Who exhibited excellent service
In the illustrious ministries of Foreign Affairs and Justice
And in the Imperial embassies at Paris and Vienna and Petersburg
But has now departed for the Abode of Eternity
Muharrem 1296 [the month from 26 December 1878 to 25 January 1879]

Sadullah Pasha. Ambassador. E118

Born in Erzurum in 1838, son of a governor (and poet) who claimed descent from the Prophet Muhammad, Sadullah Rami completed his studies in Istanbul, mastering French. The young man launched his government career in the tax revenue office, followed quickly by appointments to, among other departments during the reign of Sultan Abdülaziz, the Translation Bureau of the Sublime Porte, the Council of State (serving as Senior

Secretary, in 1870), the Imperial Chancery (serving as translator), the Ministry of Public Instruction, and the Imperial Registry Office. Excelling at the written word, during his tenure as secretary at these various posts Sadullah contributed greatly to reforming the heretofore abstruse and opaque writing style of official Ottoman documents. As Undersecretary of Public Instruction, he took the lead in reforming high schools and opening a public library.

In June 1876 Sadullah was appointed Private Secretary to the new sultan Murad V. When that monarch was deposed after his brief reign of three months, the next sovereign, Abdülhamid II, appointed Sadullah Minister of Commerce briefly, but the Pasha's service to Murad V did not sit well with Abdülhamid II; Sadullah could continue in high government service, but only far from the capital, in a kind of gilded banish-

Ambassador to Austria-Hungary, where he met his untimely demise, Sadullah Pasha would surely rather have spent his days composing prose and poetry than navigating the minefields of diplomacy.

ment. From 1877 to 1883 he was ambassador to Germany, joining in the treaty negotiations at the Congress of Berlin that followed the Russo-Turkish War. In 1883 he transferred to Vienna as ambassador to the Habsburg Court, a post he occupied until his death. Meanwhile the Sultan showered Sadullah with the great orders and decorations of the empire, raising him to the highest civil rank, *vizier*, in 1883, and dispatching him to Berlin in 1888 to represent him at the funeral of the German emperor Wilhelm I. All the while, for some fourteen years, his wife remained behind in Istanbul.

Alongside his official duties, Sadullah took up the pen as a poet and literary translator. While many of his works have not survived, his visit to the Paris World's Fair of 1878 inspired his most noted poem, *The Nineteenth Century*. The work is celebrated in Ottoman literature not for poetic perfection but for its daring theme, the triumph of Western scientific and technological progress, proclaimed in its opening couplet:

> Insight's light scaled the peak of perfection,
> Unimaginable reached the rank of possible.

After years as ambassador in Vienna, Sadullah Pasha began an affair with a young Austrian woman employed at the embassy. When she became pregnant, Sadullah grew despondent, apparently at the impending scandal. On 19 January 1891 he took his own life, by gas asphyxiation, in the embassy. His body was returned to Istanbul via the *Orient Express* for the elaborate state funeral organized for the Pasha's remains. Given the controversial nature of his death, however, only after reinstatement of the Constitution in 1909 could his biography appear in print, authored by a former secretary in the Vienna embassy and plaintively entitled *Sadullah Pasha: A Cry from the Grave*.

The demise under such mysterious circumstances of the well-known figure spawnted a barrage of articles in the capital's English journal of the day, which of course was not apprised of the real circumstances of his death:

SADOULLAH PASHA

—

Following the news which came yesterday morning by telegram to the effect that Sadoullah Pasha, Ottoman ambassador to Vienna, was slightly unwell, there came a despatch in the afternoon, which says that the state of Sadoullah Pasha had changed for the worse. . . .

THE LATE SADOULLAH PASHA

—

Saadoullah Pasha, Ottoman ambassador to Vienna, whose illness we announced on Saturday, expired shortly after one o'-

clock on Sunday morning. The story of his end is sad and strange. For some time past his Excellency had suffered greatly from mental depression, accompanied by sleeplessness, for which he was under medical treatment. This condition is attributed to distress at the state of health of his wife, increased by the fact that her malady was mental and had been aggravated by their separation. Saadoullah Pasha had, under medical advice, tried several remedies for the insomnia that afflicted him, but without obtaining the desired result. Last Thursday night, worn out by want of sleep, if appears that he left his bedroom and went into an adjoining cabinet, where there was a gas-burner, set low on the wall. From this he inhaled carbureted hydrogen, which rendered him insensible, and he was found lying unconscious in the same room next morning, the gas still turned on. From this comatose condition he never rallied, and yesterday morning an hour after midnight he breathed his last.

Saadoullah Pasha had made many friends in Vienna and received many marks of sympathy in his last hours. It is not believed that he had any suicidal intention but that he resorted to the strange experiment of inhaling coal gas merely as a desperate attempt to procure the sleep which other remedies had failed to bring him.

THE LATE SAADOULLAH PASHA
—

Nasri Bey has been entrusted with the affairs of the Ottoman embassy in Vienna, until the appointment of an ambassador to succeed the late Saadoullah Pasha. Among those who paid visits of condolence at the Ottoman embassy in Vienna were: Count Kalnoky, all the Austrian and Common Ministers of the Monarchy, the Hungarian Minister, the German ambassador and the Princess Reuss; several other members of the diplomatic body, and Prince Gustav of Saxe-Weimar.

On an order of his Imperial Majesty the Sultan the remains of the late Saadoullah Pasha are to be brought to Constantinople for interment. . . . On their arrival they will, by order of his Im-

Sadullah's tomb, unique in the garden for the poignant aphorism he himself composed, on the footstone (left).

perial Majesty the Sultan, be conveyed to the mausoleum of Sultan Mahmoud, at Stamboul. . . . All the expenses connected therewith will be borne by the Sultan's Privy Purse.

THE LATE SAADOULLAH PASHA
—

As already stated, the body of the late Saadoullah Pasha arrived yesterday by the ordinary train. His Excellency Ridvan Bey, Prefect of Stamboul, several functionaries of his department, accompanied by a detachment of gendarmes and police agents, were in waiting at the railway station. The coffin was temporarily deposed in the Custom House at the station and shortly before mid-day was conveyed to the mosque of St. Sophia. The funeral cortege, which consisted of the relations of the deceased and a large number of State officials, was preceded by several Sheikhs, and was brought up in the rear by a large body of police agents and ushers from the Foreign Office. Among the State functionaries who attended were Aziz Bey, member of the council of State; . . . Ebouzzia Tevfik Effendi, director of the school of Arts and Professions; Shevki Bey, member of the Court of Cassation; Reshad Bey, sub-director of the Land Registry Office and Tahsin Bey, director of the Census Department at the Home Office. After the performance of the usual ceremony at St. Sophia, the remains of Saadoullah Pasha were taken to and deposited in the mausoleum of Sultan Mahmoud.[8]

The elegant 18th-century seaside mansion on the Asian shore of the Bosphorus that Sadullah purchased in 1872, but could only inhabit five years before he was sent abroad, still bears his name today.

HEADSTONE
He is The Eternal One, The Creator
The Fatiha
For the soul of the departed and the divinely pardoned seyyid
Sadullah Pasha
Acknowledged vizier of the Exalted Sultanate
And minister of the Sublime State
Who journeyed to the Abode of Eternity
While Ambassador at Vienna
Noble son of the late Esad Pasha
Former Governor-General of Kurdistan
Of the pure lineage of His Excellency Bünyamin Ayaşi
Polestar of learned men
May his noble grave be hallowed
1308 [1890-1891]

FOOTSTONE
Be what ye may, such is life's end on this earth
Sadullah

The shocking cause of Sadullah's demise (Islam disapproves strongly of suicide) is nowhere mentioned on his headstone, although the aphorism on the footstone could be read by those in the know, as no doubt was intended, as alluding poignantly to his tragic end.

Tevfik Pasha (Ahmed Tevfik Pasha). Ambassador, Field Marshal. D88

The future Tevfik Pasha was born in Istanbul in 1858 to a family already in government service, as his father was an administrator at the Imperial Pious Foundations offices. The young man graduated from the Military Academy in 1881 and began his career with the army, his family's sobriquet *Saraylızâde* ("Son of the Courtier") distinguishing him from others of the same name. His assignments as a lower-level officer took him around the empire from Albania to Egypt, before returning to the capital as aide-de-camp at the Court of Abdülhamid II. In this capacity Tevfik's duties introduced him to protocol: welcoming royal visitors to Yıldız Palace, accompanying the gifts presented by Abdülhamid to the Austrian Crown Prince Rudolf in 1884, or to King Carol of Romania in 1886, and attending international army maneuvers. During these years he married Nudiye Hanım, the daughter of Abdülhamid II's Senior Chamberlain Osman Zeki Bey, who had founded the Osmaniye Press publishing house and is also buried in this garden.

From here lay only a short leap for the young officer into the diplomatic world, and in 1888 Tevfik became military attaché at the Paris embassy, followed by promotion in rank and posting as ambassador to Montenegro from 1889 to 1891, then ambassador to Serbia from 1893 to 1897. Rising to Divisional General and then Field Marshal, for over ten years Marshal Tevfik Pasha served as ambassador at Berlin, from 1897 to 1908—rather confusingly following another Ahmed Tevfik Pasha who had served as ambassador to Germany from 1885 to 1895.

The overthrow of his old patron Abdülhamid II in 1909 left Marshal Saraylızâde Ahmed Tevfik Pasha high and dry, as subsequent governments proved unwilling to appoint him to further posts. The next eleven years he lived in quiet retirement in Istanbul until his death in 1920, aged only 61. The Field Marshal's wife Nudiye Hanım and daughter Pervin Hanım are buried with him here.

TOMBSTONE

God   He
Illustrious Field Marshal
Former Ambassador at Berlin
Member of the General Staff
Ahmed Tevfik Pasha
In the year 25 Rebiülahir 1338
4 Kânun-ı sâni 335 [17 January 1920]

Artists and Artisans

Abdülfettah Efendi. Engraver, Calligrapher. D92

Greek by origin, the gifted future calligrapher was born on the island of Chios in 1815. As a young boy, possibly orphaned, he was taken into the household of the grandee Husrev Pasha in Istanbul, converted to Islam, and given the name Abdülfettah. During his education the young man took to calligraphy, taking lessons from the great calligraphers of the day to master the art. When his patron Husrev Pasha became Grand Vizier of the empire in 1839, Abdülfettah found doors open to him and after working in the Grand Vizierate offices he embarked upon a series of increasingly important appointments in administration in the provinces. At the same time he furthered his training in calligraphy, in 1847 receiving a certificate from Yesarizâde Mustafa İzzet Efendi, the celebrated master who, among his many other works, calligraphed the verses over the ornamental gates into this graveyard.

Graceful yet dynamic: Abdülfettah's superb calligraphy for the headstone of Harem Supervisor Şevknihal Usta, 1860.

Returning to Istanbul from the provinces in 1858, the capable Abdülfettah took up the post of Chief Engraver at the Imperial Mint, in charge of producing coins and presentation medals, and designing templates for the paper banknotes that the Ottoman Empire now began to issue. Training stints at the mints in Vienna and Paris allowed Abdülfettah to perfect his skills.

Alongside his engraving work at the Mint, the talented artist continued to pursue his first love, calligraphy. His calligraphic oeuvre adorns a wide range of mosques, tombs, and palaces throughout Istanbul as well as in Edirne, Bursa, Damascus, and Crete—including one example in this graveyard, the tombstone of the palace lady Şevknihal. His many services to the state saw Abdülfettah promoted to the second-highest civil rank, *Bâlâ*. From his honorary title *el-Hac*, "the Pilgrim," we know that he performed the pilgrimage to Mecca at least once.

Abdülfettah Efendi died at his seaside villa at Vaniköy, on the Asian shore of the Bosphorus, in 1896, aged approximately 81. We don't know who drew his epitaph, but whoever it was must have felt honor at designing the tombstone of such a master fellow artist.

TOMBSTONE
He is The Eternal One
The Fatiha for the noble soul of
The Hajji Abdülfettah Efendi
Chief Engraver to His Imperial Majesty
Member of the ranks of eminent High Officials of the Sublime State
Holder of the civil rank of *Bâlâ*
8 Rebiülahir 1314 [16 September 1896]

Halim Pasha. Egyptian Prince, State Councillor, Artist. C73

Son of Muhammad Ali, the Ottoman governor of Egypt who founded the royal line of khedives and kings of Egypt, Muhammad Abdülhalim was born in Cairo around 1829. As an adult he entered Ottoman state service, attaining the highest civil rank, *vizier*, in 1857. He should have inherited the khedival title according to the rules of succession in Egypt, but in 1866 his nephew, the reigning khedive Ismail, obtained Sultan Abdülaziz's approval to alter the succession so that Ismail's own son would inherit the Egyptian throne. The Sultan's acquiescence did not endear him to Halim Pasha.

Halim purchased a classic seaside villa in Istanbul, settling there, and served on various high councils of the Ottoman state, but his real love was art and he demonstrated notable skill as a painter. When he died unexpectedly on 2 June 1894, aged about 65, the capital's English newspaper marked the event in a lengthy obituary:

All those who were acquainted with Halim Pasha will learn with deep sorrow of his death, which occurred on Saturday evening at Alem-Dagh [in the countryside east of the Bosphorus] where he went about a fortnight ago for change of air. The deceased was the fourth and youngest son of Mehmed Ali Pasha, and though not more than 63 or 64 years of age was uncle of his Highness Ismail Pasha, great-uncle of the late Tewfik Pasha, and great-great-uncle of the present Khedive. Halim Pasha was a man of great intelligence and culture; he had read a great deal, and although leading a life of seclusion was well informed on all the topics of the day. He was a keen sportsman in his younger days, and was a worshipper of art in all its forms. His character was one of great truth and single-mindedness; his disposition was amiable, his temperament cheerful, his manner kind and winning, and his retired and modest life was graced by a large and open-handed beneficence.

The simplest element on Halim Pasha's exuberant tomb, far outshining the catafalques of Ottoman royalty inside the mausoleum, is the fez atop the left-hand cylinder.

His Imperial Majesty the Sultan was deeply affected by the sad news of the death of Halim Pasha. The Sovereign ordered that the remains be interred within the precincts of the mausoleum of Sultan Mahmoud II. in Stam-

boul. The body was accordingly conveyed to the residence of
the deceased at Bebek and thence on board a Shirket steamer
[the Bosphorus steamship company Şirket-i Hayriye] to
Sirkedji. There the funeral cortege was formed and proceeded
to the St. Sophia mosque where the funeral service was held. In
the cortege were the relatives of the deceased, a large number
of Ottoman and Egyptian superior functionaries, and sheikhs
and ulemas. A body of gendarmes, municipal agents, and police
agents walked in front, and another detachment brought up the
rear. After the prayers for the dead in the mosque, the body was
transferred to the mausoleum and interred. Among those who
attended the funeral were . . . the sons of the deceased: Abbas
Pasha, Mehemmed Ali Pasha, and Ibrahim Pasha; Reshid Bey,
Referendary of the Imperial Divan; Munir Bey, secretary-general of the Ministry for Foreign Affairs; Fethi Bey, deputy Grand
Master of Ceremonies of the Imperial Divan; Brigadier General
Sherif Pasha, son of the Minister for Foreign Affairs, and son-
in-law of the deceased.[9]

Halim Pasha's son Said Halim Pasha, later Grand Vizier of the Ottoman
Empire, is also buried in this garden.

TOMBSTONE
He is The Eternal One, The Creator
*For the sake of God—may His name be exalted—*the Fatiha
For the noble soul of
The late and divinely pardoned son
Of the former Governor-General of Egypt, Muhammad Ali Pasha
His Highness the Most Excellent Halim Pasha
Whose abode is Paradise, who dwells in Heaven
June 1894 of the European calendar
Zilhicce 1312 [incorrectly; correct date is Zilkade 1311]

Necib Pasha, Yesarizâde. Musician. A24

Born in 1813 to the famed calligrapher Yesarizâde Mustafa İzzet Efendi, who calligraphed the verses adorning the gates into the garden, Necib trained as a young man in service at Topkapı Palace, after which his musical talents landed him in the Imperial Corps of Music. Over time, under Sultan Abdülmecid, he rose through the ranks to command the Corps, which provided musical entertainment at Court and during parades. Discharged from the post when Abdülaziz became sultan in 1861, he worked for the Customs Administration, but returned to palace service when Abdülhamid II came to the throne in 1876, with a high posting in the Palace Chancery and his old position back as Commandant of the Imperial Corps of Music.

Necib Pasha's most famous composition is undoubtedly the *Hamidiye March*, which he composed for his new master Abdülhamid II in 1876, and which served as national anthem for the Ottoman Empire until Abdülhamid's deposition in 1909.

When Necib Pasha died in 1883, in his villa at Nişantaşı at age 70, the capital's English- language newspaper ran an obituary of the Pasha since his musical works made him well-known to the foreign community resident there:

> General Nedjib Pasha, long an influential member of the Imperial Household, died on Wednesday last of the cancerous affection of the throat which has afflicted him for many months past. Nedjib Pasha's official post was that of director of the Imperial School of Music for the training of performers in the military bands; but of late years he filled a confidential position at the Palace, being much trusted as a loyal and devoted servant of the dynasty. He was buried yesterday in the cemetery attached to the Mausoleum of Sultan Mahmoud II., with all the military honours due to his rank, and the funeral procession of officers of State and of the Imperial Household, was swelled by the students of the school over which he had presided. Nedjib Pasha entered the Palace at a very young age, and it was through his ability and intelligence that he reached the position of Chief of the Imperial Music. His death leaves unanimous regret amongst all those whose esteem and affection he had earned.[10]

TOMBSTONE
He is The Eternal One
A Fatiha for the soul of Yesarizâde Ahmed Necib Pasha
Who journeyed to the Abode of Eternity
While serving in the Imperial Palace Chancery and the Imperial Privy
Household Staff
And as one of the Noble Commandants of the Corps of Music
23 Cemaziyül'ahir 1300 [1 May 1883]

Osman Zeki Bey. Publisher, Senior Chamberlain. D82

Son of a renowned master calligrapher and grandson of an engraver, Osman Zeki was most likely born in the 1820s, probably in Istanbul. As a young man he trained with his father in calligraphy, along with receiving religious training in exegesis and in study of the hadith, during which he memorized the Koran. He married the daughter of another master calligrapher, as no doubt the two families knew each other well; both his father and father-in-law received commissions from the Imperial Family for their excellent work with the pen.

When the time came to choose a profession Osman Zeki tried his hand too at calligraphy, but soon discovered another calling where he made his mark: publishing. By the mid-1860s he had opened the Osmaniye Press (*Matbaa-ı Osmaniye*, a play on his first name, but equally readable as "The Ottoman Press," thus forming a happy allusion to the central importance of his press in Ottoman literary culture of the day) at a site near this graveyard. His family was long connected to the neighborhood since his father taught calligraphy at the Empress Mother Bezmiâlem School just behind the graveyard.

Familiar with palace circles thanks to his family's connections, Osman Zeki became close to Prince Abdülhamid, who in 1882, as Sultan, appointed him Senior Chamberlain. While retaining this post in the palace chancery, Osman Zeki opened in 1884 the new and modern plant of his publishing house.

Thanks to his palace connections, Osman Zeki received the Imperial warrant to publish the Koran—remarkable as the first-ever dispensation from the Ottoman government to print the Holy Book, and evidence of the

Sultan's great trust in his loyalty. Osman Zeki chose his own calligraphed version of the Koran to print as a lithograph. His publishing venture proved a spectacular success throughout the empire. In addition to this coup Osman Zeki expanded his publishing ventures to include government documents as well as works of literature, science, and history, along with dictionaries and grammars. Most of the publications were in Ottoman Turkish of course, but some were in Western languages. His efforts brought him great wealth, and the elegant district of Istanbul where he built mansions for himself and his children still bears his name today, Osmanbey.

When Osman Zeki died in May 1891, probably around age 70, still doubly engaged as Senior Chamberlain at the palace and manager of his publishing house, his longtime patron Abdülhamid II gave permission for his burial here in this Imperial graveyard. Quite exceptionally for this graveyard, not only the celebrated publisher but also his wife Zehra, three sons Cevad, Ömer Vasfi, and Saim, and granddaughter Gılman are all buried close to one another here, while his daughter Nudiye lies interred across the garden path, beside her husband, Tevfik Pasha. Typical of the modesty expected for females in Ottoman culture, the epitaphs upon the ladies' tombstones describe the men in their family in more depth than they do the deceased ladies themselves.

TOMBSTONE
He is The Eternal One, The Creator
Here is the tomb of
The late, divinely pardoned scholar in exegesis and hadith, and famed
calligrapher
The Hajji and Hafiz Osman Zeki Bey
Who is in need of the mercy of his God, the Pardoner
And who journeyed to the Abode of Eternity
While serving as Senior Chamberlain to His Imperial Majesty
A Fatiha for his noble soul
1308 [August 1890-August 1891]

Cabinet Ministers and Grand Viziers

Cavid Bey. Member of the Council of State, Grand Vizier's Son. C77

Only son of Halil Rifat Pasha, later Grand Vizier under Abdülhamid II, İbrahim Cavid Bey was born in today's Ruse, Bulgaria, in 1860. Following his father into government service, the young Cavid graduated from the School of Civil Service in Istanbul in 1885 and began work as secretary at various administrative offices. Thanks no doubt to his father, now Grand Vizier, in 1896 Cavid was appointed to the prestigious Council of State, with concomitant promotion to the rank of *Bâlâ*, the second highest in civil service.

However, the young man's perceived arrogance and meddling behavior began to earn him enemies, and even a reprimand from the Sultan. One such rival and enemy, by the name of Gani, along with his cohorts, attempted several times unsuccessfully to assault Cavid. In reprisal, Gani was murdered, possibly on the Grand Vizier's orders. Seeking revenge in turn, Gani's friends arranged to have Cavid shot the evening of 8 October 1899, at the Golden Horn bridge pier as he approached the steamer to return to his home in the Princes Islands. The stricken young man was carried to the small mosque at the pier, where he expired. He was 39 years of age.

The electrifying news—murder of the Grand Vizier's son—rocked the capital:

> An atrocious crime, which has thrown into mourning the family of the Grand Vizier, was perpetrated on Saturday afternoon. His Excellency Djavid Bey, son of his Highness and member of the Council of State, met with a tragic death on Galata Bridge under the following circumstances. At half-past three P.M. Djavid Bey left the Sublime Porte and drove to the bridge, intending to take the boat for Prinkipo, where he resided. . . . As Djavid Bey was going down the three steps of the gangway a man came up to him, and pointing a revolver of large calibre, fired twice. Djavid Bey turned round in a vain endeavour to escape, when the murderer shot him a third time in the back, and Djavid Bey then fell. The assassin fired a fourth shot, grazing the leg of Nassuh Bey,

who had advanced to arrest him. The murderer, throwing away his weapon, then tried to escape, but the report of the shots had brought the police to the spot, and he was arrested at once by Nassuh Bey, . . . the policeman Ali Riza, and the gendarme Abdullah. He offered some resistance, and thereupon a naval officer, Sami Bey, dealt him a blow on the head with his sword, and wounded him slightly.

At the time the murder took place the bridge and Karakeui were quite crowded, and great excitement prevailed, which did not subside until the exact nature of the event was ascertained. In the meantime, Djavid Bey was taken to a room adjoining the toll-office of the bridge and serving as a mosque. . . . He was still breathing, but the doctors at once saw that the case was hopeless, and ten minutes later Djavid Bey expired, without having uttered a word since he received his death wounds. . . .

The murderer was taken to the toll-office, and examined. . . . His replies were at first contradictory, but he ultimately confessed that he is an Albanian named Hadji Mustapha, although he stoutly denied his guilt. . . . He arrived in Constantinople on the 19th August. . . . Mustapha, whose remarkable coolness and calm are undisturbed, alleges that he came to this city in hopes of finding employment. To many of the questions put to him he declined to reply. A considerable sum was found in his possession. After this preliminary examination he was taken in a cab to the prison of Galata Serai.

The Grand Vizier was at the Porte when the murder took place. He was not at first told the whole truth, but was informed that his son was wounded. His Highness at once went to Djavid Bey's konak [villa], which he reached at the very moment the body of his deceased son was brought there. The unhappy father then understood the full extent of his misfortune, and broke down. . . .

On leaving the konak of his son the Grand Vizier returned to his residence at Nishan Tash, where Vice-Admiral Hadji Rifat Pasha and Marshal Shakir Pasha, chief of the Military Household of the Sultan, called shortly afterwards, bearing a message of condolence from his Imperial Majesty to his Highness. A little later the Sultan invited the Grand Vizier to the Palace and received him in audience to assure him of his sympathy in his affliction. In the evening his Majesty sent two civil doctors, with Marshal Zeky Pasha, Grand Master of Ordnance, to draw up another medical report.

The examination of the murderer was resumed in Pera. . . . He speaks no language but Albanian, and professes total ignorance of the murder. . . . The witnesses, however, are quite positive about his identity.[11]

The Sultan ordered his Grand Vizier's son interred in this Imperial graveyard, with burial expenses paid from the Privy Purse. Given the sensational crime, when the funeral took place the morning after the murder a huge crowd accompanied the body the short distance from the Sultan Ahmed Mosque to this graveyard.

The funeral of the late Djavid Bey took place yesterday morning. Headed by the Sheikhs and their subordinates of the Tekke of Sunbul Sinan and other monasteries in Stambul, and escorted by commissaries and orderlies of the police force, the funeral procession left the konak of the deceased in the Binbir Direk quarter, where the body had been previously conveyed, and proceeded to the mosque of Sultan Ahmed, where a large congregation awaited it. Here prayers were said, and when they were concluded, the coffin was borne to the Mausoleum of Sultan Mahmud, where, in accordance with Imperial orders, the remains of the murdered man were laid. The melancholy ceremony was attended by a vast number of persons belonging to Court and official circles.

Yesterday his Highness the Grand Vizier, on the occasion of his bereavement, received cards, messages, or visits of condolence from the members of the official hierarchy, the spiritual chiefs of the several communities, and the dragomans of the foreign Embassies and Legations.[12]

The murderer received a sentence of life imprisonment. Shaken by his son's death, Halil Rifat Pasha sought numerous times to resign his post as Grand Vizier but on each occasion Abdülhamid II refused the request. As a result the Pasha continued as Grand Vizier until his own death two years after his son's, in 1901, at which the newspaper reported, "The death of his only son, Djavid Bey, was a heavy blow to him, and he never recovered from its effects."[13]

TOMBSTONE
He is The Eternal One
The illustrious son of the merciful Chief Minister Halil Pasha
—adornment of the Grand Vizierate—
The erudite, skilled, highly accomplished and provident gentleman Cavid
—Oh! and Alas!—
A culprit merciless and cruel and wicked—Ah!—did martyr
Thus wronged, his death plunged old and young into sorrow
From earth the groan of vexation soared heavenward
O God, may the two grandsons of the Most Generous Friend
Seek intercession for the gentleman İbrahim Cavid at the Last Judgment
The compassionate reed, in sorrow and grief, pens a date at his death:
"Devoted to the Prophet's Family, Cavid departed a martyr, Ah!"
The year 1317 [1899-1900]

The epitaph is a poem that rhymes at every other line in the original. "The two grandsons of the Most Generous Friend" refers to Hassan and Hussein, grandsons of the Prophet Muhammad. The chronogram at the last line of the verse totals 1,317, the year of Cavid Bey's death in the Muslim calendar.

Derviş Pasha. Field Marshal, Governor-General, Cabinet Minister. C51

Hailing from a prominent family in Lofça (today's Lovech, Bulgaria), Derviş was born around 1816 and embarked upon a military career. Rising through the ranks, in the 1850s he served as A.D.C. to the Generalissimo of the Army, Ömer Pasha, and rose to Divisional General during the Crimean War.

Following his service in the war with Montenegro, in 1862 Derviş was promoted to Field Marshal, whereupon he also embarked upon a career in the civil service, becoming Governor-General of Yannina (in today's Greece) in 1863 as well as commander of the Fourth Army Corps. Other Governor-Generalships around the empire followed in the 1860s, at Kurdistan, Shkodra (Albania), then Bosnia and Monastir in the 1870s. In between these posts he served as commander of various army corps and on military commissions. Late 1875 found the Pasha back in the capital as Minister of Marine, 1876 as Minister of War, albeit briefly, before returning to the Balkan provinces as commander, followed in 1877 by Governor-General at Salonica, then back in the capital the next year as Chief of the Military Staff.

The prestigious appointments continued, including posting in Egypt as inspector general, A.D.C. to the Sultan at Yıldız Palace, and greatly honored

General, statesman, and Sufi, Derviş Pasha's illustrious career earned his son a princess's hand in marriage.

by Abdülhamid II as "Commander Extraordinary" in charge of all forces in the Balkan provinces. After this dizzying career Marshal Derviş Pasha retired to Istanbul, showered with decorations both domestic and foreign. As supreme gesture of the Marshal's many years of eminent service to the state, in 1889 his son Halid Pasha was given the hand in marriage of Princess Nâzıme, daughter of the late Sultan Abdülaziz and the lady Hayranıdil (both buried in the mausoleum).

Alongside his high-flying professional career, Derviş Pasha cultivated his spiritual life as a longtime member of the Nakşbendi order of Sufis. Typical of the Ottoman elite, he established a wide patronage network among members of this order as well as among other rising men throughout Ottoman society.

When the well-known Pasha died in Istanbul in 1896, around age 80, he merited a lengthy obituary in the capital's English newspaper:

> Marshal Dervish Pasha, senior marshal of the Turkish Empire, and aide-de-camp-general of the Sultan, who has been in failing health for a long time, died on Saturday in his konak at Yuksek-Kalderim, Stamboul. The deceased was born at Lescovotz, in 1816, and was therefore ninety years of age [*sic*]. He joined the army as a volunteer when still a mere boy, and soon distinguished himself by his bravery, energy, and intelligence. He was quickly promoted and held the rank of Colonel when the Crimean War broke out, and that of General of Division in 1862. In that year he was entrusted with the command of the army operating in Montenegro and was rewarded for his successful conduct of the campaign by promotion to the grade of Marshal. During the Russo-Turkish War he commanded the army occupying Batoum, and notwithstanding the weakness of the fortifications he successfully defended that town against the greatly superior Russian forces and their heavy artillery. A few years later he was sent, with the late Djevdet Pasha, to superintend the execution of reforms in Albania, and in the following year he went as Extraordinary Commissioner to Egypt. On his return to Constantinople he received the appointment of governor-general of Diarbekir, and subsequently of Salonica. In recognition of his many services the Sultan conferred upon him the title of Commander Extraordinary in Roumelia [European Turkey]. He also held for a brief period the office of Minister of War, and afterwards that of Marine. He was also for some time commander of the Imperial Guard.
>
> Besides numerous foreign decorations and the commemorative medals of all the campaigns in which he took part, Dervish Pasha was a Grand Officer of the *Medjidieh*, *Osmanieh*, *Imtiaz*, and *Iftihar*.
>
> The interment took place yesterday afternoon, the funeral

charges being defrayed by his Majesty the Sultan. The cortege left the deceased's residence at one o'clock and proceeded to the mosque of Sultan Bayazid, where the burial service was performed. Detachments of infantry, gendarmes, policemen, and municipal agents marched at the head of the procession, and were followed by sheikhs and dervishes singing hymns. At the conclusion of the religious ceremony the coffin, which was enveloped in a Turkish flag, was conveyed to Ak-Serai and interred in the courtyard of the mausoleum of Sultan Mahmoud. His Majesty the Sultan was represented at the funeral by Marshal Hakki Pasha, vice-president of the High Military Commission at the Palace, Marshal Shakir Pasha, chief of the Sultan's Military Household, and the Chamberlains Faik Bey and Loutfi Bey. The mourners also included Khalid Pasha, son-in-law of the Sultan and son of Dervish Pasha; Ahmed Pasha, second son of the deceased . . . Ismail Kemal Bey, formerly governor-general of Tripoli in Barbary . . . Youssouf Pasha, commander of the Hamidieh Regiment; . . . Brigadier-Generals Tahsin Pasha, Saadi Pasha, and Kiamil Pasha; . . . Tahir Pasha, formerly governor of Mossul; Sheikh Zafer Effendi and his sons. . . .

His Imperial Majesty, who was much pained by the loss of his old and faithful servant, sent Loutfi Bey on Saturday to express his condolence with the bereaved family.[14]

Marshal Derviş Pasha was remembered kindly after his death as "courageous, intelligent, well-spoken, experienced in battle, wealthy in riches and in good fortune."[15]

TOMBSTONE

He is The Eternal One, The Creator
A Fatiha, *for the sake of God*, for the soul of
İbrahim Derviş Pasha of Lofça
Illustrious Field Marshal and Noble Warrior
Of the Exalted Sultanate
General Commanding Officer Extraordinary
In the European Provinces

Date of his death, 10 Muharrem the Sacred,
in the year 1314 [21 June 1896]

Edib Efendi. Minister of Finance, Customs Official. E117

Born around 1832, Edib was the son of İshak Nureddin Efendi, the accountant who had converted from Judaism to Islam and risen to become Director
of Finance with the army. Edib followed his father's career path. Trained
at the Ministry of Finance, in the 1860s the young accountant served as
financial director of the provinces of Yemen, Vidin (in today's Bulgaria),
and the Danube. By 1872 he was back in the capital as Undersecretary at
the Ministry of Finance. His accounting skills brought him to the Council
of State in 1872 under Sultan Abdülaziz, followed by prestigious appointment at the palace as Superintendent of the Privy Purse.

Edib's career continued to rise in the early years of Sultan Abdülhamid's
reign, becoming President of the Court of Audit in 1877, followed in 1879
by appointment as Minister of Finance and promotion to the second-highest
civil rank, *Bâlâ*. But his heart did not seem to be in the Cabinet minister
business, and he resigned the following year, becoming Superintendent
of Customs instead. Again appointed Minister of Finance in 1882, he
requested to be excused from taking up the post, and continued his work at
the Customs office.

In 1887 Edib Efendi purchased the splendid eighteenth-century wooden
seaside villa at Üsküdar that bears his name today. However he could enjoy
it but a short while before his untimely demise on 11 April 1889, still in
office, aged around 57. The villa passed to his two sons and subsequently
fell into disrepair, but has been restored today to its original glory.

Subsequent to his death Edib Efendi was described in just the way a
financial man would choose to be remembered: "well versed in accounting,
systematic, upright, diligent."[16]

TOMBSTONE
He is The Eternal One
A Fatiha for the soul of İbrahim Edib Efendi
Who died having served nine years as Superintendent of Customs
Following his resignation as Minister of Finance

And who served as Director of Finances of the Danube and Yemen
Undersecretary at the Ministry of Finance
President of the Court of Audit and of the Civil Service Division
of the Council of State
And Director of the Imperial Land Registry Office
As well as on numerous commissions and councils
The son of İshak Nureddin Efendi
Who departed this life in 1270 [1853-1854]
While Director of Finances of the Batum Army Corps
1305 [Rumî year], 1306 [Muslim calendar year] [1888-1889]

Fethi Pasha (Ahmed Fethi Pasha). Grand Master of Artillery, Imperial
Son-in-Law. A2

Born in Istanbul in 1801-02, a few months after his father's death, to a family that hailed from the island of Rhodes, as a lad of about seven Fethi entered service as apprentice in the personal household of Mahmud II at
Topkapı Palace. Remaining at Court seventeen years, in 1826 the young
Fethi embarked upon a military career in the new army founded by Mahmud that year to replace the Janissary Corps. His excellent performance in
the 1828-29 war with Russia led to rapid promotions that brought him to
Divisional General by 1831. In 1835 the Sultan honored Fethi—known
from his family's place of origin as *Rodosî* or Rhodian Fethi—by dispatching him to Vienna as special envoy to convey felicitations to Emperor Fer-
dinand I upon ascending the Austrian throne. The next year saw his official
appointment as ambassador to the Habsburg Court.

Mahmud II further honored his former palace servant by elevating him
to the highest civil rank, *vizier*, in 1837, then raising his military rank to
Field Marshal and appointing him Governor-General of the province of
Aydın, followed the next year by posting to London as ambassador and, a
few months later, ambassador at Paris. In 1839 Fethi Pasha represented
Mahmud II at the coronation of Queen Victoria at Westminster Abbey, although as fate would have it illness forced him to miss the ceremony itself.
Events continued to move quickly for the favored Marshal, as later
that year the Sultan recalled him to Istanbul with appointment to the advisory Supreme Council, followed in January 1840 with his first Cabinet

appointment, as Minister of Commerce, under the newly enthroned Sultan Abdülmecid.

Invoking the traditional token of great Imperial favor, in 1840 Abdülmecid presented Fethi Pasha the hand in marriage of the Sultan's sister Princess Atiye. The Princess was 16 at the time (the Sultan himself was only 17) whereas the Pasha was 39, and required by the dynastic law of the Imperial House to divorce his first wife, the lady Şemsinur. The spectacular week-long wedding celebrations, which foreign ambassadors attended, constituted the social event of the year. With the Princess he had two daughters, in addition to the sons and daughters he already had by his previous wife.

In 1843 the favored Imperial Son-in-Law became President of the Supreme Council, followed in 1845 by appointment as Commandant of the Tophane Imperial Gun Foundry, or "Grand Master of Artillery" as foreigners generally called the post. The job was far more prestigious than its Ottoman name implied; ever since the Artillery Corps enabled Mahmud II to crush the rebellious Janissaries in 1826, monarchs appointed their particular confidants to the post. This position Fethi retained, with brief interruptions, for the rest of his life.

During these latter years the Pasha formed a particularly close bond with Sultan Abdülmecid, as affectionate mentor to the young ruler some twenty-two years his junior. Newspapers of the day abound with accounts of the two visiting each other, of the Pasha accompanying the Sultan on official visits around town, or of the Pasha carrying out official duties at the monarch's behest. Alongside his other work, Fethi founded the first Ottoman public museum, the army museum on the grounds of Topkapı Palace, thus contributing significantly to the establishment of modern museums in the empire. The Sultan also entrusted his good friend with purchasing furnishings and decorations for the palaces, including the newly built Dolmabahçe Palace, leading wits to dub him *Bezirgân Paşa*—Shopkeeper Pasha.[17]

Fethi's wife Princess Atiye died in 1850 of tuberculosis, aged only 26, and is interred in the main chamber of the mausoleum. She left the Pasha with their two small daughters, one of whom, Princess Seniye, was interred in the side chamber of the mausoleum at her own death in 1911.

Family lore has it that Fethi Pasha returned to his first wife after Atiye's death.[18] The renowned Pasha himself died in 1858, aged about 56. As we've noted earlier, he was only the second person to be buried in this garden— a mark of his status as Imperial Son-in-Law and close friend of the Sultan. Even *The Times* of London noted his passing, with the correspondent invoking a strong flight of fancy when speculating as to the secret of his success:

> Another important personage, the Grand Master of Artillery, Fethi Ahmed Pasha, the Sultan's brother-in-law, and most intimate confidant, is dead. He had been suffering for some time from a heart complaint which, after several crises, carried him off suddenly four days ago. His place in the Ordnance Department has been given to Mehmed Rushdi, lately at the head of the War Department, but it will take a long time before anyone else will acquire his position with the Sultan. For years the latter used to come every day to the Kiosk of Tophane [the Imperial villa at the artillery barracks] and spend his evenings in company with the Grand Master of Artillery, who in this intimate daily intercourse gained an influence over the Sultan such as no man ever had, or is likely to have. His secret consisted in never asking for anything, and in being very cautious in his suggestions.[19]

Years after his death one biographical dictionary recalled the monarch's favorite rather laconically: "Combining, as he did, knowledge and intelligence, eloquent speech, and polished manners, he did not fail to attract the Sultan's attention. He was overweight and suffered from asthma."[20]

Three months after Fethi's death, and in posthumous recognition of the Pasha's many services to the state and of the Sultan's affection for him, his son by his first marriage, Mahmud Celâleddin Pasha, received the hand in marriage of Sultan Abdülmecid's daughter, Princess Cemile. This son's life ended tragically in 1884, when he was strangled in remote exile in Arabia, having been arrested at the instance of his brother-in-law Abdülhamid II and convicted, under dubious circumstances, of complicity in the alleged murder of Sultan Abdülaziz.

Three of Fethi's sons-in-law are buried in this garden—İngiliz Said

Pasha, who married a daughter by his first wife, and Hüseyin Hüsnü Pasha and Nedim Pasha, who married the two royal daughters of his second marriage. One grandson-in-law, Kâmil Pasha, is also buried here.

Fethi Pasha's traditional seaside villa still stands at Üsküdar on the Asian side of the Bosphorus.

TOMBSTONE

God   He

There is no god but the one God, and Muhammad is the Prophet of God
The Fatiha for the noble soul
Of the late, divinely pardoned Ahmed Fethi Pasha
Who is in Need of the Mercy of his God, the Pardoner
Illustrious minister of the Exalted Sultanate
Who attained the honor of relationship by marriage to
His Imperial Majesty
And who journeyed to the Abode of Eternity
While serving as Commandant of the Imperial Gun Foundry
1 Receb 1274 [15 February 1858]

Fethi Pasha's sarcophagus is the only one in this garden inscribed on all four sides, quite in addition to the short epitaph on the cylindrical headstone. The delightfully elegant and exceedingly lengthy inscription by the calligrapher Rifat—a marble résumé, complete with dates, of the deceased's impressive career—rolls around the sarcophagus in High Ottoman prose: long phrases linked together by conjunctions, bejeweled by lofty vocabulary and grammar the average citizen of today would find impenetrable, and ornamented with clever internal rhymes, all in a display of literary virtuosity that earns the reader's admiration, as it was designed to do. "On the last day of Cemaziyül'ahir of that year [1274, so 14 February 1858]," the synopsis ends, just before the two lines that describe the Pasha's charitable works, "a Sunday evening that harbored the hour of bitterness for the numbered breaths of life, he journeyed to the Abode of Eternity, and was buried in the garden of the tomb of His Majesty the Paradise-dwelling Monarch." Intriguingly, the headstone and the sarcophagus give different dates of death for Fethi Pasha, but the conflicting dates are only one day apart.

Fevzi Bey. Manager of the Debt Administration. E127

Born probably in the 1860s, we know little of Fevzi's youth, but his qualities ensured that he married well: his bride, the lady İffet, was daughter to Galib Pasha, the eminent Governor-General and Cabinet Minister under both Abdülaziz and Abdülhamid II. Most likely Galib Pasha had been the young Fevzi's patron beforehand.

Undoubtedly it was Fevzi's illustrious marriage, alongside his own talents, that landed him his position as Senior Manager with the Ottoman Public Debt Administration, the body established in 1881 at the demand of the empire's foreign creditors to ensure payment of the huge Ottoman foreign debt. Fevzi Bey oversaw the revenue stamps issued by the O.P.D.A., mandatory on a range of everyday products in order to generate income to service the debt.

Fevzi's son Fahir contracted an even more prestigious marriage when Abdülhamid II granted him the hand of his daughter Princess Şadiye in 1910 (a match only slightly dimmed as the Princess's father had been deposed). Sadly, as Fevzi's tombstone tells us, the son predeceased the father, and was buried here. At his own death some four years later, Fevzi was buried beside his son, while at her death five decades later his daughter-in-law Princess Şadiye was interred within the mausoleum. Fevzi Bey's father-in-law Galib Pasha is also buried in this garden, nearby.

TOMBSTONE
O Visitor
The person interred here is Mustafa Fevzi Bey
Senior Manager of the Special Revenues Stamp Office
Son-in-law of the late Galib Pasha, the former Minister of
Pious Foundations
This gentleman was honorable and upright
And possessed of high moral qualities
Unable to bear the wound inflicted upon his heart
At the sudden passing of his young son, who lies next to him
He departed this life
Leaving his afflicted widow burdened with anguish
In unending sorrow and despair

A Fatiha for his soul
1344 [22 July 1925-12 July 1926]

Galib Bey. Civil Servant, Senator, Poet. Gravesite unknown.

Evidently because his grave lacks a tombstone, Galib Bey does not appear on previous lists of persons interred here. His biography in the reputable dictionary of poets, *Son Asır Türk Şairleri*, however, insists that he was interred in this garden when he died in 1915, and so he is included in this list.

Galib Bey was born in central Anatolia's Niğde province in 1853-54, the son of Şerifefendizâde Mehmed Said Efendi, a local judge. In 1869, still a teenager, he received appointment as assistant secretary in the Muş correspondence office. The next year he came to Istanbul to work in the correspondence office of the Ministry of Finance, then went on to the secretariat of the Court of Appeals in Baghdad. Over the following decades Galib received appointments as chief judicial inspector in a variety of provinces around the empire. Over time he received promotions up the civil service ladder to First Rank, First Class, the third highest rank in the bureaucracy.

His work life aside, Galib Bey was an accomplished poet, publishing rhyming verses (rich in vocabulary that would send today's citizens to the dictionary) in Ottoman newspapers in Egypt, Paris, and Monastir under the pen name Fikrî ("The Thinker"). In addition he was a member of the Masonic Lodge in Salonica, where he was living as of 1908. His Masonic brothers there included several leaders of the C.U.P., and after the Constitution was restored in 1908 and the C.U.P. came to power, he was appointed to the reconvened Senate by the C.U.P. government.

When Galib died in Istanbul 6 February 1915, aged about 61, although no pasha he was buried in this elite graveyard presumably thanks to his friends in government, leading the eminent biographer of poets İnal to put it rather unkindly years later, alluding to the celebrated line of verse by Namık Kemal: "Quite contrary to the wisdom inherent in *First below ground, as first above, is your place*, he was interred in the courtyard of the Sultan Mahmud Mausoleum, which heretofore had been set aside for great men at their deaths."[21] His wife and five sons survived him.

There is no tombstone.

Galib Pasha. Governor-General, Cabinet Minister. D93

Born in Istanbul around 1829, Galib was raised by his brother, an Egyptian merchant who placed him in school and saw to it that he learned Arabic, Persian, and French. At a tender age, probably around 1840, he began his long career at the Ministry of Finance, emerging eventually as accountant of the Imperial Army in the Crimea, member of the Board of Customs, then Chief Accountant of that Board, all while making his way up the ranks of the civil service. Branching out, in 1860 the rising Galib received appointment as Undersecretary at the War Ministry, followed by the same post back at the Finance Ministry, and then Director-General of Customs.

Now a Pasha, Galib began his highest-level government posts as Minister of Finance in 1872. There followed terms as Governor-General of provinces around the empire, in the typical rather dizzying succession, including Bursa (twice), Trabzon, Aleppo, Salonica (twice), and the Aegean Archipelago. In between these appointments he served for the second time as Minister of Finance during the tumultuous "Year of Three Sultans," 1876, the next year appointed Prefect (Mayor) of Istanbul, followed by more appointments as Governor-General in the provinces. Returning to the Imperial capital in 1891, Galib Pasha took up his longest appointment—indicative of the trust Abdülhamid II placed in him—as Minister of Pious Foundations, from 1891 to 1904, during which time he simultaneously served on the advisory Council of State.

Galib Pasha's long career in the highest ranks of government service earned him burial here.

Galib Pasha's health was not good in his latter years, and six months after retiring he died in his villa on the Asian shore of the Sea of Marmara, in 1905, aged about 76. The capital's English newspaper noted:

Ghalib Pasha, formerly Minister of the Evkaf [Pious Foundations] and Member of the Council of State, died yesterday morning in his residence at Erenkeui, after a long illness.

The funeral takes place to-day; the remains will be conveyed by a special train to Haidar Pasha [the railway station on the Asian shore of the Bosphorus], and by Imperial Order will be buried within the precincts of the Mausoleum of Sultan Mahmud. The funeral expenses have been defrayed by the Privy Purse.[22]

Some five years after his death, Galib Pasha's loyalty to the Imperial House was posthumously awarded when Abdülhamid II betrothed his daughter Princess Şadiye to the Pasha's grandson Fahir Bey (son of his daughter İffet). In the 1920s both this grandson, and his son-in-law Fevzi Bey, would be interred in this graveyard as well.

His villa, and the mosque that Galib Pasha built in 1897 in Kadıköy during his tenure at the Pious Foundations ministry, and which bears his name, still stand.

TOMBSTONE
He is The Eternal One, The Creator
Here is the spiritual resting place of the late Abdullah Galib Pasha
Who rendered worthy service in a wide range of ministries
and governorships
And as Minister of Pious Foundations for fourteen years
With his superb character and integrity
An illustrious and eminent minister and vizier of the Exalted Sultanate
For his noble soul, the Fatiha
6 Zilkade 1322 [12 January 1905]
Mehmed Zühdi [Calligrapher]

Hakkı Pasha, Arab. Governor-General, Cabinet Minister. E131

Born in 1842 in Mosul (today's northern Iraq) as the son of a Pasha native to that town, and who claimed descent from the Prophet, throughout his life this statesman was known as "Arab Hakkı" in reference to his origins, and "Emiroğlu" or "son of the emir" in reference to his father. Arab Hakkı's knowledge of Arabic as well as Turkish no doubt served him well in his career. He followed his father into government service, beginning as secretary in a government office at Damascus while still a young teenager. Thanks to his father's influence, he came to Istanbul in 1859, only 17, to work in the Protocol Office of the advisory Supreme Council.

Promotions up the ranks of the civil service, accompanied by increasingly important appointments, came Hakkı's way over the 1860s, followed in the 1870s by even higher postings around the empire as District Governor at Tripoli in Syria, San'a in Yemen, and various posts in Anatolia. Recalled to the Imperial capital, for six months in 1879-1880 Arab Hakkı Pasha served as Minister of Commerce, during which period he was also rather taxingly appointed Governor-General of Sivas province. Now followed the dizzying series of typically brief appointments to the top rank of provincial postings, Governor-General, in provinces across the empire: Ankara, Salonica, the Aegean Archipelago, Izmir, Bursa, the Hijaz, and Erzurum.

Leaving that last Governor-Generalship in 1895, Hakkı Pasha did not work again, although he was only in his 50s; probably ill health caused his retirement. He died at his seaside home in Istanbul some eight years later, on 29 January 1904, aged 61, his death and funeral meriting notice in the capital's French newspaper:

> Hadji Hakki Pasha, formerly Governor-General of the province of Erzeroum, has died in his yali at Boyadji-keuy. His obsequies took place Saturday, at the expense of the Privy Purse of the Sovereign. After the prayers for the dead, recited in the mosque of St. Sophia, the remains were transported and inhumed within the environs of the Mausoleum of Sultan Mahmoud.[23]

From his honorific title of *Hajji*, we know that Hakkı Pasha performed the pilgrimage to Mecca at least once. Quite apart from his government work and religious observations, the talented Pasha also took up the pen, publishing works of literature and history in the Arabic language.

The unusual "modern" shape of the headstone, the Ottoman script outside any traditional school of calligraphy, and the two bottom lines in Modern Turkish all lead to the conclusion that Hakkı Pasha's tombstone was added decades after his death.

TOMBSTONE

The vizier and former Governor-General of the Hijaz,
The seyyid Hajji İsmail Hakkı Pasha Emiroğlu
1258 [1842]. 1319 [1903-1904, Rumî calendar]
[In Modern Turkish script:]
Died 1903. Hajji İsmail Hakkı Pasha Emiroğlu

İbşir Mustafa Pasha. Grand Vizier. B43

During the chaotic years of the mid-seventeenth century, this Pasha's wife Princess Ayşe (sister of Sultan Mehmed IV) secured his appointment as one of the string of that monarch's Grand Viziers. However, the hapless Pasha served in the post barely seven months when he was beheaded by the Janissaries at the behest of his successor in office, in 1655. He was approximately 48 years old.

Originally buried in the tomb beside the theological school at Parmakkapı (near the Grand Bazaar), when that tomb and school were demolished in 1957 İbşir Mustafa Pasha's remains were transferred here.

There is no inscription on the tombstone.

Mazhar Pasha. Mayor, Governor-General. E121

Son of Hasib Ağa, an official in service at Topkapı Palace, Mazhar was born in Istanbul in 1834 and began his government career at age 18 as a secretary in the Grand Vizier's offices, then in the secretarial office to the Supreme Council, the advisory body to the monarch. In 1871 he was appointed head of the district of Gemlik, rising in 1872 to District Governor of Sofia (in today's Bulgaria).

In 1876 Mazhar moved up the bureaucratic ladder to become Governor-General of the newly constituted province of Nish and Sofia (straddling today's Serbia and Bulgaria)—and simultaneously raised to the topmost rank, *vizier*—followed by appointment the next year as Governor-General of Bosnia. These two appointments demonstrated the government's confidence in Mazhar Pasha's abilities, since they occurred during the Balkan crisis and war with Russia in these years.

Leaving the Bosnia post in 1878, Mazhar took up a slightly different career path as superintendent of police at Aleppo, and indeed his career was noted for his aggressive pursuit of brigands. At last he returned to the capital, as Chairman of the Refugees Commission that dealt with the large influx of Balkan Muslims into Istanbul and Anatolia following the 1877-78 war.

In 1880 the versatile Mazhar was appointed Prefect (Mayor) of the City of Istanbul, serving for ten years (another mark of Imperial favor), until chronic ill health finally forced his resignation in December 1890. He died three months later, aged 57, hailed later as "generous, noble, a wise administrator, a man of taste."[24] His lengthy obituary in the English-language newspaper of the day reflected the Pasha's renown even among the foreign residents of the capital:

DEATH OF MAZHAR PASHA

Mazhar Pasha, ex-Prefect of the City, who had been ailing for a long time past, died on Monday night at his residence in Beshik-tash. The funeral took place yesterday, being very largely attended. The procession went from the residence of the deceased to the shore whence the mourners were conveyed in boats to Sirkedji. Here the body was landed and taken to the St. Sophia mosque, where the burial service was celebrated. The remains were afterwards transferred to the mausoleum of Sultan Mahmoud and interred in a special vault there. As ordered by the Sultan the expenses of the funeral were defrayed by the Privy Purse. Among those present were: Sheikh Zafer Effendi; their Excellencies Nazim Bey, Minister of Police; Redvan Bey, Prefect of Stamboul; Djemal Pasha, commander of the gendarmerie of Constantinople. . . . In recognition of his numerous services to the State, his Excellency had been decorated with the grand cordon of the Osmanieh in brilliants, the grand cordon of the Medjidieh, and the gold and silver medals of the Imtiaz.[25]

TOMBSTONE
Every soul shall taste of death
He was Prefect of the City, truly nurturing of justice,
given to benevolence
From this world he departed with perfect sincerity and purity
I have spoken his date; bejeweled it is with grief in great measure:
"His Excellency Mazhar obeyed the command, *Return!*"
Here is the grave of the late Prefect of the City, Ahmed Mazhar Pasha
From the tongues and hearts of all brothers of the Faith, a Fatiha
19 February 1306 [3 March 1891]

The chronogram alludes to the Koran, chapter 89:28, "O soul at peace, return unto thy Lord, well-pleased, well-pleasing!" The word *bejeweled* in the previous line alerts us to count only the letters bearing dots when deciphering the chronogram. Following this instruction, we arrive at 1,308 —the year in the Muslim lunar calendar of Mazhar Pasha's death, corresponding to 1306 in the Rumî calendar and 1891 in the Western calendar. The day of 19 February is the Julian date, then in use in the Rumî calendar, corresponding to 3 March in the Gregorian calendar that prevails in most of the world today.

Mehmed Pasha, *Kıbrıslı*. Grand Vizier, Field Marshal. A1

Born to a prominent family on the island of Cyprus in 1813, the young Mehmed came to the Imperial capital for schooling thanks to his uncle, a steward at the Imperial Treasury. He spent time at Paris and London in his twenties before returning to Istanbul when Sultan Abdülmecid came to the throne in 1839, at which time he worked, with the rank of colonel, at the Imperial Gun Foundry at Tophane.

Known by the sobriquet *Kıbrıslı*, "the Cypriot," to distinguish him from others of his name, the soon-to-be Pasha saw his talents for administration

Cypriot Mehmed Pasha occupied virtually
all the highest-ranking positions in
Ottoman state and military service.

rewarded with increasingly higher posts around the empire. By 1844 he was commandant at Akka in the Levant, then Governor-General at Jerusalem, followed by Belgrade. In 1848 he was named ambassador at London, aged but 35, a post he retained two years, until the government sent him to Aleppo, in Syria, to quell the revolt that broke out there in 1850. Mission accomplished, the following year Cypriot Mehmed Pasha took the reins as commandant of the army in the Arab provinces, with promotion to the rank of Field Marshal.

Henceforth the eminent Cypriot assumed a series of high-level civil and military appointments over the 1850s—some more than once, and all rather short-lived as was the custom of the day—including Governor-General at Edirne, Admiral of the Fleet, President of the Council of Reforms, and ambassador extraordinary at St. Petersburg. In between these posts he served as Grand Vizier three times to Sultan Abdülmecid, leaving the post for the last time when the Sultan died in 1861. After this highest of civil positions the Marshal returned to the provinces as Governor-General once again at Edirne, returning to the capital in 1865 to sit on various high-level councils, culminating in his appointment as President of the influential Supreme Council.

Marshal Kıbrıslı Mehmed Pasha died in 1871, aged 58, at his Bosphorus villa, which remains in the family to this day. His last illness and death made *The Times* of London, however briefly:

Constantinople, Sept. 6. Kubrysly Mehemed Pasha remains in a precarious state. Sept. 9. Mehemet Kibrisli Pasha is dead.[26]

And the next year:

> The obituary of high personages has been unfortunately extensive in Turkey during the last 13 months. Aali Pasha, the greatest statesman of the Turkish Empire, was followed to the tomb by Mehemmed Kibrisli Pasha, another clever and patriotic functionary, who had been several times Grand Vizier.[27]

Shortly after his death his divorced wife published in Europe a sensationalist memoir of her life that appeared under the English title *Thirty Years in the Harem or, the Autobiography of Melek-Hanum, Wife of H.H. Kibrizli-Mehemet-Pasha.*

TOMBSTONE

He is The Eternal One

The Cypriot vizier has passed away

Old and young have grieved and wept

Three times he assumed the Grand Vizierate

And carried out his turns of duty

For zeal and truth and ardor was he famed

Among ministers and grandees

At length he passed from the world

May the Lord make his abode Paradise

On the stone of his tomb has been written out a date:

"To Paradise went Mehmed Pasha"

22 C. [Cemaziyül'ahir] 1288 [8 September 1871]

The epitaph consists entirely of verse that rhymes at every other line. The chronogram in the last line of the verse totals 1,288, the year of the Pasha's death in the Muslim calendar.

Mehmed Ali Bey. Mayor. E115

Son of the future Minister of Marine Moralı İbrahim Pasha, or "Morean İbrahim," from the family's origins in the Morea (today's Greece), Mehmed Ali was born about 1860 when his father was still a rising naval officer.

Mehmed Ali followed his father into government work, serving as mayor of Kadıköy, the Istanbul suburb where the family had settled on the Asian shore of the Bosphorus. His children left their mark on society. His older son, the army colonel Naci, married Princess Vicdan of Egypt. His second son, Selaheddin Ali, married the Ottoman princess Âdile and is buried beside him here. Of his two daughters, the musically gifted Melek's husband Şevket Keçeci became ambassador to Egypt and Belgium in the 1940s, while her older sister Hasene's husband Salah Cimcoz served in the Turkish parliament.[28]

At his death in 1909, Mehmed Ali Bey was laid to rest here beside his father.

TOMBSTONE
The Fatiha
Mehmed Ali Bey
Son of the former Minister of Marine
Moralı İbrahim Pasha
Died 1327 [1909]. Born 1277 [1860-1861]

Receb Pasha. Field Marshal, War Minister. C55

Born to Albanian parents in 1841-42 in Debre (today in Macedonia), in his early twenties Receb graduated from the Imperial War College and embarked upon a successful career in the military. During the 1877-78 war with Russia he served as major general, to be promoted shortly thereafter to Divisional General, and in 1884 to Field Marshal, commanding various army corps.

For the twelve years from 1896 to 1908, Marshal Receb Pasha served as military commander and governor in Tripoli of Barbary (today's Libya)—a somewhat notorious post, since that province served as a major place of banishment for those who fell afoul of Abdülhamid II. But Receb Pasha treated the exiles with consideration, turning a blind eye when they escaped to Europe. At the reinstatement of the Constitution in Summer 1908 his leniency toward Abdülhamid's foes was rewarded by the new powers that be, who summoned him back to the capital to serve as War Minister. Crowds warmly greeted Receb upon his return, but only days into his new post he suffered an attack of shortness of breath and collapsed, dead, at age 66.

The English-language newspaper obituary points out two noteworthy aspects (one traditional, the other innovative) to Receb's death and funeral: first, the surprising demise of the new national hero in the heady days of the Constitutional era triggered rumors—completely unsubstantiated—of poisoning by unnamed foes of liberty; second, his death occasioned the first-ever Ottoman application of the European practice of half-masting the national flag at important deaths.

Death of Marshal Redjeb Pasha

—

The Ottoman Nation was plunged into mourning last Sunday by the sudden death of Marshal Redjeb Pasha, who succumbed to heart disease two days after having taken up his new office of Minister of War. The Marshal, who was 55 years of age [*sic*], was a brave soldier and perhaps the most popular officer in Turkey, and his death constitutes a most serious loss to the Army and to the country in general.

As soon as the sad news became known, malevolent people were found to spread alarming rumours to the effect that the Marshal had been the victim of foul play, and an immense crowd assembled on Monday outside the Ministry of War, where a post mortem was held, to learn the truth about the gallant soldier's death. The post mortem was attended by the doctors of the several Embassies and the directors of the English, French, Italian and German hospitals. As soon as it was over, bulletins explaining the true cause of death were distributed to the impatient crowd, which dispersed reassured.

The funeral of the much-lamented Marshal, which took place on Monday afternoon, was attended by thousands and thousands of mourners including the Sheikh-ul-Islam, the sons-in-law of H.I.M. the Sultan, the Cabinet Ministers, all the superior officers of the army and the high officials of the Government.

For the first time on record Turkish flags were half masted and all the shops in the streets through which the funeral procession passed were closed.

The Late Redjeb Pasha

The story is circulating about the following curious coincidence concerning the late Redjeb Pasha, Minister of War. Redjeb Pasha was named to his post during the Arab month of Redjeb. He took possession of his post and died during the same month, and it is quite probable that he was born during this month, because according to an ancient custom the Albanians give their children the name of the month in which they came into the world.[29]

HEADSTONE

He

Visitor, here is the tranquil eternal resting place of Marshal Receb Pasha
The first War Minister in the Ottoman era of liberty
The deceased dedicated his personal life to justice and virtue
His political life to liberty in the face of despotism
His military life to service with the Ottoman Army that shall serve
As stuff of glorious legend
Every nation, in every era, takes pride in a handful of great men
Receb Pasha was one of those great men
As you cast your perceptive glance over this awe-invoking pillar
Do not forget to pay your respects
By offering a holy Fatiha
For his pure soul
Died 19 Receb 1326 [17 August 1908]
Entered the War College 1279 [1862-63]
Born 1257 [1841-42], at 5 o'clock on a Sunday

FOOTSTONE

The country and its army again assumed black robes of mourning
As a moon of unequaled enlightenment entered eclipse
I, Hakkı, recited the Ihlas thrice and spoke out his date:
"With the country's sorrow, to the next world passed Receb Pasha"

The Ihlas sura (Koran 112) is recited particularly for the dead. The chronogram in the last line of verse on the footstone totals 1,323. Heeding the poet Hakkı's clue in the preceding line, one adds 3 to this total so as to yield 1,326, the year of Receb Pasha's death in the Muslim calendar.

Rıza Pasha. Governor-General, Cabinet Minister. A9

Born around 1809 as son of a perfumer, and educated by his uncle, as a youth Rıza began an apprenticeship in the Egyptian bazaar before taking up as apprentice in the chancery at Topkapı Palace in the reign of Mahmud II. His talents came to light and lifted him through the ranks eventually to become Senior Chamberlain to the monarch. When Mahmud's son Abdülmecid ascended the throne in 1839, he appointed Rıza, now holder of the highest civil rank and hence a Pasha, as head of his chancery at Topkapı Palace. All this by age 30.

In 1841 the rising bureaucrat broadened his career with postings in the provinces, beginning with Governor-General at Bursa, but by 1843 he was back in the capital as Minister of War. This would be the first of eight appointments to that position (nine, according to his tombstone, six according to his obituary) over Rıza Pasha's long career, interspersed with brilliant appointments in the top ranks of the Ottoman bureaucracy as Minister of other Cabinet posts and Governor-General of various provinces. Mere recitation of his posts is dizzying indeed, for alongside the multiple appointments as Minister of War (including during the Crimean War of the 1850s), Rıza Pasha's posts over the 1850s, 1860s, and early 1870s included, chronologically: Minister of Commerce (twice), Governor-General of Salonica province, Admiral of the Fleet, Commandant of the Imperial Gun Foundry (three times), Governor-General at Aleppo, then at Izmir, then at Konya, and Minister of Marine (four times), in addition to serving more than once on the Supreme Council that advised the Sultan. As peerless token of Rıza's high standing in Imperial favor, in 1861 Sultan Abdülmecid gave the hand of his widowed teenage daughter Princess Münire in marriage to Rıza's son İbrahim Pasha.

Filling what must have seemed the only job he hadn't done, in March 1877 Rıza Pasha served as senator in the first Ottoman Parliament. When he died in November that year, aged about 68, the capital's English newspaper paid somewhat combative tribute to the man it saw as a quaint relic in the much-changed Ottoman world of the later nineteenth century:

The once prominent figure in Turkish political life, Riza Pasha, who died on Friday last at about 70 years of age, almost a nonentity, at his residence in Kadikeui, was one of the few remaining links attaching the Turkey of the present to the Turkey of the past, —men whose early lives wore a romance, and who rose from nothing to power, fame, and great riches. A little Arab slave boy, brought from Egypt in the early years of the present century by a high functionary of the Turkish palace, and fairly educated by his master as Turkish education then went, he attracted the attention of Sultan Mahmoud, the father of Abdul-Medjid and of the late Sultan Abdul-Aziz, and grandfather of the present Sultan, —the famous Sultan Mahmoud, who crushed the Janissaries, and was in his way, one of "the world's workers." Young Riza's career up fortune's ladder was thereafter rapid, for to good luck he added good guidance, and was a shrewd and capable as well as a favoured man. He was not only a supple courtier, by who knows what peculiar paths, as one in a Turkish palace bred and well mured in all its ways, but an intelligent discerner and a hard-worker—never, under the mask of his quiet and silky manners, losing sight of the main chance. Palace Chamberlain under Sultan Mahmoud, he became Master of the Imperial Household under Abdul-Medjid, and afterwards figured in a military capacity and became commander of the Imperial Guard. His subsequent career from 1840 to the time of the Crimean War was one round of provincial governor-generalships in those vanished and halcyon days when to be vali of a Turkish province was the readiest way of acting upon Iago's advice and "putting money in thy purse." When, at later period, that Andrew Marvell of Turkish public life, Ahmet Vefyk Pasha, became governor-general of Broussa, deep was the feud which arose between him and Riza Pasha, because he dared to bluntly intimate that the ex-vali had derived more from the province than he could justify, and demanded . . . that he "should render his accounts."

Thirty-five years ago, in 1842, Riza Pasha was first appointed Minister of War; but he became a European personage when he filled the same high office during the Crimean War, in the latter part of which, after the disaster at Sinope, he was also appointed Minister of Marine. It is on record, and the matter was referred to in recent debates in the British Parliament, that Sir Henry Bulwer, when he succeeded Lord Stratford de Redcliffe as British ambassador at Constantinople, took occasion to send home a despatch animadverting in strong terms upon the financial character of Riza Pasha's administration. Be that as it may; —however he may have benefited himself, or however others may have benefited through him, —and countless are the fortunes which were made at that time, several of which have since vanished into thin air, —certain it is that, in that great historic crisis, Riza Pasha was a most capable and energetic Minister; and, side by side with the English, French, and Sardinian troops before Sebastopol, in Omer Pasha's expedition to Mingrelia, in the Turkish naval operations in the Black Sea, he caused the Turkish troops and the Turkish fleet to be well-equipped, well-provided, and to make their mark. He himself was a man of mark; having been, in all, six times Minister of War, thrice Minister of Marine, and thrice Grand Master of Artillery. He was head of the War Office at several critical periods of Turkish history, —after the Hungarian insurrection, when the refuge given by Turkey to Kossuth and his co-fugitives caused a European commotion—during the Crimean war—during the Syrian massacres, and European occupation—during the insurrection in Crete. On State occasions, his breast bore not only the highest Turkish Orders of the Osmanié and the Medjidié, and the Persian Order of the Lion and Sun, but the Order of the Bath [British] and the Legion of Honour [French], of the Austrian St. Leopold, and of the Iron Crown of Italy.

Amongst statesmen, as among ordinary men, the older gradually gives way to the younger race, and of late years Riza Pasha has not been so prominent a public figure as he was of yore, though he was more or less in harness to the last, having died a senator and a member of the Imperial Divan as Minister without portfolio.

For some time past, Riza Pasha has suffered from that most insidious and debilitating of maladies, disease of the heart, which at length carried him off, at the sufficiently ripe old age, however, of about 70. He died in the well-known mansion at Kadikeui, where he has lived for long years past, —overlooking the Bosphorus and the Sea of Marmora, and the minarets and domes of Stamboul. Riza Pasha has left several children, one of his sons being connected by marriage with the Imperial Family. He always exercised great influence—at any rate, until the present Sultan's time—at the Palace, both amongst the male and female inmates of its gilded saloons. He has enjoyed the reputation of being one of the richest men in Turkey ; like many men of his stamp, he was not ostentatious in point of charity, and has endured many reproaches on that score; but he is understood to have done many quiet acts of good-hearted benevolence, and to have lent a helping hand to many necessitous families, in an unobtrusive but not less effectual way. A man of middle height and unpretending appearance, scarcely looking all his age, with a quiet thoughtful face lit up by pensive but penetrating eyes, —a stranger would scarcely have recognised, at the first blush, in the plain Turkish gentleman who every day, in the fine weather, walked down from his house on the seashore to the tree-shaded avenue at Moda Point, looking over the rippling bay to the Fanaraki lighthouse, and tranquilly smoked his tchibouque [tobacco pipe] there, the once famous Riza Pasha, —the celebrated Turkish Seraskier [War Minister] of the time of the Crimean War. He was one of the *suaviter in modo, fortiter in re* [gentle in manner, resolute in execution]; rich in Turkish and Arabic, but speaking no European language, though understanding a little French; great in experience, great in knowledge of men and events; sought for and sagacious in council, —a memorable Turkish magnate of days fading into history who has gone.[30]

Posthumously, an Ottoman biographer remembered Rıza far more succinctly as "intelligent, quick to comprehend, of moderate education, a friend to the indigent, wealthy."[31]

TOMBSTONE
He is The Eternal One, The Creator
A Fatiha for the soul of the late, divinely pardoned Hasan Rıza Pasha
And for the souls of all people of the Faith
Who served nine times in the illustrious post of Minister of War
And who took leave of the transitory world while a member of the Senate
17 Zilkade 1294 [23 November 1877]
Calligrapher Şevki

Safvet Pasha. Ambassador, Cabinet Minister, Grand Vizier. A7

Named Mehmed Esad at his birth in Istanbul in 1815 to a family in government work, the future Grand Vizier embarked on his illustrious career

in service to four sultans by taking up an apprenticeship in the offices of the Imperial Council at age 15. Here he was given the name Safvet, perhaps to distinguish him from others of his same original name. Transferring the following year, 1831, to the government's Translation Bureau, Safvet learned enough French to assume oversight in 1839 of the French edition of the government's official press organ, *Takvim-i Vekayi* ("Calendar of Events"), rising the next year to become translator to the Imperial Council.

Safvet's career blossomed in 1842 with the first of his postings to the provinces, as inspector at Wallachia (today's Romania), followed three years later by appointment back in Istanbul as secretary at the Foreign Office, then in 1855

Occupant of the highest posts in state service, congenial Safvet Pasha won the affection of the British ambassador.

as member of the Supreme Council of Reforms and undersecretary at the Foreign Office, followed in 1856 as undersecretary at the Sublime Porte, all during the reign of Sultan Abdülmecid.

For the remainder of his career Safvet Pasha filled a bewildering range of top-ranking posts, some of them several times over, which even he must have been hard-pressed to recall chronologically in later years. Quite apart from his travels to Europe on government business on numerous occasions, Safvet Pasha served, under Sultan Abdülaziz in the 1860s and 1870s, as Minister of Commerce, member of the Supreme Council, ambassador to Paris, Minister of Public Instruction, member (and then President) of the Council of State, Foreign Minister, and Minister of Justice.

The new sultan Abdülhamid II in 1877 named him Minister of Public Works, then in February 1878 Foreign Minister (for the fourth time). During this tenure Safvet Pasha signed the Treaty of San Stefano that ended the lost war with Russia and would have effectively expelled the Ottoman state from nearly all of Europe, had the European powers not modified it. In June that year Abdülhamid II brought the Pasha to the copestone of his career with appointment as Grand Vizier, if only briefly, for the Sultan found him dilatory (in the British ambassador's opinion).

By December 1878 Safvet Pasha was back in Paris as ambassador, but only for six months, probably because of increasing ill health. Mid-1879 found him again in the Imperial capital as Foreign Minister yet once more, but just briefly, as he transferred to a kind of inspector-generalship. November 1882 saw him as Foreign Minister for the sixth time, but only for three days as he resigned due to failing health, taking on instead the far lighter role (probably a sinecure) of councilor to the Sultan, with the title "Inspector of Ministries."

The busy Pasha's star faded only when he died of cancer in 1883, aged 68. The international press, including *The Times* of London, noted his passing, while the local English-language newspaper's fulsome obituary on the long-serving statesman—so well-known among the foreign residents of the capital—paid tribute to him in surprisingly candid language as symbol of a passing era:

> After a long illness Safvet Pasha died early on Saturday morn-
> ing. His Highness was one of the last of the school of public

functionaries created during the reign of Sultan Mahmoud, under the regime of the great Reschid Pasha. Safvet Pasha's career although not brilliant was eminently respectable. Every office he held he filled with credit to himself and advantage to his country, and although he was often reproached in the later years of his career with lack of courage, it is probable that he might have fared worse had he been less cautious, without accomplishing more than he did. He was the contemporary of A'ali, Fuad, Kibrisli-Mehmet [also buried in this garden], Mahmoud-Nedim, and Hussein-Avni—a class of men now extinct in the Ottoman official hierarchy. . . .

In his official career Safvet Pasha was uniformly upright, and he leaves a stainless name. He was eminently conciliatory, and although apt, through a certain want of decision, to temporise, was truthful and trustworthy. In diplomacy he was respected both for his virtues and his abilities. Although an advanced liberal in his views as a politician, he was a loyal servant of the dynasty. In his private relations he was amiable, and never forgot a service rendered. His tastes and habits of life were refined, and literature was his relaxation. He was every inch a gentleman, quiet, considerate, consistent, and dignified.

Safvet Pasha was buried on Saturday afternoon with all the pomp due to his rank. From his mansion at Sheikhzadé-bashi, the coffin was taken to the Mosque of Bayazid, where a funeral service was performed, and thence to the mausoleum of Sultan Mahmoud, the Ottoman Westminster Abbey, where by Imperial order the late statesman was interred. The funeral was attended by a vast procession of Ministers and public functionaries, and by a guard of honour consisting of gendarmes and troops of the line. All honour was shown to the deceased statesman, whose life had been devoted to the service of his country and of his Sovereign, and who, although he had filled the highest offices of State for twenty years almost without intermission, had never amassed wealth, and leaves but a very modest inheritance to his numerous family.

Safvet Pasha was a knight of the [British] Order of the Star

of India, the Grand Cross of that order having been conferred
upon him for the Treaty of June 4, 1878.[32]

Writing after Safvet's death, the British ambassador to the Porte fondly
recalled the Pasha's character:

> I had for some time previous perceived that the Sultan was
> dissatisfied with Safvet. . . . When, on the occasion of the Coun-
> cil . . . Safvet sat in his normal silent manner with his hands
> joined in front of him and his eyes closed, H.M. observed, more
> than once, with some irritation, "See, even now when matters
> of so much importance are being discussed and examined he is
> asleep." It was undoubtedly true that Safvet was deserving of
> the charge made against him by the Sultan and that he was want-
> ing in the qualities required to direct the affairs of an Empire
> which was threatening to fall to pieces and which required a
> man of extraordinary and exceptional power to conduct them.
> . . . But he had, on the other hand, qualities and virtues which
> were rarely found amongst Turkish statesmen and which ren-
> dered him eminently deserving of the confidence of his sover-
> eign, which he for a long time enjoyed.
> He spoke French correctly and with fluency. . . . In manner
> he was dignified, courteous, and gentle, but he suffered from a
> nervous twitch of the muscles of his face which caused him to
> make incessant grimaces. . . . I found him honest, truthful, and
> just . . . and, at the same time, sincerely liberal and enlightened
> in his political and religious opinions. He was as much of a pa-
> triot as an Osmanli Turk of the governing class could be, and
> always endeavoured to uphold, in his quiet way, the dignity and
> independence of his country. . . . From my long and close inter-
> course with him, I came to entertain a real friendship, I may
> almost say affection, for him.[33]

TOMBSTONE
All that dwells upon the earth is perishing [Koran 55:26]
The Fatiha, *for the sake of God*
For the soul of the late and divinely pardoned
Mehmed Esad Safvet Pasha
Grand Vizier and former Foreign Minister
16 Muharrem the Sacred in the year 1301 [17 November 1883]

SARCOPHAGUS
(in rhyming verse)
Paragon of the Viziers, His Excellency Safvet Pasha
Obeyed the divine command, *"Return!"*

Serving with veracity four great monarchs
Favor and praise honored him at every instance

Like his good character, his span of years attained perfection
Possessed of excellence was he; to pronounce his name is
honorable mention indeed

The departed's death has plunged all into grief
May the Lord God gladden his soul with pardon and mercy

He had not lived to become Doyen of Viziers, and yet
Who would not grant the Chief Minister worthy of the esteem

The monarch of the age—may his days increase—enhanced his dignity
Through the lofty post of the Grand Viziership

Leaning ever toward amity and advancement
Even should his adversary rise in agitation never would he condone
injuring him

With tears of grief write out his date, Münif:
"To this world bade Safvet Pasha farewell"
1301 [1883]

The first stanza on the sarcophagus refers to Koran 89:28, "O soul at peace, return unto thy Lord, well-pleased, well-pleasing!" The chronogram in the last line of verse totals 1,301, the year of Safvet Pasha's death in the Muslim calendar.

Said Pasha, İngiliz. Cabinet Minister, Governor-General. C53

Born in Istanbul in 1830 to a family that claimed descent from the Prophet Muhammad, the young Said studied for seven years in Britain, which bequeathed him the moniker by which he was thereafter known among his compatriots, *İngiliz Said*, "English Said." Returning to the Ottoman capital in 1860, the young man took up a post in administration of the navy, then rose to the supervisory Naval Council, and appointment as Commandant of the Naval Academy. Domestically, he concluded a brilliant marriage with Güzide, daughter of Fethi Pasha, Sultan Abdülmecid's longtime favorite who is also buried in this garden. The marriage brought him a kind of connection to the Imperial Family, as his wife's brother Celâleddin had married Abdülmecid's daughter Princess Cemile and her father had married (as a second marriage) Princess Atiye, Mahmud II's daughter. The couple had five children.

Having established cordial relations with sort-of-relative-by-marriage Prince Abdülhamid, when the latter ascended the throne in 1876 English Said Pasha saw his career star rise dramatically. The new Sultan appointed him Marshal of the Palace Chancery and Minister of Marine. As an ally to Abdülhamid in gathering power to the throne, Said Pasha assisted in the dismissal and fall of the liberal Grand Vizier Midhat Pasha and the suspension of Parliament. Unnerved by the bloody Ali Suavi coup attempt in 1878, however, and likely incited by Said Pasha's enemies at Court, the suspicious Sultan quite suddenly lost his confidence in the Pasha, unjustifiably so, and precipitously dispatched him away from the palace to postings as Governor-General of various provinces around the empire, including Ankara, Kastamonu, Aleppo, and Konya. He left his last post at Konya, in 1887, entered retirement, and died in Istanbul some nine years later, aged about 66. As a mark of his esteem, however, the Sultan ordered his longtime loyal emissary interred in this Imperial graveyard.

The English newspaper of the capital ran a short funeral notice on the prominent bureaucrat, who retained his naval title all his life:

> The funeral of the late Admiral Saïd Pasha, formerly governor-general of Konieh, took place on Saturday amid a large concourse of officers of the army and navy and civil functionaries. The body was conveyed from the residence of the deceased at Sali-Bazar to the St. Sophia mosque where the funeral service took place. The remains were afterwards removed to the mausoleum of Sultan Mahmoud, within the precincts of which they were interred. The expenses of the funeral were defrayed by the Sovereign's Privy Purse.[34]

The British ambassador in the early years of Abdülhamid's reign recalled English Said Pasha fondly:

> Said Pasha was then at the head of H.M.'s military household and enjoyed his entire confidence. And he was well worthy of it, for a more loyal and honest and devoted servant H.M. had never possessed. He had studied for some years in the Royal Military College of Woolwich where he had acquired a knowledge of the English language, which he spoke and wrote with ease. . . . Although not a man of commanding abilities, he was so thoroughly trustworthy, so straight-forward, patriotic and liberal in his views, and possessed so much good and practical common sense that the Sultan could not have had a better adviser. . . . It would have been well for the Sultan if he had possessed and listened to such advisors as Said, and for Turkey if she had possessed a few more like him.[35]

Quite outside his career in government, English Said Pasha penned several books that reflected his active mind, including (in English translations of their titles) *Fundamentals of Geometry, Principles of Arithmetic,* and *The Science of Architecture.*

TOMBSTONE
Every soul shall taste of death
The Fatiha for the noble soul of His Excellency
The renowned seyyid Mehmed Said Pasha
Retired minister of the state
And most illustrious noble vizier
Formerly Governor-General at Konya
Who passed his lifetime in humaneness
Truly endowed with an excess of integrity and public spirit and fortitude
And earnestness and knowledge and virtue
Friday, 7 Ramazan 1313 [21 February 1896]
Calligrapher Hajji Ârif

Said Pasha. Ambassador, Cabinet Minister, State Councillor. D96

The illustrious diplomat Said Pasha was born at Süleymaniye, in west-central Anatolia, around 1832, son of Hüseyin, the local majordomo of Kurdish descent who later rose to Pasha rank himself and is also buried in this graveyard. Embarking upon government service as a teenager, the young Said followed a typical path that began with work in the Translation Bureau and eventually led, thanks to his talents, up the ranks to posting decades later as ambassador to Germany from 1883 to 1885, and culminated in his appointment as Foreign Minister. The latter exalted post Said Pasha occupied a remarkable ten years, from 1885 to 1895, which demonstrates the great trust Abdülhamid II placed in him, as does his appointment by the Sultan to the presidency of the prestigious Council of State for a full twelve years, from 1895 to his death on 29 October 1907.

When the eminent Pasha died in his villa in the Istanbul district of Nişantaşı, aged around 75, he was buried here just across the garden path from the tomb of his father. The capital's English newspaper ran a full obituary and funeral notice that recapped Said's lengthy career in Ottoman government service:

Death of H.E. Said Pasha
—

We deeply regret to announce the death of H.E. Said Pasha,

President of the Council of State, which occurred at nine o'clock yesterday morning at Nishan Tash.

The sad news was immediately conveyed to H.I.M. the Sultan, who was deeply grieved at the loss of his faithful servant.

His Imperial Majesty announced that he would defray the expense of the funeral and at the same time gave orders for the remains to be buried in the precincts of the Mausoleum of Sultan Mahmoud, Stamboul. The Sovereign further sent a message of condolence to the deceased's family through H.E. Nouri Pasha, Court Chamberlain.

The funeral took place yesterday afternoon and was a very impressive ceremony. The arrangements for the funeral were made by T.E. Memdouh Pasha, Prefect of the City, Shefik Pasha, Minister of Police, and Marshal Saadeddin Pasha, Military Commander of Constantinople and Commander of the First Division of the Imperial Guard.

General Fouad Pasha, A.D.C. of his Majesty, went to the Imperial Palace last evening to express his deep gratitude to the Sovereign for the honour paid to the memory of his deceased father.

Said Pasha was born in 1832 at Suleimanié. He entered the service of the Government at the age of sixteen, being first attached to the Translator's Office at the Sublime Porte and eight years later he held the important office of chief translator. He successively held the offices of president and vice-president of the Board of Commerce and in 1864 was named director of political affairs in the vilayet [province] of Syria. The following year he was named governor of the sandjak [sub-province] of Janina. In 1878 he was appointed Inspector of Anatolia and after occupying that office for a year he was summoned to Constantinople and made a member of the commission for Public Works.

In the course of the next twelve months he received the office of Governor-General of the Archipelago. In 1881 he was named Minister of the Interior and a few months later Minister for Foreign Affairs. Shortly after he was sent as Ambassador to Berlin.

A year afterwards he was again appointed Minister for Foreign Affairs and occupied that office for ten years. He was at the same time President of the Board of Health and for six years Vice-President of the Council of State. In 1894 he resigned all his functions but a year later was named Foreign Minister for the third time, and held that portfolio till he was named President of the Council of State a few months later.

Said Pasha possessed a great number of Ottoman and Foreign Orders including the Grand Cordons with star in brilliants of the *Osmanieh*, the *Medjidieh*, the *Iftihar*, and *Imtiaz*.

Among the cortege at his funeral, one noted: H.H. Said Pasha, formerly Grand Vizier, H.H. Kiamil Pasha, formerly Grand Vizier and formerly Governor-General of the province of Aydin; T.E. Tevfik Pasha, Foreign Minister; Memdouh Pasha, Interior Minister; Hashim Pasha, Minister of Public Instruction; Mehmed Pasha, son-in-law of H.I.M. the Sultan; . . . Mehmed Ali Pasha, secretary of the Grand Vizierate; Reshid Pasha, Prefect of the City; Shefik Pasha, Minister of Police; Marshal Saadeddin Pasha, Military Commander of Constantinople; . . . numerous functionaries of the War Ministry; Marshal Dr Hadji Nafiz Pasha, physician to H.I.M. the Sultan; . . . numerous magistrates and superior functionaries at the Ministry of Justice; Husni Pasha, director of the School of Medicine; Nouri Bey, Secretary-general at the Foreign Ministry, with numerous other functionaries of this department, several Councillors of State, and delegates from numerous government offices.

H.H. Prince Mirza Riza Khan, Ambassador of Persia, also attended the funeral along with his First Dragoman, Ohannes Khan. In addition, dragomans of the Foreign Missions went to the villa of the deceased and expressed their condolences to his son, Divisional General Fouad Pasha.[36]

TOMBSTONE
He is The Eternal One
The Fatiha for the soul of
Mehmed Said Pasha

Vizier of the Ottoman State
Who rendered extended service as Foreign Minister
And as President of the Council of State
Distinguished for the renown of his many acts of virtuous beneficence
23 Ramazan 1325 [30 October 1907; correct date should be
22 Ramazan, 29 October]

Said Halim Pasha. Grand Vizier, Political Theorist. C66

Scion of the khedival family that ruled Egypt, Said Halim was born in Cairo in 1866. His father, Halim Pasha (who is also buried in this graveyard), brought the family to Istanbul in 1870, where the young Said Halim finished private schooling, mastering French and English in addition to Arabic and Persian. He completed university studies in political science in Switzerland, returning to Istanbul where he began his illustrious government career when Abdülhamid II appointed him to the Council of State in 1888, then to the Governor-Generalship of the Balkan provinces in 1900. His seaside home in Istanbul became a center of culture and art.

Said Halim took up with the Young Turks, the movement opposed to what they saw as the autocratic rule of Abdülhamid II. As a result, he had to leave Istanbul in 1903, making his way to Europe where he supported the Young Turks financially and through his brilliant treatises on political reform in the Muslim world. In 1908, at the reinstatement of the Constitution, he returned to Istanbul with the other Young Turks, serving in the Senate, then as President of the Council of State in 1912, Foreign Minister, and General Secretary of the C.U.P. In 1913, the C.U.P. rewarded Said Halim Pasha's long services by installing him as Grand Vizier. His tenure in this highest political post in the empire coincided with the dramatic era of the Second Balkan War and the Ottoman entry into World War One. Still publishing his political writings, he remained as Grand Vizier throughout most of the latter war, resigning the post only in February 1917, citing poor health.

Two years later, following the end of hostilities, a special tribunal exiled Said Halim to Malta for complicity in involving the empire in the lost war. Freed in 1921, he went to Italy and sought to return to Istanbul but the government of the day refused him entry. In Rome on 6 December 1921, he was assassinated by an Armenian activist in retribution for his perceived role in the government's directives against Ottoman Armenians during the war. He was 55 years of age.

In death, Said Halim was finally allowed to return to Istanbul. Newspapers recorded the elaborate funeral that began as soon as the ship carrying

Cultured Said Halim Pasha photographed in splendor under the portrait of his illustrious ancestor Muhammad Ali Pasha, founder of the Egyptian Royal Family.

the coffin docked, a nationalist demonstration accompanying the murdered Pasha's remains uphill through a sea of mourners to burial in this Imperial graveyard next to the tomb of his father.[37]

Elaborately carved in neo-Islamic motifs and culminating in the traditional shape of a Muslim coffin, Said Halim Pasha's exceptional sarcophagus, quite modern in its day, further stands out by its complete lack of the customary epitaph describing and praising the deceased.

SARCOPHAGUS

921 [1921] Said Halim Pasha 866 [1866]

Şakir Pasha. Field Marshal, Imperial A.D.C., Cabinet Minister. F145

Descendant of a notable Georgian family at Batum, Şakir was born in that Eastern Anatolian province in 1853. He came to Istanbul after completing his primary education, through connections securing a place in the Military High School. Continuing at the Military College, the young Şakir graduated in 1876 with the rank of captain in the army. He was fortunate to be sent to Germany to complete his military training, remaining there five years.

Back in the Imperial capital in the early 1880s, Şakir took up duties as instructor at the Military School. By 1888 he was assigned to the offices of the General Staff, rising to the rank of Divisional General by 1896. In 1900 he began serving around the empire: in the Balkan provinces as commander of forces in Albania and Kosovo, then to Yemen in 1905 to suppress the rebellion there. Success in the latter task led to promotion to Field Marshal and appointment to the Military Inspections Commission back in the capital.

When the army revolt broke out in July 1908, Şakir Pasha was appointed Chief of the General Staff and Senior A.D.C. to Abdülhamid II. These palace connections did not sit well with the C.U.P. rebels who overthrew Abdülhamid in Spring 1909, and Şakir found himself demoted and exiled to the island of Mytilene in the Aegean. There he sat out the ensuing turbulent years until pardon came in early 1913, along with restoration of his rank and permission to return to Istanbul. Appointed to command the Seventh Army Corps to suppress yet another revolt in Yemen, Şakir was about to depart when he fell afoul of Enver Pasha, the new C.U.P. Minister of

War. Enver had Şakir arrested on suspicion of involvement in the assassination of Grand Vizier Mahmud Şevket Pasha in June 1913, and again Şakir was exiled, this time to the town of Gemlik on the Sea of Marmara. There he sat out World War One, returning to Istanbul only with the Ottoman surrender in November 1918 and the collapse of his old antagonists, the C.U.P.

Seemingly against all odds, Şakir's star now rose again. In early 1919, during the tumultuous era following the empire's defeat in the Great War, despite his poor health Şakir accepted appointment as Minister of Marine and then Minister of War in the Cabinet of Sultan Mehmed VI's Grand Vizier. The political situation was grim, given the occupation of the Imperial capital by Allied forces and the landing of Greek troops in Izmir with the intention of conquering Anatolia. Doubtless, Şakir's most famous deed during his short term as Minister of War was to secretly dispatch war hero Mustafa Kemal Pasha by ship to Samsun on the Black Sea in May 1919; from his base in Anatolia, Mustafa Kemal Pasha (the later Atatürk) went on, of course, to rally the Turkish army and nation against the occupiers.

Now quite ill, but convinced (according to his son's account) that sending Mustafa Kemal was the last and best duty he could render the country,[38] Şakir resigned the War Ministry that month of May 1919. He died but a few weeks later, aged 66. By outliving his old antagonists, the C.U.P. government—even if by only eight months—Şakir's tumultuous career received its final honor of burial in this Imperial/national graveyard.

TOMBSTONE
He is The Eternal One, The Creator
A Fatiha for the soul of the late
Field Marshal Şakir Pasha
Former Minister of War
Son of the Georgian Nu'man Tahir Efendi
Of the notable house of Batum
17 Haziran 1335 [17 June 1919]
Made by Kadri

Sami Pasha. Poet, author, governor-general, minister. A5

Born in 1795 to a prominent family in the Morea (today's southern Greece), Sami's father, a sheikh of the Halveti dervish order, perished in the Greek revolution of the 1820s, whereupon Sami and his family departed for the province of Egypt, which was rapidly developing at the time and offered opportunity. The young man began as secretary in the household of İbrahim Pasha, son of the Governor-General, rising to the upper echelons of the civil bureaucracy.

In 1849, in his mid-50s, Sami forsook Egyptian service for the Imperial capital, where under Sultan Abdülmecid he was soon appointed Governor-General in diverse posts around the empire including Bosnia, Trabzon, Vidin (Bulgaria), and Edirne. Returning to Istanbul, from 1857 to 1861 he was Minister of Public Instruction (the first to serve in the newly created post), serving simultaneously as Governor-General of Crete.

Shortly after Abdülaziz came to the throne in 1861, Sami Pasha resigned the Ministry and revisited Egypt, but returned to Istanbul the following year when the Sultan appointed him to the Supreme Council, the body that advised the monarch. Some months later Sami retired to his home in Istanbul, in his late 60s. But the Pasha did not sit idly in retreat; he continued to produce poetry in the traditional Ottoman style, as well as prose works, and a significant tome on philosophy. He remained active as a practicing Sufi with the Halveti dervishes.

Emerging from "retirement" after fourteen years, now in his 80s, Sami capped his long career in government with appointment to the new Ottoman Senate in 1877, but returned to retirement after the dismissal of Parliament the following year. Shortly thereafter, in 1879, in further honor to the veteran statesman, Abdülhamid II gave his younger sister Princess Mediha in marriage to Sami's son Necib, tying the family to the Imperial House it had so long served.

Sami Pasha died 24 April (or alternatively, 23 May) 1881, aged 86, and was buried in this garden where his accomplished Morean cousin Admiral İbrahim Pasha would also be buried eight years later. After his death Sami Pasha was recalled as "of medium height, rather gaunt, a gentleman of saintly appearance. He was learned, virtuous, a poet, thoughtful, eloquent, generous, and wealthy. He gathered within himself wealth in knowledge, religion, and consciousness of God, and his sons Subhi Pasha, Necib Pasha, Hasan Bey, Baki Bey, and Halim Bey are all fine men in their own right."[39]

Sami's son Subhi, the accomplished scholar who followed him in death only five years later, is buried in this graveyard as well.

TOMBSTONE

He is The Eternal One, The Creator
O Visitor endowed with life
Quit your love for ones like you
No one keeps to this world
God is enough, desire for Him eternal

Pronouncer of truth-seeking verse, the eminent Minister
Abdurrahman Sami Pasha
Whom all did admit as distinguished by spiritual manifestations
Expert in the secrets of the *Mesnevi*
Master at ornamentation in poetry and prose
Beloved of the hearts of the superior and the adept
And whom adepts agree fully capable of penning the perfections
in *Rumuzu'l-Hikem*

At the age of eighty-nine, of choice work a master
Cloaked in luminous mystery of spiritual aspect
His soul, laden with divine gifts
In obedience to the command, *"Return!"*
Attained the abode of the Illiyin
While his blessed remains, in accordance with his faithful vision
Received interment in this verdant graveyard of tranquil earth
The divinely pardoned deceased
Having earned the esteem of high and low in this world
And having attained a life and livelihood in every way joyous
Achieved contentment
From his firm faith and moral virtues it is hoped that in the
next world too
He shall receive the kind favors of the Lord of Humankind
May God extend copious mercies upon him
1298 [1881]
Calligrapher Aziz

Fittingly, Sami Pasha's epitaph begins with the first four lines of the rhyming elegy he himself composed in 1868 at the death of former Grand Vizier Fuad Pasha.[40] The remainder of the epitaph, while not in verse, sparkles with numerous internal rhymes—one of the delights of intricate Ottoman prose. *Rumuzu'l-Hikem* ("The Symbols of Inner Meanings"), Sami's work on philosophy, was published in 1870. "Return!" alludes to the Koran 89:28: "O soul at peace, return unto thy Lord, well-pleased, well-pleasing!" "Illiyin," the highest level of Paradise mentioned in the Koran, is the abode of the most righteous.

Server Pasha. Ambassador, Cabinet Minister. A29

Born in 1821, the future Server Pasha rose to the highest echelons in civil service apart from that of Grand Vizier itself. His marriage to Ayşe Sıdıka, daughter of Halil Rifat Pasha, who in a second marriage had wed Princess Saliha, Mahmud II's daughter (interred, at her death, in the mausoleum), gave Server Pasha a kind of kinship by marriage to the Imperial Family, which no doubt stood him in good stead when climbing the professional ladder.

His government career achieved its first truly prominent note in 1868 when, aged around 47, Server was appointed Prefect (Mayor) of Istanbul. Three years later, in 1871, he became Foreign Minister under Sultan Abdülaziz, followed in quick succession by rapidly rotating posts (usually lasting one to two years, and some of which he occupied more than once), each brilliant: ambassador to Paris, Minister of Public Works, President of the Council of State, Senator, Foreign Minister again in the early reign of Abdülhamid II, Justice Minister, Minister of the Interior, capping his career (as Death would decree) with a second appointment as Justice Minister, in September 1885.

When he died unexpectedly in office in 1886, aged about 65, the capital's English newspaper noted the indefatigable Minister's passing:

DEATH OF SERVER PASHA

—

We regret greatly to announce the death of H.E. Server Pasha, Minister of Justice, which occurred yesterday afternoon. His

Excellency has succumbed to the illness by which he was suddenly attacked on the eve of the day settled for his mission to
Livadia [in the Crimea, by which the Sultan annually paid respects to the Tsar]. The funeral will take place today with all the
honours due to the rank of the deceased gentleman.

Server Pasha belonged to the school of the late Aali Pasha
[former Grand Vizier], whom he accompanied to Paris in 1856
to the Congress convoked to settle the Crimean peace. . . . Returning from Paris, Server Pasha discovered a brilliant career
opening out before him. He was successively Under-Secretary
of State at the Ministry of Foreign Affairs, Minister several
times of this department, ambassador to Paris, in addition to filling with rare ability many other distinguished posts at the capital, in the interior, and abroad. Server Pasha married the
daughter of the late Halil Pasha, brother-in-law of the Sultan
Abdul-Medjid, who played a great rôle during the reign of this
monarch as during that of the late Sultan Mahmoud II, of illustrious memory.

THE FUNERAL OF SERVER PASHA

—

The mortal remains of Server Pasha were taken yesterday by
a launch from the deceased's country-house at Erenkeuy to
Sirkedji. The procession was of a very imposing character.
H.I.M. the Sultan [Abdülhamid II] was represented by H.E.
Ghazi Osman Pasha, Grand Marshal of the Palace, and by H.H.
Mahmoud Djelaleddin Pasha, his son-in-law. Nearly all the
Ministers and high State functionaries were present to render a
last tribute to their colleague and friend. The way to the Sublime
Porte was kept by a line of soldiers. A few minutes later, H.H.
the Sheik-ul-Islam presided over the funeral ceremony within
the enclosure of the mosque of St. Sofia; the cortège afterwards
proceeding to the mausoleum of Sultan Mahmoud where the
body of Server Pasha was placed beside the tomb of Subhi
Pasha, in life a close friend. The *Tarik* [Ottoman newspaper of
the day] cannot help remarking upon the strange coincidence of

the death in the same year of two statesmen fifteen years ago simultaneously created viziers of the Empire. H.I.M. the Sultan defrays the funeral expenses out of the privy purse.[41]

TOMBSTONE
He is The Eternal One
A Fatiha for the soul of
The late and divinely pardoned
Mahmud Server Pasha
Illustrious Cabinet Minister of the Exalted Sultanate
Minister of Justice and Religious Affairs
Eighth Day of Noble Ramazan in the year 1303 [10 June 1886]

Generals, Admirals, and Governors

Ahmed Eyyûb Pasha. Field Marshal. A4

Born around 1833, the future Pasha graduated from the military school in the capital in 1854 with the rank of Staff Captain and rose quickly through the hierarchy thanks to his abilities. In 1870 he was appointed Brigadier General, followed shortly by appointment as Divisional General; his distinguished dual career then took off as both leading military officer and governor of provinces throughout the empire.

From 1873 to 1875, under Sultan Abdülaziz, Ahmed Eyyûb Pasha served as governor of Yemen. In 1876, now a Field Marshal, the Pasha commanded the Ottoman forces seeking to put down rebellion in the Balkans, during which his dispatches back to the capital consistently made the newspapers. During the ensuing war with Russia in 1877-78, Ahmed Eyyûb Pasha commanded the Eastern Army Corps along the Danube. The years following the war, under Abdülhamid II, saw the Pasha commanding army corps mostly in the Balkans, where he served also as governor of Monastir (today's Bitola, in Macedonia) and then of Kosovo until his retirement in 1890.

Two years later Abdülhamid II called the Pasha out of retirement for one final, elegant mission:

Marshal Ahmed Eyyûb Pasha late in life, honored with the major Ottoman decorations. His granddaughter became the last person interred inside the mausoleum.

Marshal Ahmed Eyoub Pasha, who has been selected by the Sultan to bear the firman of investiture and the Grand Cordon of the order of the *Medjidieh* to the new Khedive of Egypt, his Highness Abbas Hilmi Pasha, embarked yesterday evening on board the yacht *Izzeddin* for Alexandria. Previously the Marshal had gone to the Sublime Porte to take leave of the Grand Vizier, and afterwards proceeded to the Palace to receive the final instructions of his Imperial Majesty the Sultan. The *Izzeddin* steamed out of the port at half-past six in the evening and passed the Dardanelles at the same hour this morning. Marshal Ahmed Pasha's suite is composed of twelve persons.

The British fleet which is now at anchor in Souda Bay has orders to return to Alexandria to salute the Sultan's messenger on this stately errand.[42]

Learning private details about Ottoman families from public sources is difficult at best, but on one sad occasion in 1891 Ahmed Eyyûb Pasha's family made the papers:

The medical commission constituted to examine the case of Dr. Kondopoulos, charged of having caused the death of the daughter of Marshal Ahmed Eyoub Pasha by an overdose of chloroform, will meet to-day and decide whether proceedings should be taken against the accused.[43]

The prominent dignitary's precipitous death in 1893, aged about 60, merited him an obituary in the capital's English-language newspaper.

Ahmed Eyoub Pasha, one of the oldest Marshals of the Empire, died on Saturday morning in his kiosk at Kizil Toprak, near Kadikeui. The Marshal, who was suffering from heart disease, was present at the Selamlik [the Sultan's Friday mosque procession] on the previous day. On Saturday morning he was taken suddenly ill soon after getting up. A physician inhabiting the neighborhood, Dr. Ibrahim Bey, was called in, but the Marshal passed away shortly after. The news of the death of Marshal Ahmed Eyoub Pasha was communicated to the Sultan, who was deeply affected by it. His Imperial Majesty transmitted his condolences to the family of the Marshal and to Ahmed Atif Pasha, member of the Superior Military Commission, and son-in-law of the deceased.

The funeral of the late Marshal took place on Saturday afternoon with great pomp. The coffin, which was wrapped in an Ottoman flag, was conveyed in a special steamer to Sirkedji, whence the mourners proceeded to the St. Sophia mosque, where the funeral service was held. The cortège was preceded by a battalion of sharpshooters with reversed rifles. Then came the sheiks and dervishes reciting prayers, the marshals, generals, and other superior officers, the relatives and friends of the deceased, and detachments of Palace ushers, gendarmes, policemen, and municipal agents. After the prayers for the dead, the body was conveyed to the Mausoleum of Sultan Mahmoud where it was interred.

Among those who attended the funeral were: The Minister of War, his Excellency Riza Pasha; the Minister of Public Works, his Excellency Tewfik Pasha; Marshal Fuad Pasha; his Excellency Redvan Pasha, Prefect of the City; the Minister of Police, his Excellency Nazim Bey . . . Kiazim Pasha, Military Commander of Constantinople; Ghalib Bey, Deputy Introducer of Ambassadors . . . Djemal Pasha, Commander of the Gendarmery. . . .

Deceased was an active, intelligent, and honest State servant, and has left traces of his good and enlightened administration wherever he has been. He possessed the Order of the *Imtiaz* with the star in brilliants, the gold and silver medals of the same decoration, and the Grand Cordons of the *Osmanieh* and the *Medjidieh*, also with the stars in brilliants.[44]

As a mark of esteem at Ahmed Eyyûb's death, Abdülhamid II took the Pasha's seven-year-old son Ali Fuad into the palace to be educated alongside his own sons. This young man eventually received the hand in marriage of Abdülhamid's daughter Princess Refia. In turn, their daughter Princess Rebia—granddaughter of both Abdülhamid II and Ahmed Eyyûb Pasha—became the last person to be interred within the mausoleum upon her own death in 1988.

Fittingly for the distinguished Field Marshal, Ahmed Eyyûb's headstone is a draped Ottoman flag complete with tassels and crescent atop the "flagpole."

TOMBSTONE
He is The Eternal One, The Creator
The Fatiha for the soul of the famed commander Ahmed Eyyûb Pasha
Who, as a most illustrious military Field Marshal
Waging all battles with consideration and shrewdness, valor and courage
Was distinguished with victory
Bowed his neck at last in surrender to the talons of death
17 Zilkade 1310 [incorrectly; should be 11 Zilkade 1310, 27 May 1893]

Ali Sâib Pasha. Field Marshal, Governor-General, Minister of War. C72

Known by the sobriquet "the Georgian," indicating his descent, Ali Sâib Pasha followed the typical Ottoman career trajectory of military officer serving also in administrative posts. He was born in the Anatolian town of Talas, near Kayseri, probably around 1820, entered the War College in Istanbul in 1840, from which he graduated, and advanced through the ranks to Divisional General by 1870. The high-ranking officer now held a seat on the Council of the Ministry of War—the administrative department of the Ottoman War Office—of which he served as President in 1871. Subsequently he returned to the field as commander of the forces at Vidin (Bulgaria) and then, in 1872, quite briefly, as commandant of the gendarmerie.

Given the tense political situation in the Balkan provinces of the empire, the mid-1870s proved momentous for Ali Sâib Pasha—and undoubtedly fatiguing, given that he was in his fifties. The year 1873 began with assignments in quick succession as Governor-General of Shkodra (Albania), then as Commandant of the Imperial Gun Foundry back in the capital, followed by elevation to the highest civil and military ranks, the latter as Field Marshal in command of the Third Army Corps. The year 1874 continued in the same vein with his appointment as Governor-General at Monastir (Macedonia)—while still Commandant of the Third Army Corps —and then Deputy Minister of War, followed in 1875 by elevation to Minister of War. The latter post lasted but eight months, with the Pasha returning to his old job as Commandant of the Imperial Gun Foundry, for only three days, then back to the Balkan provinces as

Ali Sâib Pasha received the unusual honor in 1886 of having the newest Ottoman steamship named for him.

Governor-General of Monastir and Commandant of his old Third Army Corps—this during the disastrous 1877-78 war with Russia.

After the war Ali Sâib returned to posts he had occupied before, namely Commandant of the Imperial Gun Foundry, in 1879, then Minister of War, in 1885—serving simultaneously in both. His multi-tasking talents earned him regard in foreign circles as well, for example in 1887:

> The German Emperor has conferred the Grand Cordon of the Order of the Red Eagle on his Excellency Ali Saib Pasha, the Minister of War, and Grand Master of Artillery. On Wednesday last, M. de Radowitz, the German ambassador, proceeded to the Seraskierate [War Ministry], and handed to the Minister the insignia of the decoration, and congratulated his Excellency Ali Saib Pasha, on the honour conferred upon him.[45]

The busy Pasha was still serving in the two latter appointments at his death of a heart attack on 20 August 1891, aged around 70. He was remembered as "a knowledgeable and good administrator, mild-mannered, a heroic warrior."[46] His son Sa'di Pasha—also buried in this graveyard—carried on his father's army traditions with his own service as military A.D.C. at the palace.

In 1886, during his second tenure as Minister of War, Ali Sâib Pasha erected the mosque and fountain that bear his name in his hometown of Talas. That same year the Ottoman state shipping line honored the Minister by christening its newest steamer the *Ali Sâib Pasha.*

When he died, the prominent general/statesman rated a lengthy obituary in the English newspaper of the capital:

THE DEATH OF ALI SAIB PASHA
—

The heart disease from which his Excellency Ali Saib Pasha, Minister of War, had been suffering for some time past, took a fatal issue yesterday morning. On rising his Excellency had a sudden attack, and in spite of everything that was done he passed away at about half-past ten.

The funeral took place yesterday afternoon in the presence

of a large concourse of people and of high officials and functionaries of the Empire. From the late Minister's waterside residence at Ortakeuy, the remains were transferred into a steam-launch and brought to Sirkedji. Here, the funeral procession formed and slowly took its way to the St. Sophia mosque in the following order. First came the commissioners of the municipalities and police agents, followed by a detachment of gendarmes, with arms reversed; then a number of sheikhs, chanting selections from the Holy Book. These were immediately followed by the coffin, surrounded by the relations of the deceased and high functionaries of State. At the St. Sophia mosque the usual prayers for the dead were offered. The body was then taken into the precincts of the Mausoleum of Sultan Mahmoud and buried in a private vault.

Among those present were Aarifi Pasha, president of the Council of State; the Ministers of Marine, the Interior, and Evkaf . . . Arif Pasha, military commander of Constantinople . . . General Ibrahim Pasha . . . Generals Ahmed Pasha and Ahmed Arif Pasha . . . General Eumer Pasha, chief of the Staff of the Imperial Guard . . . and many other functionaries, civil and military. His Imperial Majesty the Sultan was represented by Mehemmed Pasha Damad, aide-de-camp-general to his Majesty; General Ahmed Ali Pasha, and Colonel Talat bey. Saadi Pasha, aide-de-camp to his

Axes, pikes, spears, drum, and helmet with star and crescent: a fitting mélange for Field Marshal Ali Sâib Pasha.

Majesty, and son of the deceased, acted as chief mourner. By
order of his Majesty, the expenses of the funeral were defrayed
by the Privy Purse.

Ali Saib Pasha was a native of Talas, near Caesarea, in
Capadoccia . . . During the course of his career, his Imperial
Majesty was pleased to confer upon the deceased Minister the
decorations in brilliants of the *Osmanieh* and *Medjidieh*, the
medals in gold and silver of the *Imtiaz*, and the Cretan medal in
gold. His Excellency had also several foreign decorations.[47]

TOMBSTONE

He is The Eternal One, The Creator

My God, my God, what an inauspicious day

When—ah!—a woesome wail befell Istanbul

"Oh, what predicament is this," I asked, "what disaster?"

They answered, "Alas, Ali Sâib Pasha has passed away."

That is to say, the Minister of War, covered in glory, whom the
Emperor of the World

Held in abundant regard

One day, suddenly, entirely, disappeared from contemplation

The price for entry to the Mansion of Felicity

Is, alack, the coffin of death

Seven years he held the lofty office of commander

Glory and greatness were his, embellishing zeal was he

The rising of the light of dignity served as splint for the times

With wisdom of rectitude he managed affairs

At war valiant he was, at fêtes congenial

In battle the very shadow of the victory-dispensing sword

No feelings did he injure

His goodness of character charmed old and young

In many a work in his native land was he successful

Building mosque and fountain, constructing schools

Pleased with his service was the great Sultan

May Almighty God approve Paradise as his shelter

LOWER PORTION OF HEADSTONE
He himself departed, but his good name remained in the world
May God bless his soul for all eternity
Muhtar sighed as he penned this date
"Sâib Pasha journeyed to the fete of Naim"
1309 [1891-92]

In the last two lines, Muhtar is the poet who composed the rhyming verse, while Naim is the fourth of the eight paradises that the Koran mentions. The letters in the chronogram of the last line of verse total 1,309, the year of Ali Sâib Pasha's death in the Muslim calendar.

Alyanak Mustafa Pasha. Field Marshal, Governor-General. E100

Son of one Ahmed Pasha, this future top-ranking military officer and statesman was born around 1812 and most likely acquired the distinguishing first part of his name, *Alyanak*—"ruddy cheek"—as a youth. He began work in civil service but soon transferred to the military as a battalion secretary. Alyanak Mustafa's star rose quickly after he married the daughter of Grand Vizier Mehmed Emin Rauf Pasha—which demonstrates that his talents were already in evidence, for such an illustrious statesman to offer the young officer his daughter's hand. Promoted to Divisional General, he served long years on the Council of the Ministry of War. Raised in 1854 to Field Marshal, the newly created Alyanak Mustafa *Pasha* commanded the Batum Army Corps during the Crimean War, followed by his first appointments as Governor-General, at Aydın and then Edirne.

Other Governor-Generalships around the empire followed into the 1860s—Skopje (Macedonia), Kurdistan, and Diyarbakir—succeeded by brief tenures as commanding officer of the Fifth Army Corps in the late 1860s and as commandant of the gendarmerie. In 1871 Sultan Abdülaziz appointed the Marshal to the advisory Council of State and the Council of Military Reforms. Capping his long service in high officialdom was his tenure as Governor-General of Shkodra (Albania) from 1876 to 1878, during the Russian invasion of the Balkans, followed by his return to the Imperial capital as a member, for the second time, of the Council of the Ministry of War, and President of the latter ministry's Judicial Commission.

When the seemingly indefatigable Pasha died in that last post in 1884, aged around 70, the capital's English newspaper ran his obituary under the headline, "Death of a Veteran":

> One of the veterans of the Ottoman army, the mushir [Field Marshal] Al-Yanak Mustapha Pasha, who until lately occupied the post of honorary president of the judicial section of the Seraskierate [Ministry of War], has just died. The deceased, who was a Marshal of the Empire for more than 30 years, took an active part in the Crimean war, being then the commander-in-chief of Batoum. When peace was concluded, he was entrusted with the administration of the province of Adrianople, and, subsequently, with that of Kurdistan. Afterwards he occupied several high military commands as well as civil offices at Constantinople. His funeral took place yesterday with all the military honours due to his high rank, and amidst a great concourse of people who followed the funeral cortège from his konak [villa] at Yuksek Caldirim to the garden near the mausoleum of Sultan Mahmoud II., where most of the eminent men of the Empire are buried.[48]

TOMBSTONE
He is The Eternal One, The Creator
A Fatiha for the soul of
Alyanak Mustafa Pasha
Eminent military Field Marshal
Formerly President of the Judicial Commission
1 Muharrem the Sacred 1302 [21 October 1884]

Hüseyin Pasha. General, State Councillor. E109

Circassian by origin, born around 1815, as a very young man Hüseyin was sent (probably as a purchased slave) to the household of the governor at Tunis, who raised him and provided him an education. He entered military service and worked for several years as superintendent of schools at Tunis before setting out for the Ottoman capital. Rising through the ranks to Divisional General, Hüseyin Pasha received appointment to the Council of

State at an unknown date, probably in the 1870s. The Pasha died in Italy in 1887-1888, with his remains brought back to Istanbul for burial in this garden.

TOMBSTONE
He is The Eternal One
The Fatiha for the soul of Hüseyin Pasha
Divisional General in the Imperial Army
And commander at Tunis
Later appointed member of the Council of State
Deserving the pardon
And meriting the forgiveness and compassion
Of the Lord God
In the year 1305 [19 September 1887-7 September 1888]

Hüsnü Bey's children Ferruh and Ruhi. A6

The grave of Ferruh and Ruhi, two (presumably young) children of Hüsnü Bey, Governor-General of Kastamonu and fiduciary of the *Halk Fırkası* or "People's Party." This was the political party founded in 1923 by Mustafa Kemal (Atatürk), so these children were probably buried here around 1925, among the last interments in this garden shortly after the end of the monarchy, although we lack the details of their deaths. Their burial here symbolizes the appropriation of this formerly Imperial graveyard for burials by the nascent Turkish Republic.

There is no tombstone.

İbrahim Pasha. Admiral, Minister of Marine, Governor-General. E116

This future admiral was born in 1818 in the Morea (today's southern Greece) as son of Tatarzâde Tâhir Bey, whose name indicates the family's Tatar descent. With the Greek revolution and independence in the 1820s, the family left the Morea and secured a position for their young son İbrahim at the Imperial Shipyard at Istanbul. Henceforth he embarked upon a sailor's life, as his nautical sepulchre so eloquently attests, participating in the Crimean War and the naval action at Crete, and rising through the ranks to the top echelons of command. In 1868, aged 50, Moralı İbrahim ("Morean İbrahim"), as he was known to distinguish him from others of his name, became naval Chief of Staff. Five years later Sultan Abdülaziz appointed him Minister of Marine, honoring him with the highest civil rank, *vizier*.

After but five months as Minister, Moralı İbrahim Pasha was reassigned to the Council of State, then to Cyprus as District Governor, rising the next year, 1874, to Governor-General of the Aegean Archipelago. After leaving that post in 1877, he was appointed senator in the newly born Ottoman Parliament, followed the next year by a second turn as Minister of Marine, if only for four months, whereupon he retired at the age of 60.

When İbrahim died in his villa at Kadıköy in 1889, aged 72, the capital's English and French newspaper noted his passing:

DEATH OF AN EX-MINISTER OF MARINE
—

Ibrahim Pasha, a former Minister of Marine, died on Monday night in his residence at Kadikeui, at the age of seventy-two years. By order of the Sultan, the expenses of the funeral were defrayed from his Imperial Majesty's privy purse. The body was interred near Sultan Mahmoud's tomb. His mortal remains were transported to Sirkedji on board a steam launch, and inhumed in the vault prepared for this purpose. The funeral was very largely attended, among those present being Hassan Pasha, Minister of Marine, several high functionaries of the Ministry of Marine, Eyoub Sabri Pasha, Mehmed Pasha, commander of the Imperial fleet, Hassan Pasha of Salonica, and a large number of naval functionaries and officers.[49]

İbrahim's son Mehmed Ali and grandson Selaheddin Ali are also buried in this graveyard, alongside him. All three lie across the garden from where their distinguished Morean cousin, Sami Pasha, had been buried at his own death in 1881. İbrahim's exuberantly nautical sepulchre follows a certain model—that of another admiral, Ateş Mehmed Pasha, erected in 1865 in the graveyard at Istanbul's Ali Pasha Mosque.[50]

Delightful nautical motifs (with the epitaph inscribed onto the "sail")
make İbrahim Pasha's tomb the perfect fit for the late admiral.

TOMBSTONE

He is The Eternal One, The Everliving One
For the sake of God, the Fatiha for the soul of
İbrahim Pasha
Member of Parliament, former Minister of Marine
Son of Tâhir Bey of the Morean family well-known as the Tatarzâde
Who in the year 45 [1829-1830] embarked upon his illustrious
career in the military
And who after that time demonstrated courage and loyalty in battles
And in the other services he rendered to the Exalted Sultanate
Thereby winning the praise of his peers and equals
17 Receb 1306 [19 March 1889]

İbrahim Şükrü Pasha. Governor-General, Senator. D90

Son of Major General Süleyman Pasha, İbrahim Şükrü was born in Istanbul in 1857. After completing his education, including learning French, he began work as a secretary in various government offices, including the Council of State. By the later 1880s and through the 1890s he had begun serving as Chief Secretary in a variety of commissions and councils—the Budget Commission and the Civil Registry Commission as just two examples—earning honors and decorations along the way. One of his honors was the hand in marriage of the daughter of Halil Rifat Pasha, the prominent Grand Vizier under Abdülhamid II from 1895 to 1901; his murdered brother-in-law Cavid Bey (brother of his wife) is buried in this graveyard as well.

In 1905 İbrahim Şükrü's career advanced with appointment as Vice-Governor of the Aegean Archipelago, followed the next year with promotion to Governor-General of the province of Syria, and the highest civil rank, *vizier*. In late 1908 he was dismissed from the Syrian post, but after some three years was appointed a Senator, in 1912. He suffered a fatal stroke in his home 22 November 1918, aged 61.

At the time of his death, İbrahim Şükrü's brother Lütfi Simavi was Senior Chamberlain at the Court of Sultan Mehmed V Reşad. He described the Pasha's demise in his memoirs:

22 November 1918. I was busy with my official duties at the Imperial Palace Chancery when a telephone call came through from Rauf Ahmed Bey, son-in-law of my brother İbrahim Şükrü Pasha. He told me that my brother suffered a mild stroke while getting himself ready to go to Parliament. I was beside myself with anxiety and rushed to his house. Two hours later he died, leaving me distraught with grief. . . .

The next day we held an elaborate funeral for my dear brother. By Imperial command, he was laid to rest in the garden graveyard at the Sultan Mahmud Mausoleum. His Majesty most graciously sent the Second Chamberlain, the Chief Physician, and other palace officials to represent him at the services. A large number of ministers and senators also came to pay last respects and to take their leave of my brother.[51]

We have one other reference to the family of İbrahim Şükrü: rarely enough for Ottoman letters, it is to his daughter Fatma. At the state visit of Bulgaria's king and queen to the Ottoman capital in 1910, the young girl carried out a special task:

For the duties of translator and guide to the Queen in the palace, the Senior Chamberlain's niece Fatma (granddaughter of the former Grand Vizier Halil Rifat Pasha) and the Senior Secretary's daughter Bihin were appointed. In later years hundreds of distinguished and intellectual Turkish girls would be up to this task, and under the republic thousands, but in the preceding generation there were but few. Though still young enough to be called schoolgirls, Fatma and Bihin proved alert little ladies who spoke French and English with ease, were thoroughly versed in music, polite behavior, and etiquette, and knew how to dress elegantly and comport themselves properly.

When it was over they told us the visit had come off well. The Senior Consort carried out her duties properly, the hazinedars in the Imperial Harem rendered impeccable service, and as a result the Queen left the Imperial Harem with delightful impressions that she had not anticipated.[52]

TOMBSTONE
He is The Eternal One, The Creator
İbrahim Şükrü Pasha
Illustrious vizier of the Exalted Sultanate
Distinguished senator
Son-in-law to Halil Rifat Pasha
Son of Süleyman Pasha
The Fatiha
1334 [1918-1919]

Mahmud Hamdi Pasha, Macar. Field Marshal. C62

Born in Hungary in 1828 with the surname Freund, as a young man of 20 this future Ottoman general joined the 1848-49 Hungarian revolt against Habsburg authority. With the suppression of that revolt in 1849 he fled to the Ottoman Empire, as did quite a number of Hungarian rebels at the time. Converting to Islam and adopting the name Mahmud Hamdi, he took up service as an officer in the Ottoman army. His battle experience was soon put to good use, for as A.D.C. to the generalissimo of the Ottoman forces during the Crimean War he helped defeat his old adversaries, the Russians (who had put down the Hungarian revolution of 1848-49).

Promoted over the ensuing years in Ottoman service to Field Marshal, Mahmud Hamdi Pasha—known by the epithet *Macar*, "the Hungarian"—ran into trouble in 1876 as commander at Shkodra (in today's Albania) during the Balkan insurrections that year, when his defeat at the hand of Montenegrin troops at the Battle of Medun led to his dismissal. The irony is ripe, with the former Hungarian rebel against the Habsburg Empire assisting, years later and however unsuccessfully, in suppressing the revolt of Montenegrin rebels against the Ottoman Empire.

After this reversal, the Hungarian Pasha served on the Military Investigatory Commission before appointment to the Privy Council, the military and political leaders at Yıldız Palace who advised Abdülhamid II. As swan song to his long career in Ottoman service, from 1891 to 1895 Marshal Mahmud Hamdi Pasha, who was also known particularly in the Western press as General Freund from his original surname, commanded the Second Army Corps, at Edirne.

The Hungarian Marshal's death in 1898 at age 70 made the European newspapers, including *The Times* of London:

The death is announced of Marshal Mahmoud Hamdi Pasha, member of the High Military Commission which sits at Yildiz, and Aide-de-Camp General to the Sultan. The late Marshal, who was of Hungarian origin, came to Constantinople in 1849, and, embracing the creed of Islam, entered the Turkish army.[53]

TOMBSTONE
He is The Eternal One, The Creator
Field Marshal of the Imperial Second Army Corps
Mahmud Hamdi Pasha
Who was deeply bound to the Imperial House
And gloried in his abundant loyalty and devotion to it
The military ranks that he obtained
As high as that of Field Marshal
He earned through his jihad-embracing discharge of duty
On all fields of battle
May God gladden his soul
The Fatiha
4 August 1314 [Rumî calendar]
28 Cumadelûlâ 1316 [incorrect month; should be Rebiülevvel]
[16 August 1898]
Calligrapher [name illegible; allegedly Hüsnü Efendi[54]]

Mehmed Emin Pasha, Pepe. Field Marshal of the Gendarmerie, Governor-General. A8

Born to a poor family in the Eyüp district of Istanbul around 1771, the future Pasha began his rise to eminence thanks to training as a young protégé in the household of Grand Vizier Abdullah Hamdullah Pasha, which is probably where his speaking difficulties earned him the distinctive nickname *Pepe*, "The Stutterer." Around 1824 he began assuming managerial positions—superintendent of a barracks, then of repairs at a fortress—followed by supervisory posts at the Imperial stables. The year 1837 saw him rise to Supervisor of Market Regulations, followed in 1841, around the age of 70, by appointment as Director of Finances for the province of Bolu, then the next year as Governor-General of Bolu with the highest civil rank, *vizier*.

Advanced age notwithstanding, in 1842 Pepe Mehmed Emin Pasha sailed for what is today Libya to take up the post of Governor-General of the province of Tripoli of Barbary. Four years later he was back in the capital as Supervisor of Market Regulations again, then back to the provinces for a series of appointments as Governor-General over the 1850s and into the 1860s: among others Crete, Tırhala (in today's northern Greece), Bosnia, Yanina (Greece again), then back to Crete, and on to Damascus. Between these posts he served twice as Field Marshal of the Gendarmerie.

By this time the indefatigable Pasha was in his 90s, but still his career went on. In 1863 Sultan Abdülaziz recognized the loyal bureaucrat's talents by appointing him to the advisory Supreme Council as well as, for the third time, Field Marshal of the Gendarmerie. Sitting in his chair at the Gendarmerie headquarters in 1867, Pepe Mehmed Emin Pasha suffered what was probably a stroke, immediately fatal. He was some 96 years of age, over 100 by the Muslim calendar.

Years after his death the long-lived Pasha was lauded as "strong of constitution, hardworking, diligent, and of undiminished mental faculties despite having reached 100 years of age, so that he truly could still manage the affairs of the Gendarmerie office. He had difficulty in speaking. His good deeds touched many people,"[55] the last statement a nod to his generosity in helping several young men rise in their careers, just as he himself had been helped in his own youth. Among his sons, Pepe Salih Pasha was the first appointee to the newly created post of Prefect (Mayor) of the City of Istanbul, in 1855.

TOMBSTONE

God   He

A Fatiha for the soul of Mehmed Emin Pasha
Descendant of the Prophet, Commandant of the Gendarmerie
11 Şevval 1283 [16 February 1867]
Calligrapher Mehmed Şevki

Tevfik Pasha. Governor-General, Doyen of Viziers. C57

Born in 1815, Tevfik went by the patronymic sobriquet *Taşçızâde* ("Son of the Stonemason") to distinguish himself from others of his same name. He rose to lofty rank in 1860 with his appointment, at age 45, as Finance Minister, followed shortly by promotion to the highest civil rank, *vizier*. Subsequently, over the 1860s and 1870s, his career followed the typical bureaucratic path of one- to two-year appointments, in Tevfik's case as Governor-General in the Balkan and Anatolian provinces of Hüdavendigâr (Bursa), Rumeli (approximately today's Bulgaria), Kastamonu, and Adana.

Taşçızâde Tevfik Pasha completed his posting at Adana in 1878, returning to the capital where, after 1883, nearly 70 years of age, he served as Director of both the Civil and the Military Pension Funds. He lived two more decades, into the new century, his last years in poor health, until his death 11 June 1902, aged 88, at his home in the Kızıl Toprak district on the Asian side of the Bosphorus. By that point Tevfik bore the honorary title *Şeyhülvüzera*, "Doyen of Viziers," bestowed upon the eldest living holder of that highest civil rank in the empire.

The Doyen's passing merited mention in the capital's English newspaper:

The Late Tewfik Pasha

—

The funeral of Tewfik Pasha, late Director of the Civil and Military Pensions, took place yesterday, and was attended by the Ministers of the Evkaf [Pious Foundations], Public Works, and Finance, State Councillors Namyk Bey and Feizi Bey, Halim Bey, President of the Board of Audit, and many other State officials. The remains were removed from Kizil Toprak to Stambul, and after the service in St. Sophia, were interred in the graveyard attached to the Mausoleum of Sultan Mahmud. Detachments of infantry, gendarmery, and police were in attendance.

Tewfik Pasha was 88 years of age, and was raised to the Viziership more than forty years ago, being the senior Vizier of the Empire. He entered the State service in early youth and rose rapidly. . . . He was decorated with the *Osmanieh* in brilliants, the Grand Cordon of the *Medjidieh*, and the gold and silver *Imtiaz*.[56]

TOMBSTONE
He is The Eternal One
Mehmed Tevfik Pasha
Former Minister of Finance
Former Minister of the Civil and Military Retirement Funds
Doyen of Viziers
May God pardon his sins
The Fatiha, *for the sake of God*
Rebiülevvel 1320 [8 June-7 July 1902]
Calligrapher Ârif

National Heroes

Includes those buried here because their deaths, or their fame (or that of a family member), warranted national honor; also includes the few burials held here because the site was thought prestigious.

Ahmed Samim. Journalist. F140

Born in Prizren, Kosovo, in 1884, Ahmed Samim graduated from Robert College, the famed English-language academy in Istanbul. He found his calling as a journalist, first with the newspaper *Osmanlı* ("The Ottoman"), then with *Hilal* ("The Crescent") in 1909, and finally as editor-in-chief of *Sadâ-yı Millet* ("Voice of the Nation") in 1910. Ahmed Samim adhered to the literary school *Fecr-i Âti* ("Dawn of the New Age") that flourished in the early twentieth-century, and his published editorials vociferously opposed what he saw as the dictatorial policies of the C.U.P., the military-backed party that largely took over the government after 1908.

Despite the C.U.P.-orchestrated murder in 1909 of fellow journalist Hasan Fehmi (also buried in this garden), Samim refused to moderate his fiery anti-C.U.P. stance. The night of 9 June 1910 he was shot dead in the Bahçekapı district of Istanbul, his alleged assailant one Abdülkadir, an extremist adherent of the C.U.P. The deceased journalist was 26 years of age. He thus became the second Turkish journalist (after Hasan Fehmi) to die because of his writings.

The murder shocked the capital and led the government to honor the new martyr to liberty by interring his remains within the precincts of this national graveyard, although hastily and under heavy police escort.

The liberal press, including the capital's English newspaper, quickly led the assault on what it saw as the dangerously autocratic ways of the C.U.P.:

Turkish Journalist Murdered

—

It is with deep sorrow that we record a ghastly crime which was committed in Stamboul last night. Ahmed Samim Bey, chief editor of the *Sedai Millet* was murdered while on the way from his office to the Karakeui Bridge.

Ahmed Samim Bey left the offices of the *Sedai Millet* towards nine o'clock, accompanied by Ahmed Fazil Bey, of the *Tanine* [pro-C.U.P. newspaper]. As they passed before a bakery at Baghtché Kapou three shots were fired at Ahmed Samim Bey, who fell dead. The murderer disappeared in the darkness.

One of the bullets wounded a certain Seraphim Bedros. Both this man and Ahmed Fazil Bey declared to the police that they saw nothing of the murderer.

The body of the unfortunate journalist was removed by the police to a Mosque in the neighbourhood.

Ahmed Samim Bey was thirty years of age [*sic*]. He made excellent studies at the Lyceum of Galata Serai and Robert College and he took to journalism after the revival of the Constitution. He was an ardent supporter of the cause of liberty and he displayed remarkable courage at the time of the counter revolution.

The Late Ahmed Samim Bey

—

The funeral of Ahmed Samim Bey, chief editor of the *Sedai Millet*, who was murdered in Stamboul on Thursday night, took place yesterday. The relatives of the deceased had arranged for the funeral to take place to-day but the Court Martial decided otherwise. Towards six o'clock last evening the remains were taken from the Hilal printing establishment, whither they had been removed, and after a short service in the Mosque of St. Sophia they were buried in the precincts of the Mausoleum of Sultan Ahmed [*sic*].

The coffin was surrounded by troops and every precaution was taken to avoid disorders.

The police enquiry into the crime has so far given no result and no clue of the murderer has been found.

Cosmidi Effendi, M.P. for Constantinople and proprietor of the *Sedai Millet*, telegraphically informed the Sultan of the crime and begged to be excused from attending the fête champêtre given yesterday by His Imperial Majesty in the grounds of the Palace of Beylerbey.

The *Tanine* this morning gives expression to its deep regret at the untimely death of Ahmed Samim Bey whose political views, adds our contemporary, differed entirely from its own. The *Tanine* then asks if it is forbidden to express an opinion and if a similar fate awaits all those who for one reason or another do not share the views of the majority. The *Tanine* calls upon the Government to elucidate the crime which, it may be inferred, was perpetrated by one of Ahmed Samim Bey's political opponents. In conclusion the *Tanine* draws a comparison between Thursday night's crime and the murder last year of Hassan Fehmi Effendi, of the *Serbesti*.[57]

The Late Ahmed Samim Bey
—

The Sultan has sent a message of condolence to the widow of the late Ahmed Samim Bey, chief editor of the *Sedai Millet*. His Majesty has further given £t. 25 in favour of the deceased's children who will be educated in Government schools. . . .

Halil Bey, leader of the Union and Progress Party, is reported by the "Agence Ottomane" to have said that he considered the

murder of Ahmed Samim Bey to constitute a crime of high trea-
son against the country as it has been committed at a moment
when it is more than ever necessary to strengthen the ties uniting
Ottomans.[58]

The murder was never solved, but it served to roundly damage the
C.U.P.'s reputation and rally the opposition.

The slain journalist's fame led to the subsequent burial here of two family members: his father Mehmed Tevfik Bey, a retired Lieutenant Colonel
who died in 1919, and his grandmother Emine Hanım, who was interred
between her son and her grandson at her own death in 1921.

TOMBSTONE
The martyr
Ahmed Samim
Lies buried here
2 Cemaziyül'ahir 1328 [11 June 1910], Friday

The tombstone date apparently refers to his burial, as he died on 1
Cemaziyül'ahir. Discrepancy on the date probably stems from the fact that
since the Ottoman day began at sunset, Ahmed Samim's death occurred on
Thursday evening in the Western calendar, Friday morning in the Ottoman.

Bedreddin, Sheikh. Sufi Author and Sheikh, Rebel Leader. A40

Born around 1359 to a judge in the town of Simavna (today Kyprinos,
Greece), Bedreddin received his education (in religion, Islamic jurispru-
dence, and logic) at Edirne, Bursa, and eventually Cairo, where he took up
work as instructor in the palace of the ruling Mamluk sultan, and married
a palace concubine. While in Cairo Bedreddin came to embrace Sufism,
the more mystical expression of Islam, eventually becoming a sheikh or
leader of a Sufi convent.

In the early 1400s the now-Sheikh Bedreddin returned to Edirne, at the
time still the Ottoman capital. It was the Interregnum—the struggle for the
Ottoman throne in 1402-1413 among the sons of the deceased Sultan
Bayezid—and Bedreddin cast his lot with one of the sons, Prince Musa.

This placed him at odds with Musa's brother Mehmed, the ultimate victor in the struggle. Sheikh Bedreddin inspired a great revolt against the now-Sultan Mehmed, whom he saw as representing centralized state authority as opposed to the looser Sufi ties of Turkish nomads. Bedreddin and his comrades in arms posed a major threat to Mehmed, who sent a large force that defeated and captured him. In 1420 the rebellious Sheikh was executed and buried at Serez (today Serres, Greece).

Some 500 years later, in 1924, during the population exchange between Turkey and Greece, Muslims forced to leave Greece for Turkey brought Bedreddin's bones with them. Given at some point thereafter to Topkapı Palace Museum, which probably did not know quite what to do with them, finally in 1961 the bones were interred here.

During his lifetime, Bedreddin's highly influential writings encompassed a range of theological issues, including Sufism. His colleagues-in-rebellion advanced calls for the abolition of private property and the sharing of all goods (Bedreddin's own writings not being clear on the subject), leading some observers in later centuries to view the heterodox Bedreddin as a kind of early Socialist.

TOMBSTONE

The Fatiha for the soul of
Sheikh Bedreddin, *may his grave be hallowed*
Son of the judge at Simavna
Born in the year 760 of the Hegira (1359)
Executed at Serez in the year 820 of the Hegira (1418)
Conveyed to this site 29 November 1961

Cezmi. Grandson of Namık Kemal. A38

Born in 1896, this young gentleman stemmed from one of the most eminent families in Ottoman literary circles. His paternal grandfather was Namık Kemal, celebrated author and poet whose nationalist play *Vatan* ("Homeland") revolutionized Ottoman culture of the later nineteenth century. Cezmi's father was Ali Ekrem (1867-1937, later surname Bolayır), the distinguished author and poet in his own right who also served as secretary in the palace chancery of Abdülhamid II and as Governor-General of two provinces, and taught Ottoman literature at university in the capital. Cezmi's mother Zeyneb Celile Hanım was daughter of Kavalalı Ahmed Celâl Pasha, an aide-de-camp to Abdülhamid II.

The young man's suicide on 6 March 1917 at age 20 shook his parents deeply. He was their only son. Certainly his burial here was in deference to his grandfather's illustrious stature in late Ottoman culture.

TOMBSTONE

The Fatiha, for the sake of God
Here is the grave of
Mehmed Cezmi
Son of Ali Ekrem Bey, the son of Namık Kemal
Born in 1313 [1895-1896]
Died in 1335 [1916-1917]
Calligrapher Hamid

Erşed Bey. Civil Official. F135
Nihai Bey. Soldier. F134

These two brothers were killed by Ottoman-Greek brigands, as Erşed Bey's tombstone describes their attackers, on the Asian side of the Bosphorus in 1919, during the turmoil following the armistice that ended World War One. Their burial here reflects the evolution of this graveyard into a place of interment for men seen as martyrs, to either liberty (at the time of the Constitutional era, after 1908) or to the independence of the Turkish nation following defeat in World War One.

TOMBSTONE (LEFT)

In the Name of God, the Compassionate, the Merciful
A Fatiha for the soul of
Erşed Bey
Official in the Foreign Ministry
Who was murdered in 1919
On Kılavuz Meadow at Bostancı
By Ottoman-Greek brigands

TOMBSTONE (RIGHT)
In the Name of God, the Compassionate, the Merciful
A Fatiha for the soul of
Nihai Bey
Who was murdered in 1919
On Kılavuz Meadow at Bostancı
Along with his brother Erşed Bey

Hasan Fehmi. Journalist. A34

Born in 1874, the well-educated Hasan Fehmi graduated from the School
of Civil Service in Istanbul. Opposed to what he saw as the oppressive rule
of Abdülhamid II, when he graduated he lived for a time in France (traditional home to those fleeing Abdülhamid's rule) and Egypt, working as a
journalist. At the reintroduction of the Constitution in 1908 he returned to
Istanbul and pursued his career, notably as chief columnist for *Serbesti*
("Freedom"), the most sharply anti-C.U.P. newspaper of the day.

In his editorials Hasan Fehmi came to vocally oppose what he saw as
the dictatorial tendencies of the C.U.P., the party that largely took over the
government after the 1908 revolution. Warned several times by the more
virulent members of the C.U.P., the young journalist continued writing. At
last, an unknown assailant gunned him down as he walked with a friend
along the Galata Bridge, 6 April 1909. He was 35 years of age.

Reacting appropriately to the public shock at the crime, in one of the
last acts of his reign Abdülhamid II ordered the journalist's inhumation at
this Imperial graveyard in the shadow of the Imperial Family's tomb. The
appalling murder ensured a vast crowd at the young man's funeral, which
became a kind of political statement against the C.U.P. As the local French
newspaper reported:

> Rarely has one seen a funeral as large as that on Friday for Has-
> san Fehmi Bey, the first martyr to liberty. A dense crowd gath-
> ered in front of the offices of the *Serbesti*, around the mosque
> of St. Sophia, and in the neighbouring streets. Towards 10
> o'clock the cortege departed the offices of the *Serbesti* . . . where
> the body had been carried the previous evening.

One could see the representatives of the local and foreign press, members of various clubs, and numerous persons belonging to all faiths. Marching at the head, Marshal Fouad Pasha, the press representatives, students of the higher schools, then various persons carrying smoking incense burners, after which followed an immense crowd and the coffin covered in a silk cloth embroidered over red satin and bearing inscribed on it a verse of the Prophet relative to the martyr. Sheiks were reciting moving chants. . . .

Arriving before the Sublime Porte, the cortege was further enlarged by students of theology, mullahs, and other persons.

The large square before St. Sophia was completely filled with perhaps 20,000 persons. After the funeral ceremony the convoy departed to head in the same order toward the mausoleum of Sultan Mahmoud, where the inhumation took place with the authorization of the Sultan. Everything transpired in the most perfect order.[59]

One witness to the funeral procession was the famed novelist Halide Edib, who described it years later in her memoirs:

The political passion reached its climax . . . when Hassan Fehmy, a journalist on an opposition paper, was shot on the Galata Bridge. This was the first political murder of the new régime, and it had a very bad effect on everyone. The opposition used the funeral as a demonstration against the Unionists. From the corner of my house I saw a bier wrapped in a Persian shawl, with the Arabic verse from the Koran, "One martyr is enough for Allah," written in large letters over the coffin and a white-turbaned crowd following it like an immense daisy-field. The ominous silence gave me the impression of what it must have been like in the old days of Fatih [the Istanbul district with numerous religious schools], when thousands of theological students with their white turbans rose and broke up the reforming tendencies before these tendencies were ripe.[60]

Despite the fact that the murderer was never identified, Hasan Fehmi's death fanned the flames of outrage at the C.U.P.'s perceived trampling of the precious ideals of liberty attained only the previous summer, and contributed to the counter-revolution that broke out in the capital the following week. The crime set off a firestorm in the liberal Ottoman press opposed to the C.U.P. Said the newspaper *İkdam* two days after the young journalist's death:

> In this battle—the battle for liberty—the victor is Hasan Fehmi, he of the pure soul. Utter defeat is the fate of his opponents, for by reverting to guns in this cowardly way when they could not defeat him by the pen, they have served no purpose beyond inflicting yet another act of humiliation.
>
> Alas, though these contemptible bullets bring freedom at last to a youth who until recently spent his life in exile, has not the reinvigoration of this country hurled headlong into a vast barrier squarely blocking its path?[61]

For its part, the newspaper *Volkan* used the young man's death to further fan the flames in its edition one day before the Counter-revolution began:

> O Ottomans, do we love our nation and ourselves? If so, let us prove it. Atrocities and despotism are on the loose again, plain for all to see. Is not freedom of thought needed to put them in their place? Plain as well to see, constitutional government and liberty are also among us. If we submit to these atrocities, to that despotism—wielded by the dirty, filthy hands at Sheref Street [headquarters of the C.U.P.]—then the world will know we are but a nation of cowards, and vile insult will assail our national pride. Let us not submit! On no account should we submit to these crimes![62]

Hasan Fehmi was the first journalist in the history of the Turkish press to die for his opinions. He was also the first simple civilian, not connected to the government, laid to rest here, reflecting the transition of this Imperial graveyard into a kind of national shrine. Since his tombstone is inscribed in Latin letters and uses Gregorian dates, clearly it was erected several decades after his death to replace the original Ottoman stone, if there was one.

TOMBSTONE
A Fatiha for the soul of
The first martyr of the Turkish press
Hasan Fehmi
(1874-1909)
Chief Editor of the journal *Serbesti*
Who was martyred on the Galata Bridge
For the sake of Freedom of the Press

Kara Mustafa Pasha. Admiral, Grand Vizier. B41b

Born around 1592 in today's Albania, as a young man the future Kara Mustafa Pasha was forcibly inducted into the Janissary Corps and brought to Istanbul for training. His skill at archery earned him the sobriquet *Kemankeş*, "the Bowman," while his overall qualities assured his rise through the ranks to Grand Admiral of the Fleet and commander at the successful re-conquest of Baghdad from the Persians in 1638. Kara Mustafa's strong showing during that campaign led to his appointment as Grand Vizier under Sultan Murad IV, a political role he continued under Murad's successor İbrahim. A beneficent and competent reforming statesman, during these years Kara Mustafa Pasha also built mosques, schools, and water fountains.

The Pasha ran afoul of the palace intrigues that characterized his era, however, and was executed by strangulation at İbrahim's orders on 22 February 1644, at the age of about 52. He was buried in the tomb beside the theological school he had founded, which stood near the entrance to the Grand Bazaar until 1957. In that year the area was leveled to improve public transit access to the bazaar, and the Pasha's remains were transferred to this graveyard, as were the two graves next to his.

There is no inscription on the tombstone.

Şekip, Ali Haydar. Bank Officer, Football Team Manager. B46

Only 28 years of age at his death in 1925, Haydar served as a manager at one of the country's leading banks, as his tombstone tells us, but he is better remembered now as president of the Galatasaray Football Club in the year he died, about which his tombstone is silent. Given the prominence of the bank emblem on the stone, one wonders if the bank paid for the stone, but at any event, the use of the Latin alphabet employed on it tells us that the stone was put in place after Turkey switched to that new alphabet, in 1928.

One of the last interments here before the forty-year hiatus that ended in the 1960s, Haydar's decidedly surprising burial in this garden no doubt stems from the turmoil of the times in which he died, when monarchs were no longer deciding who would be interred at this prestigious location. One could even interpret his burial here as an opening shift in the evolving national allegiance, from sultans and pashas, to football.

TOMBSTONE
Haydar Şekip
Manager at the Istanbul İş Bankası
1896-1925

Ziya Gökalp. Sociologist, Writer. B45

A controversial intellectual and sociologist, the so-called "Father of Turkish Nationalism" Ziya was, ironically enough, born to a wealthy Kurdish (or Zaza) family in Diyarbakir, southeastern Anatolia, in 1876. Having studied Islamic philosophy alongside Arabic, Persian, and French, he came to Istanbul in 1895, enrolling in veterinary school but pursuing interests in sociology, philosophy, and revolutionary politics, which landed him in prison for some months. Abandoning veterinary studies, he engaged himself in underground political movements during the latter years of Abdülhamid II's reign, joining the C.U.P.

Following the advent of constitutional government in 1908, Ziya emerged as a strong articulator of the Turkish nationalist principles then in the air. In books, newspaper articles, and poetry, Ziya espoused "Turkishness," a strong sense of Turkish identity to replace the multi-ethnicity of

The tomb of nationalist theoretician Ziya Gökalp;
on the wall behind it, the Modern Turkish version of the Ottoman epitaph.

Ottoman society. In his famous poem *Turan*, penned in 1911, he called for strong ties with Turkic peoples across the Russian Empire, outside the traditional borders of Turkey. Significantly, he adopted the name *Gökalp*, meaning "Sky Hero" in pure Turkish unadulterated (as some would see it) by Arabic or Persian.

Serving in various government and teaching posts through 1918, at the end of World War One Ziya was exiled to Malta for his close involvement with the discredited C.U.P. government. Returning to Istanbul in 1921, he resumed his teaching, government service, and writings—toning down his calls for pan-Turkish nationalism a bit, in favor of strong Turkish nationalism within Anatolian Turkey proper—when his health began to give way. He died in Istanbul in 1924, aged only 48, almost exactly one year after the birth of the Turkish Republic. He was honored by the young Republic with burial here in this Imperial/national graveyard, ironically close to— one could even say, in the shadow of—Abdülhamid II, whose policies he had opposed in life. By coincidence, his maternal uncle Pirinççizâde Mehmed Ârif, the wealthy delegate of Diyarbakir to Parliament, is also buried in this graveyard.

The great nationalist is today undoubtedly the best-known of all those buried in the garden graveyard. His epitaph (transliterated into Modern Turkish on a plaque behind the tomb so newer generations can read it) mentions the Turkish Hearth, the nationalist organization founded in 1912, and reflects the patriotic devotion it promoted:

TOMBSTONE
The great Spiritual Guide
Ziya Gökalp lies here
The day he died became a day of national mourning
The Turkish Hearth buried his dear remains
In this earth of the Fatherland that is proud to have raised him
And laid his blessed memory to rest within its own heart
Saturday, 25 Teşrinievvel 1924 [25 October 1924]
Designer Hikmet İsmet. Made in Unkapanı by Salih Sabri and
Hüseyin Avni

Palace Staff and Courtiers

Cevher Ağa. Chief Eunuch of the Imperial Household. E111

One of two high-ranking black eunuchs in service at the Imperial palace to be buried here, Cevher Ağa's origins are not well known but he was born most likely in Ethiopia, probably around 1820. He would have been captured by slave raiders at a young age, castrated, converted to Islam, and sent to the slave markets for sale to the wealthy class, who could afford eunuchs to supervise a harem. He was purchased either directly by the Imperial palace or by a wealthy figure who presented him to the palace in order to curry favor.

What we do know for certain is that Cevher Ağa (his title *ağa* signifying his high status as an Imperial eunuch) rose through the ranks of palace eunuchs to be appointed Senior Eunuch in the household of the lady Pertevniyal, mother of then-Prince Abdülaziz. When Abdülaziz ascended the throne in 1861, Cevher Ağa retained his important post at the Court of Pertevniyal, who now figured as Empress Mother, while securing appointment as one of the eunuch equerries in the household of her son, the Sultan.

Having served thirteen years in the latter post, in 1874 Cevher Ağa received promotion by the Sultan to Imperial Hazinedar, the high-ranking supervisory post in the Privy Household of the palace. In March 1876, upon the death of his colleague Talha Ağa, who is also buried in this graveyard, Cevher received appointment as Chief Eunuch of the Imperial Household, with the grand title of the position, Constable of the Noble Abode of Felicity, and its rank as a Minister of State. His lofty post lasted barely two months, however, as the overthrow of Abdülaziz in June 1876 brought in its wake the replacement of Abdülaziz's senior palace officials by those of the new sultan, Murad V.

Having lost his patron, Cevher Ağa withdrew to his house in Istanbul. His retirement from palace service lasted eleven years, until his death in 1887, probably in his 60s. As a mark of respect to his uncle's Chief Eunuch, Abdülhamid II ordered Cevher's remains interred in this Imperial graveyard, near his old master in the adjoining mausoleum. He was the second and last Court Eunuch buried here, as this graveyard evolved into a device for honoring top-ranking men of the state and military rather than palace personnel.

Cevher Ağa was described posthumously as "of provident mind, and possessed of great dignity."[63]

TOMBSTONE

He
For the sake of God, a Fatiha for the soul of the late and
divinely pardoned
Mehmed Cevher Ağa
Who is in Need of the Mercy of his God, the Pardoner
Constable of the Noble Abode of Felicity to
His Majesty Sultan Abdülaziz Khan
Whose abode is Paradise, who dwells in Heaven
17 Zilhicce 1304 [6 September 1887]
Calligrapher Ârif

Edib Bey. Palace Secretary. A32

Upon his death in 1900, Edib Bey was employed as a younger secretary in the palace chancery of Abdülhamid II. He was probably in his thirties. Edib's illustrious father, Süreyya Pasha, no doubt had secured him the post since Süreyya Pasha served as Senior Secretary at the palace under Abdülhamid II for ten years until his death in 1894. Edib's father and an unidentified brother are also buried in this graveyard, although not adjacent to one another.

TOMBSTONE

He is The Eternal One
A Fatiha for the soul of Ahmed Edib Bey
Secretary in the Imperial Palace Chancery
Who journeyed to the Abode of Eternity while still quite young
Eldest son of the late Süreyya Pasha, Senior Secretary in the Chancery
of the Imperial Palace
1 Temmuz 1316, 17 Rebiülevvel 1318 [15 July 1900]

Eser Kalfa. Senior Secretary at the Imperial Harem. D86

The lady Eser Kalfa (*kalfa* being the term for female supervisors in the harem) occupied the high post of Senior Secretary in the Imperial harem of Abdülhamid II. As such she would have been responsible for official correspondence and other paperwork concerning the harem. As with her sisters in Imperial harem service buried here, we have few other details on her life, but may presume she was Circassian in origin and most likely sold or presented to the harem of Sultan Abdülmecid when a young girl, at which point she would have been given her name, meaning "work of art."

Most probably Eser Kalfa entered service in the entourage of Abdülhamid II in the years before he came to the throne. Having not been selected as a concubine once Abdülhamid became sultan, thanks to her skills the young woman rose through the ranks of administrators in the harem until she achieved appointment as Senior Secretary. The only date we know for certain about Eser Kalfa is her death, and even then we know only the year, 1301 in the Muslim calendar, or 1883-1884.

TOMBSTONE

He is The Eternal One
O God, may the glory of that blessed, pure name
And the honor of the Prophet—the Pride of the World,
The Shah of the Corporeal and the Spiritual—
Make of my grave the Garden of Paradise, O God of the Worlds
Day and night, may the houris and attendants render service
The Fatiha for the soul of the late, divinely pardoned Eser Kalfa
Senior Secretary of the Imperial Harem
1301 [2 November 1883-20 October 1884]

Fazıl Pasha. Courtier. C76

Descendant of the Prophet Muhammad, Fazıl Pasha was born in India in 1825 to an illustrious Arab family long settled along India's Arabian Sea coastline. Around 1855 he moved to Mecca, then on to Istanbul. Due ostensibly to his usefulness in advising the Court on matters relating to Ottoman Arabia, along with his genealogy and congeniality, the well-educated

Fazıl gained the favor of Abdülhamid II, who eventually granted
him the highest civil rank, *vizier,*
with its title of *Pasha.*

At his death in 1900, the venerable seyyid received one last token
of Imperial esteem when Abdülhamid II ordered his burial in this
graveyard, at Privy Purse expense.
Fazıl Pasha's passing merited mention in the capital's English newspaper:

> Seid [Seyyid] Fazıl Pasha,
> who has been ill for some
> time past, died yesterday in
> the residence of his son, Sehil
> [Süheyl] Pasha, at Matchka.
> The funeral takes place to-
> day, and by the desire of his
> Majesty the Sultan, who de-
> frays its cost, the religious
> service will be performed in
> the Mosque of St. Sophia and
> the remains will be interred in
> the Mausoleum of Sultan
> Mahmud at Stambul.

Fazıl Pasha's stately tomb, with its
cylindrical headstone and epitaph
entirely in Arabic.

The deceased was a de-
scendant of the Prophet Ma-
homet, and was born at
Malabar, in India, where his
ancestors had emigrated from
Mecca some generations ago. His father, Arif Billal Seid Ulvi
bin Mehmed bin Sehil, watched with great care over the education of his son, who, forty-five years ago, removed to Mecca
and afterwards to Constantinople. His Majesty the Sultan con-

ferred upon him the title of Vizier, and many decorations. Fazil
Pasha, who leaves a numerous progeny, was seventy-five years
of age.

The funeral of the late Seid Fazil Pasha, whose death was announced on Saturday, took place that afternoon. The procession
from the residence at Matchka, escorted by ushers of the Palace,
gendarmes, and policemen, crossed in ten-oared caiques from
Dolma Baghtche to Sirkedji, where it was re-formed, and pro-
ceeded to the mosque of Saint Sophia, in which the religious
ceremony was performed. By the express desire of H. M. the
Sultan the body was entombed in the mausoleum of Sultan
Ahmed [*sic*]. Among those present at the ceremony were: —H.
H. Abdurrahman Pasha, Minister of Justice; H. E. Hassan Fehmi
Pasha, President of the Board of Audit; Redvan Pasha, Prefect
of the City; Shefik Bey, Minister of Police; Hussein Hassib Bey,
Post-master-general, and Sherif Abdullah Pasha; the Sheikh
Zafer Effendi, Ziver Bey, Director of Public Worship; Ahmed
Ata Effendi, representing the Holy Land; Dr. Nazif Pasha . . .
Sehil Pasha, son, and Hassan Pasha, Mehmed Pasha, Yussuf
Bey, and Ahmed Bey, grandsons, of the deceased.[64]

Fittingly, the Arab seyyid's tombstone is entirely in Arabic.

TOMBSTONE

Glory to The Eternal One, The Creator
This is the tomb of the exemplar of the Prophet's family
(and of his descendant
Fatima, the Radiant, the Immaculate), the fully observant scholar
And consummate friend of God, the famed seyyid and eminent emir
The emir of Zufar, His Lordship Fazıl Pasha the Alawite
May Almighty God bless him and benefit us
May the Compassionate One water the grave that he entered
He is noble, he has no equal among men
The sanctuary of the God-fearing and the chosen one among them
And from his character a path leads to religion

He is the noble offshoot of everything good
His chosen ancestor Taha [the Prophet] *has now arrived*
And given him the good news of felicity and acceptance
The good deeds of Fazıl were chronicled

Born 22 Receb 1240 [12 March 1825]
Lifespan 78 years [by the Muslim calendar]
Died 2 Receb 1318 [26 October 1900]
A Fatiha, for the sake of God

Ferahnüma Usta. Harem Supervisor. D84

In service at the Court of Sultan Abdülaziz, the lady Ferahnüma occupied the lofty post of *Hazinedar Usta* or High Hazinedar ("Treasurer" or "Comptroller"), top-ranking among the female administrators of the Imperial harem. Numbering perhaps ten or fifteen at any given time—these harem supervisors waited personally upon the monarch, from waking him in the morning, to attending him throughout the day, to assisting him in preparing for bed at night, to standing night watch outside his door as he slept.

Typical of the staff in service at the Imperial harem, we have no details as to her birth and original name, but she was most likely Circassian and would have been given the name *Ferahnüma* ("Displayer of Joy") when she entered palace service, most likely as a young girl during the reign of Abdülaziz's father, Mahmud II. Quite probably she was assigned to the entourage of Abdülaziz shortly after his birth and thus knew him all his life. From her tombstone we know that she left palace service at some point, of her own accord; such requests usually included arranging a suitable marriage, but we do not know if such was the case for Ferahnüma.

Befitting her exalted rank at Court, when Ferahnüma died in 1870 she was honored posthumously by burial in the garden adjacent to the mausoleum of the Imperial Family she had served in life, testifying to her place in the family's affections. She was only the sixth person, and third female, to be interred in the garden. Palace archives show that after she died her personal furnishings, including kitchen effects, were sold at auction, so that if she did indeed marry after leaving Harem service, she was probably a widow at her death.

TOMBSTONE
He is The Everliving One
For the sake of God, a Fatiha
For the noble soul of the late and divinely pardoned, modest and
virtuous lady
Her Excellency Ferahnüma Usta
Who having attained the illustrious post of High Hazinedar
And performing praiseworthy service
In the harem of the sovereign Imperial Palace
Served contentedly for some time
Then subsequently left palace service
Now she has journeyed to the Abode of Eternity
30 Ramazan 1287 [24 December 1870]

Ferid Pasha. Palace Official. A10

Born in Istanbul in 1815 to a family that claimed descent from the Prophet Muhammad, the future bureaucrat Ferid began his career as apprentice at the Sublime Porte in the days of Mahmud II, rising to become a secretary in the chancery there. In 1848, aged around 33, his capable work led to appointment as Principal Secretary to Sultan Abdülmecid, a position he retained seven years.

Under Sultan Abdülaziz in the 1860s, Ferid occupied a variety of distinguished state posts, alternately Minister of Pious Foundations, Undersecretary to the Grand Vizier, member of the advisory Supreme Council, and Minister of Marine. Alongside these state positions he served the Imperial Family personally in the prestigious posts of Senior Chamberlain in the household of Princess Âdile, Sultan Abdülmecid's sister, and Senior Chamberlain to the Empress Mother Pertevniyal, mother of Sultan Abdülaziz. Having obtained the high rank of *müşir*, "marshal," the now-Pasha capped his long career with appointment as Superintendent of the Privy Purse at the Court of Sultan Abdülaziz, beginning in October 1871.

While incumbent in his posts at Abdülaziz's Court and the Sultan's mother's household, Ferid Pasha died at home in 1875, aged about 60. A week after his death, the capital's English newspaper published a lengthy obituary on the familiar, long-serving figure at the palace:

The late Ferid Pasha, who died early last week of disease of the heart at his country-house at Kourou-tchesmé, on the Bosphorus, at the age of sixty years, and who long occupied the high functions of Marshal of the Palace and Minister of the Imperial Civil List, commenced his career under the reign of Sultan Mahmoud as a writer at the Porte. During the reign of the late Sultan Abdul-Medjid, he was charged with the correspondence between the Imperial Chancellery and the Turkish representatives abroad, and the way in which he discharged these duties attracted the attention of his Sovereign, who appointed him one of his four secretaries. Shortly after, Ferid Effendi replaced Shefik Bey as first secretary to the palace, a post which he filled with great distinction for many years, only leaving it when he was appointed Under Secretary at the Ministry of War. During the first few years of the present Sultan's reign, he was Minister of Pious Foundations, and comptroller of the household to the Validé Sultana, a confidential post which he retained until the last. Some time afterwards, he was made Grand Marshal of the Palace and Minister of the Civil List. The Sultan honoured him with his particular confidence, sent him to Egypt on an important mission, and, quite lately, he was entrusted with the provisional administration of the Ministry of Marine. Ferid Pasha married a daughter of Sebib Effendi, and leaves several sons and daughters. One of his sons is secretary to the Council of State, and the daughters are all married. The house in which he died formerly belonged to Saïd Bey, and it was presented to him by the late Sultan.[65]

Posthumously Ferid Pasha was remembered as "intelligent, a man of letters, a writer, thoughtful."[66] His untimely departure spared him the ignominious overthrow of his Imperial master and mistress some fourteen months after his death.

TOMBSTONE
He
The Fatiha for the soul of the late and divinely pardoned Seyyid
Abdülhamid Ferid Pasha
Marshal of the Imperial Palace Chancery
Who journeyed to the Abode of Eternity
While serving as Superintendent of the Imperial Privy Purse
And Senior Chamberlain
Of the Sublime Cradle of the Exalted Sultanate
[the Court of the Empress Mother]
29 M. [Muharrem] 1292 [7 March 1875]

Ferruh Efendi. Master of Ceremonial. C56

Ferruh Efendi was another product of the "Household Patronage" system that supplied members of the Ottoman elite for centuries, until the later 1800s. Born about 1818 of Circassian parents, the young Ferruh was purchased on the slave markets for service in the household of the wealthy Ramazanzâde Ârif Pasha. In the Pasha's service he would have learned Turkish, if he didn't know it already, and received an education; in Ferruh's case, he also studied at an official school in Istanbul outside the household as well as with a private tutor.

By 1839, aged around 21, the young Ferruh was working at the government office that oversaw the chamber at Topkapı Palace in which the sacred mantle of the Prophet was housed. In 1850 he transferred to the Protocol Office as a lower-level functionary, then transferred out to various provinces as aide to provincial governors. But by 1861 Ferruh Efendi, now in his forties, was back in the capital with promotion at his old place of employment, the Protocol Office. Through the 1860s and 1870s he continued in various departments of the Protocol Office, rising in 1879 to Master of Ceremonial at the Imperial Council, the advisory cabinet to the monarch, in this case Abdülhamid II.

Remaining at that prestigious post through the ensuing two decades, Ferruh Efendi received the highest Ottoman orders in recognition of his work, as well as promotion to *Bâlâ*, the second-highest civil rank, in 1884, when he was about 66.

Ferruh Efendi died while still in office in 1902, aged about 84, honored for his long years in protocol service by interment here at this Imperial graveyard, at the Sultan's expense. His obituary in the English newspaper of the capital exaggerated his age:

> Ferruh Bey, Master of Ceremonies of the Imperial Divan, who has been ailing for some months past, died on Saturday evening at the age of 102. The funeral took place yesterday, its expenses being defrayed by the Civil List. The service was performed in St. Sophia, and the remains were interred in the graveyard attached to the Mausoleum of Sultan Mahmoud.
>
> On being informed of Ferruh Bey's death, his Majesty the Sultan sent a message of sympathy to his family through Ibrahim Bey, Grand Master of Ceremonies.[67]

TOMBSTONE
He is The Eternal One, The Creator
*For the sake of God—may His name be exalted—*the Fatiha
For the soul of Mehmed Ferruh Efendi
Exalted dignitary of the Sublime State
Official of the Exalted Sultanate
Master of Ceremonial at the Imperial Council
4 Şevval 1319 [14 January 1902]
Calligrapher Sami

Hamdi Pasha. Governor-General, Senior Chamberlain. A20

Georgian by descent, Çürüksulu Mahmud Hamdi (to use his full moniker) was born probably around 1810 and entered the ranks of pages at Topkapı Palace at a very tender age, quite likely as a slave purchased or presented to the palace. At Court he began service in low posts as an apprentice but advanced quickly as he matured. In 1842 Hamdi, aged around 32, was appointed Senior Chamberlain to the teenaged Sultan Abdülmecid. Having discharged his prestigious palace duties for six years, Hamdi then embarked on appointments around the provinces, including as District Governor at Amasya, then Governor-General at Kastamonu along with promotion to the highest civil rank, *vizier*. The 1850s saw Hamdi Pasha as Governor-General of the Aegean Archipelago and then at Konya. Back in the capital by 1859, he served on the advisory Supreme Council, a post he left at the death of his patron Abdülmecid in 1861.

Rotating back through the provinces in the 1860s and 70s, Hamdi Pasha once again served as Governor-General, including at Bursa, Kastamonu, and Ankara, interrupted only when Sultan Abdülaziz appointed him briefly to the Council of State in Istanbul. Settling finally in the capital, in 1878 Hamdi Pasha again became Senior Chamberlain, for the second time in his career and 36 years after his first appointment to the post, this time to the young Abdülhamid II, who had been born during Hamdi Pasha's first tenure in the role. Perhaps Abdülhamid found a measure of comfort in appointing his father's old Senior Chamberlain to the post. While in the capital the Pasha resided in his seaside villa at Kuruçeşme on the Bosphorus, not far from his workplace at Yıldız Palace.

Hamdi Pasha died in 1882 still in office, probably in his 70s. The capital's English newspaper noted his passing, since his prominent position at Court would have made him well-known indeed to the expatriate community:

> We regret to announce the death of H.E. Mahmoud Hamdi Pasha, 1st Chamberlain to H.I.M. the Sultan, which took place yesterday morning. The deceased, who had arrived at an advanced age, had only suffered a few days' illness. The funeral took place the same day, with all the honours due to his rank. The mortal remains of Hamdi Pasha were deposited within the precincts of the Mausoleum of Sultan Mahmoud II, between the tomb of the late Halil Sherif Pasha and that of Sabri Pasha, formerly director general of the Custom House. Amongst those who took part in the funeral cortège, were to be remarked Haireddin Pasha, ex-Grand Vizier, Akif Pasha, &c, &c. Hamdi Pasha was of Georgian origin. He filled the post of 1st Chamberlain, on the first occasion, during five years in the early part of the reign of the late Abdul Medjid. He was afterwards appointed to several high administrative posts in the provinces, and subsequently reappointed 1st Chamberlain, when H.M. Abdul Hamid II ascended the throne.[68]

A later biographical entry posthumously remembered Hamdi Pasha rather unkindly as "honest, loyal, ineffectual in provincial affairs as he was of middling education."[69]

Hamdi Pasha's married daughter Behice was buried in the tomb beside his when she died some eighteen years after him.

TOMBSTONE

He is The Eternal One, The Creator
The Fatiha, for the sake of Almighty God
For the soul of the late, divinely pardoned Hamdi Pasha
Illustrious vizier of the Sublime State
Who journeyed to the Abode of Eternity
While executing distinguished service as Senior Chamberlain
11 Z.a. [Zilkade] 1299 [24 September 1882]

Hüsameddin Bey*. Senior Chamberlain. C81*

The military officer Hüsameddin Bey pursued a career in service at the palace, culminating in his appointment as Senior Chamberlain to Sultan Abdülaziz in April 1873. In this high post, he oversaw the daily operation of the palace chancery—the public affairs office of the palace, responsible also for Court protocol. His term ended with the overthrow of Abdülaziz in May 1876, but he resumed palace service among the Privy Household Staff of the new sultan, Abdülhamid II. Over the following years he rose to the rank of *Miralay*, colonel.

Colonel Hüsameddin died in 1897, at an unknown age but advanced in years and probably still in palace service. His burial here, near his former Imperial master Abdülaziz, and the wording of his tombstone reflect the respect accorded by Abdülhamid II to officials who had been at the Court of his dethroned uncle, of whom he was fond.

TOMBSTONE

He is The Eternal One, The Creator
The Fatiha for the soul of Hüsameddin Bey
Of the Imperial Household Staff
Who attained the rank of Colonel

In his lofty career in service to the Imperial Privy Household
And who found great honor heretofore
In his esteemed service
As Aide-de-camp and Chamberlain and Senior Chamberlain
During the reign of His Majesty Sultan Abdülaziz Khan
Whose abode is Paradise
17 Cemaziyül'ahir 1315 [13 November 1897]

Hüseyin Pasha. Courtier, Father of Foreign Minister Said Pasha. E108

Of Kurdish origin from the region of Süleymaniye in Anatolia, where he was born probably around 1810, Hüseyin first came to attention as major-domo of the household of the provincial governor-general Babanlı Ahmed Pasha. But his renown stems not so much from his own accomplishments in government service as from the fame of his son, Said Pasha, who rose to high prominence indeed in government service under Abdülhamid II. In tribute to Hüseyin's son, the sovereign awarded Hüseyin the rank of *mir-imiran* or Governor-General, which brought with it the honorific title of *Pasha*. In reference to his place of origin, to distinguish him from other notables of the same name he was known as Süleymaniyeli Hüseyin Pasha.

When Hüseyin came down with what would prove to be his final illness, his son's connections to the palace benefitted him yet one more time:

> Upon hearing that Hussein Pasha, father of his Excellency Said Pasha, Minister for Foreign Affairs, was ill, his Imperial Majesty requested Dr. Mühlig, physician of the Palace, to attend his Excellency in concert with Dr. Mordtmann, who is the physician in ordinary to his Excellency. At the same time his Majesty desired to be daily informed of the state of the patient. Said Pasha and all the relations of Hussein Pasha have been greatly touched by this mark of solicitude on the part of the Sultan.[70]

When Hüseyin died in 1887, the capital's English newspaper noted his passing, Sultan Abdülhamid's kindness toward his bereaved son, and the obsequies organized by Mazhar Pasha, mayor of the city, who would himself be buried in this garden four years later:

DEATH OF HUSSEIN PASHA

—

We regret to learn the death of Hussein Pasha, father of His Excellency, Said Pasha, Minister for Foreign Affairs, which occurred at two o'clock a.m. yesterday morning at his son's residence, Nishan-tash. On being informed of the Pasha's decease, His Imperial Majesty the Sultan sent for Said Pasha and expressed to him personally the sorrow which he felt at his sad bereavement. With the princely generosity that distinguishes him, His Majesty ordered that the funeral expenses should be defrayed by the Civil List, and that, in accordance with his desire, the deceased should be buried in the mausoleum of the Sultan Mahmoud. The funeral obsequies were under the direction of Osman Bey of the Imperial Navy.

Yesterday afternoon, at 2 p.m. the cortege left Nishan-tash for Dolma-Bagtché, whence the coffin was transferred in an Admiralty *mouche* [steam launch] to Sirkedji. On its arrival, the procession was formed, comprising many high State functionaries who had come to pay a last tribute of respect to the departed. The way was kept by the cavasses of the Sublime Porte, followed by ulémas and sheikhs reciting verses from the Coran. Then came the bier, borne by the relatives and intimate friends of the deceased and followed by a numerous crowd. At San Sophia, prayers were offered for the deceased, when the procession formed anew, and reached the cemetery adjoining the mausoleum of Sultan Mahmoud, where the interment took place. Mazhar Pasha's arrangements for the preservation of order, as also for giving the funeral all fit solemnity, were perfect; and he deserves great praise. We beg to offer our sincere condolences to his Excellency Said Pasha in his bereavement.[71]

At his death twenty years later, Hüseyin's son Said Pasha would be buried in this garden as well.

TOMBSTONE
Every soul shall taste of death
The Fatiha for the soul of the late Hüseyin Pasha
Of the ancient line of Süleymaniye
Noble Governor-General
Father of His Excellency Said Pasha, Minister of Foreign Affairs
Sunday, 12 Şevval 1304 [4 July 1887]

Kiryalfer Usta. Harem Supervisor. E119

Despite her lofty position as High Hazinedar in the Imperial Harem of Sultan Abdülaziz, we know next to nothing about this lady, due to the seclusion in which residents of the Imperial harem carried out their duties and lived out their lives. We can say that she was most likely of Circassian origin, as were probably all the residents of the Imperial harem in her day, and that she received her new name when she entered palace service, either purchased by the palace directly or presented to the Court of Sultan Abdülmecid by a grandee seeking to curry favor.

Most likely Kiryalfer Usta entered the service of then-Prince Abdülaziz when he was a young man, or even an infant, since only after long years in service to a prince were ladies promoted to her high rank. The ladies who occupied this important Harem post waited personally upon the monarch, and as such came to know him as well as anyone might.

Apparently Kiraylafer Usta occupied this post at the time of Abdülaziz's overthrow in 1876, at which she too lost her position and was sent into retirement along with all the other ladies in harem service at Abdülaziz's Court. From the palace archives we know that in 1881 Kiryalfer Usta joined other women of rank in Harem service in a note of thanks for the decisions of the (dubious) tribunal that convicted several high figures of plotting Abdülaziz's overthrow and death.

The retired High Hazinedar died in 1891 at an unknown age but advanced in years, and was honored by Abdülhamid II with burial in this prestigious graveyard in recognition of her service at the Court of his late uncle, of whom he was fond.

The first four lines of Kiryalfer's epitaph (below the invocation) form a verse that rhymes in the original.

TOMBSTONE
He is The Eternal One
May God in his mercy forgive her sins
Take her into Paradise Most High
And make of her grave a rose garden
Until Judgment Day filled with light

The Fatiha for the noble soul of the late
Kiryalfer Usta
High Hazinedar to His Majesty Sultan Abdülaziz Khan
Whose abode is Paradise
16 Zilhicce 1308 [23 July 1891]

Mahvisal Hanım. Divorced Wife of Kayserili Ahmed Pasha. A12

We know a great deal about this lady's former husband, Kayserili Ahmed Pasha, the native of Kayseri who rose to the highest ranks in the Navy (commanding the Ottoman Black Sea fleet during the Crimean War, and Admiral of the Fleet) and who also served as Minister of Marine and governor of provinces throughout the empire up to his death in 1878. But we know precious little about his wife, the lady Mahvisal. From her tombstone we see that she had been in service at the Court of Abdülmecid, thus in the 1840s-1850s, rising to the high post of *Hazinedar*, one of the supervisors of the Imperial harem. From this we can guess that she was probably Circassian in origin (as were most of the palace slave women), and quite capable (to have risen so high), but she asked to leave palace service by having a husband found for her.

That husband was the illustrious admiral. From state records we know the lady Mahvisal was his legal wife (not a concubine), as they were divorced by 1864 when he was governor at Izmir. At that time she received a pension from the government, the archives tell us, doubtless because she was wife of such a high-ranking bureaucrat. We also know from her title *Hacce* ("Pilgrim") that Mahvisal journeyed to Mecca for the pilgrimage at least once in her lifetime.

Nor are we certain of her exact date of death, since the final numeral on her tombstone was not carved, and other evidence of her death has not surfaced—but it would have been between 1902 and 1911, probably when she was in her 70s. If the poem on her rather blunt tombstone is reliable evidence, she failed to find much happiness in life. We can only speculate as to why Mahvisal was buried in this prestigious garden, but most likely she had remained close to influential ladies at the palace who prevailed upon Abdülhamid II to authorize the burial here of this lady in former service at his late father's Court, even in this era when palace personnel were buried elsewhere.

The first four lines of Mahvisal's epitaph (below the invocation) form a verse that rhymes in the original.

TOMBSTONE
He is The Eternal One
I found no comfort in this world
And so I chose to depart
May the wise take this lesson from me
The troubles of the world are not worth its pleasures

The Fatiha for the soul of the hajji Mahvisal Hanım
Wife of Admiral of the Fleet Kayserili Ahmed Pasha
And Hazinedar to His Majesty Sultan Abdülmecid Khan,
whose abode is Paradise
132_ [the last numeral was not chiseled; 1320-1329 = 1902-1911]

Münir Pasha. Interpreter, Grand Master of Ceremonies. C78

Son of Necab Efendi, majordomo in the household of the Minister of Finance, Münir was born in Istanbul in 1844. At the tender age of 13 he began work in the offices of the Finance Ministry, thanks to his father's employer. That year he was fortunate to be sent to Paris for further education, where he remained five years, perfecting his French and obtaining work at the Paris embassy. In 1863 the young man returned to the Ottoman capital and put his French to work as clerk at the Foreign Office. Over the next two years he transferred to the Treasuries Office as a translator, then to the Translation Bureau of the Supreme Council.

The year 1866 found Münir Bey back in Paris as Third Secretary at the

Ottoman embassy. Rising through the civil bureaucracy, by 1869 he was Chief Secretary at the embassy, and by 1872, chargé d'affaires. That year he returned to Istanbul—after six years in Paris—as director of his former office, the Foreign Dispatches Bureau at the Foreign Office. In 1874 he took up the prestigious post of Official Translator at the Imperial Council, with concomitant rise in his civil rank. Three years later, in 1877, during the war with Russia, Münir became Chief Secretary at the Foreign Dispatches Bureau at the Imperial Council, which meant he was entrusted with foreign correspondence of the palace at this critical juncture. Only months later, in 1878 Münir reached the pinnacle of his career with appointment as the government's Chief of Protocol, or "Grand Master of Ceremonies" as Europeans usually termed the post. In 1884 Abdülhamid II honored his distinguished and lengthy path in civil service with the highest civil rank, *vizier,* and the title *Pasha* that came with it.

In reward for his loyal service and his prominent work as interpreter with foreign diplomats posted to the Ottoman capital, Münir Pasha received not only the highest Ottoman orders but a host of foreign decorations as well. "Few are the men who hold as many decorations as he did," commented the capital's English newspaper in his obituary, which went on to explain the reason for the honors showered upon him:

> In his capacity as Grand Master of Ceremonies and Dragoman of the Divan ["Council"], the late Pasha was present at all interviews which foreign Sovereigns, Princes, and Ambassadors had with his Imperial Master. Munir Pasha's position was thus confidential in the highest degree, and to his honour be it said that he always showed himself worthy of the unbounded trust placed in him.[72]

When the German Emperor and Empress visited Abdülhamid II in 1889, the Empress's lady-in-waiting recorded her memories of Münir Pasha:

> The conversation was conducted through . . . the Master of Ceremonies Munir Pasha, the European-educated man who undertook this tiresome task. He is said to be entirely honourable, as proven by the fact that despite his high position he has remained

quite poor. At every uttering of his sovereign as well as of the [German] Imperial couple the hapless Pasha had to execute a deep bow and extend his right hand to the floor and then to his heart, mouth, and forehead. . . .

We used the occasion to extend [the Sultan] our thanks for the Orders he sent us, most assuredly in less flowery form than he did in his reply—or was this how the good Munir Pasha embroidered it?!. . . .

The Sultan sat at the middle of the horseshoe-shaped table with the Emperor and Empress to his right and left. . . . The unfortunate Munir Pasha stood as interpreter behind his sovereign's chair and during the entire endlessly long dinner conveyed the conversation between our Majesties and the Sultan, at every sentence of which he had to repeat the above-described Turkish salutation ceremonial, not only with the Sultan but also with the Emperor and Empress.[73]

Given his well-known figure among the international community, the death of the congenial Münir Pasha at age 55 on 6 October 1899 occasioned sincere regret as well as lengthy coverage in the press:

It is with much sorrow that we fulfil the painful duty of announcing the death of Munir Pasha, Grand Master of Ceremonies, which took place this morning at Prinkipo [Büyükada, one of the Princes Islands in the Sea of Marmara] where the deceased had been spending the summer, and where he was taken seriously ill some weeks ago. Munir Pasha had long been troubled by asthma, and that chronic malady was the origin of the illness that has now proved fatal, and of which the first signs were attacks of syncope following upon failure of respiration. His death will be a source of general regret, for he was a thoroughly estimable man, of great amiability of character, always courteous and obliging, alike in his official and in his private life.[74]

———

The funeral of the late Munir Pasha took place yesterday afternoon. The remains were conveyed in a steam-tug from Prinkipo to Sirkedji, and thence to the Mausoleum of Sultan Mahmud, where they were placed in a special vault. Both at Prinkipo and Stambul the way was held by troops, police, and municipal agents. In recognition of the distinguished services of the deceased, the Sultan ordained that a State funeral should be given him. The chief mourner was Lieut.-Colonel Zia Bey, son-in-law of the late Pasha, and among those who attended were Marshals Fuad Pasha and Assaf Pasha, Turkhan Pasha, Constantine Anthropulo Pasha, Ambassador in London; Mirza Mahmud Khan, the Persian Ambassador; Ghalib Bey, Assistant-Introducer of Ambassadors; Enver Bey, Governor of Pera; Ohannes Effendi Sakiz, Minister of the Civil List; . . . Hamdi Bey, manager of the Imperial Museum; . . . Vice-Admiral Woods Pasha, Mr. O. Straus, the United States' Minister; . . . Sir Ellis Ashmead-Bartlett, . . . etc.

His Majesty the Sultan yesterday sent a message of condolence to the family of the deceased, and the heads of the Foreign Missions telegraphed messages of sympathy to Lieutenant-Colonel Zia Bey, his son-in-law.

The vacancy caused by the death of Munir Pasha has been filled by the appointment of Ibrahim Bey, Introducer of Ambassadors at the Foreign Office. . . . Ibrahim Bey is already so well known as an efficient Court functionary and as a courteous, kind-hearted gentleman, that it is not needful to say more than to record our satisfaction, which will be shared in all the upper social circles, that the late lamented Munir Pasha should have a successor in all respects so worthy of him.

—

To the Editor of the "Levant Herald"

Sir, —I wish to express my deep sense of the heavy loss which his Majesty the Sultan and the Ottoman Empire have sustained by the death of Munir Pasha.

I had the privilege of knowing the late Pasha well, and I feel his loss as a severe personal bereavement. Munir Pasha was a most faithful servant of his Majesty, and a true lover of his country. He was a man of high natural ability, and of the most kindly and sympathetic nature. In fact, he was a gentleman *in the best sense.*

When in England, during the times of 1877, as representative of the Sultan, Munir Pasha made a most favourable impression, and gained many friends.

His untimely death is mourned by many in this Empire, and by none more sincerely than by myself. —

I am, &cc.,

F. Ashmead-Bartlett.

Therapia, Oct. 6.

TOMBSTONE

He is The Eternal One, The Creator
The Fatiha, *for the sake of God*
For the soul of the late Mahmud Münir Pasha
Exalted vizier of the Sublime State
Translator at the Imperial Council
Chief of Protocol
30 ___ 1317; [Rumî] year 1315

The month is illegible, but from the obituary clearly it is Cemaziül'evvel, which yields the correct date of death of 6 October 1899.

Râşid Efendi. Harem Financial Director, City Supervisor. A31

Born around the 1820s and Circassian in origin, in his younger days Râşid served as majordomo to high-ranking pashas. Having demonstrated his talents at management, he was appointed to the directorates of the two government-run steamship lines out of Istanbul, the *Şirket-i Hayriye* and the *İdare-i Mahsusa.* Subsequently, for some twenty years Ahmed Râşid served as Supervisor of the First Ward of the city of Istanbul, as well as superintendent of financial affairs of the Imperial Harem. His services brought him to the second-highest civil rank, *Bâlâ.*

When the prominent bureaucrat and palace official died in 1893, he merited an obituary in the capital's English newspaper:

Rashid Effendi, a former president of the first municipal circle,
who was unwell for some time past, died on Monday in his summer residence at Erenkeui [Erenköy, on the Asian shore of the
Sea of Marmara]. The funeral took place yesterday, the expenses
being defrayed by his Imperial Majesty's Privy Purse. The body
was conveyed from Erenkeui to Sirkedji and thence to the St.
Sophia mosque where the prayers for the dead were said. From
St. Sophia the body was taken to the Mausoleum of Sultan Mahmoud, where it was interred. Among those who attended the funeral were the presidents of the several municipalities and
several State functionaries. Deceased held the rank of *bala* and
possessed the Grand Cordons of the *Osmanieh* and *Medjidieh*
and silver medals of the *Imtiaz*.

A posthumous short biography lauded Râşid simply as "an effective and
influential man."[75]

TOMBSTONE
He
O His Excellency Mevlana Celâleddin Rumî, *hallowed be his grave*
The Fatiha for the soul of the late Ahmed Râşid Zeynel Efendi
Civil Official of the rank *Bâlâ*
Superintendent of the Imperial Harem
Supervisor of the First Ward of the city
13 Zilhicce 1310 [incorrectly; the day should be 11,
to yield 26 June 1893]
Calligrapher Mâhir

Revnak Usta. High Hazinedar. D83

Like her colleague the lady Şevknihal, next to whom she lies in death, the
lady Revnak occupied the exalted position of *Hazinedar Usta* or High
Hazinedar, the high-ranking supervisory post among the female personnel
charged with managing the Imperial harem. As such she would have been
addressed at Court as Revnak Usta, the term *usta* meaning "superintendent." Female superintendents in the Imperial harem waited personally
upon the monarch.

We have no biographical details on Revnak, who served in the palace of Sultan Abdülaziz. Most probably she was Circassian by birth, and at a young age entered palace service where she would have been given her new name ("Splendor") and taught palace manners and customs as well as the Turkish language. Having not been selected as a concubine, her skills in management propelled her through the ranks of the harem hierarchy to finally occupy her high post, which she would have taken up at the death of her predecessor in office.

At Revnak Usta's death in 1865, Abdülaziz honored his harem superintendent by ordering her burial here, adjacent to the mausoleum of the Imperial Family she had served in life. She was only the fifth person, and the second female, to be buried in this garden—a mark of the high esteem in which she had been held during her life. Her head- and footstones reflect her position at Court, bearing as they do the sun-ray device, a symbol of the monarchy.

Revnak Usta's graceful headstone, with its Imperial sun to symbolize her exalted status as Supervisor of the palace harem.

TOMBSTONE
Every soul shall taste of death
*For the sake of God—may His name be exalted—*a Fatiha
For the noble soul of the late and divinely pardoned modest
and virtuous lady
Her Excellency Revnak Usta
Who journeyed to the Abode of Eternity
While performing praiseworthy service
In the illustrious post of High Hazinedar
In the harem of the sovereign Imperial Palace
27 R.a. [Rebiülevvel] 1282 [20 August 1865]

Sa'di Pasha. General, Imperial Aide-de-Camp. A33

Son of Ali Sâib Pasha, the noted general and Minister of War who is also buried in this graveyard, Sa'di Pasha was born probably in the late 1840s and followed his father in an army career. He rose eventually to Divisional General, no doubt helped along by his family connections, but more than held his own after his father's death in 1891, with his prestigious appointment as aide-de-camp to Abdülhamid II.

When he died at his villa in the Fatih district of the city on 3 December 1905, Sa'di Pasha was aged probably about 60. The capital's English newspaper recorded his passing:

> General Saadi Pasha, A.D.C. of His Imperial Majesty and member of the High Military Commission sitting at the Imperial Palace, died last night at his Stambul residence. He was the son of the late Ali Saib Pasha, Minister of War. The funeral is to take place today.[76]

TOMBSTONE
He is The Eternal One
The celebrated Divisional General, Imperial Aide-de-camp
Sa'di Pasha, son of Sâib
Prepared for his journey to God
His heart filled with misery at the calamity of suffering the hour of death

Suddenly he took refuge in the paradises of the Abode of Heavenly Joys
His late father was Minister of War, and lies here as well
Both of them convivial companions of the manifestation of God
Mild of speech, smiling of face, angelic in temperament was he
May God bless his soul and illumine his grave
The date of his death flowed from the pen with three of the Ihlas:
"Sa'di Pasha made the regions of Paradise a seat of beauty"
In the year 1323 [1905-1906]

The epitaph, clearly commissioned from a professional poet, rhymes at every other line. The clever chronogram at the verse's end totals 1,326. But by referring beforehand to three recitations of the *Ihlas* chapter of the Koran (chapter 112, recited particularly for the dead)—and mentioning a flowing outward while doing so—the poet clues his reader to subtract 3 from the sum, yielding 1,323, the year of Sa'di Pasha's death in the Muslim calendar.

Şevknihal Usta. High Hazinedar. D85

The third person, and first female, to be buried in the garden graveyard, the lady Şevknihal Usta was laid to rest just inside the western gate at her death in 1860. She was singled out for such high honor because of her eminent status as manager in the Imperial harem of Sultan Abdülmecid. It was her skills at administration that had earned the lady Şevknihal this rank of High Hazinedar, superintendent of the female chamberlains who waited in personal service upon the monarch. Due to her exalted position at Court, Şevknihal would have known Sultan Abdülmecid well—in fact, he would have approved her appointment to the post—and as a mark of his esteem for the lady, the Sultan ordered her interment in this garden adjacent to the Imperial mausoleum, many of whose present and future occupants she would have served in life.

As with the three other female Imperial harem supervisors interred here, regrettably we know very little of her life. Most probably she was Circassian in origin and would have entered service in the palace as a young girl either purchased or presented to the Court. At that point she would have received her new name, *Şevknihal* ("Sapling of Ardor"). Quite likely she had served in the entourage of Abdülmecid since his birth in 1823, and before that in the household of his father, Mahmud II.

As her headstone attests, Şevknihal Usta proved herself a generous donor, giving of her salary to support works of beneficence. She established the "Şevknihal Usta Primary School" for girls and young women in the Vefa district of the city. She also donated funds toward at least two water fountains in Istanbul, repairing the Ahmed Ağa street fountain in the Aksaray district and in 1858 constructing the fountain (demolished in the 1950s) named after her at the mosque in the Sancaktepe district of the capital. In one final honor for the great lady of the Court, renowned calligrapher Abdülfettah Efendi (at the time Chief Engraver at the Imperial Mint, and buried in this garden at his own death 36 years later) was commissioned to draw her tombstone (see the entry for Abdülfettah Efendi).

TOMBSTONE

Her Excellency the late and divinely pardoned Şevknihal Usta
Benefactress of pious foundations
Pride of virtuous women
Who performed most excellent service and affirmed the
assertion of integrity
With devotion and sincerity
In the Harem of the Imperial Palace
So as to attain the exalted post of High Hazinedar
And acquired dignity and honor and distinction
As the recipient of trust and esteem
May her noble soul reach God's mercy and pardon
And attain the Garden of Paradise, Amen
24 Rebiülevvel 1277, Tuesday [10 October 1860]
Abdülfettah [Calligrapher]

Süreyya Pasha. Senior Secretary in the Palace Chancery. C70

Born in Istanbul in 1845, Süreyya graduated from high school at age 17, whereupon he began his career in government service with appointment to the secretarial office of the Superior Council of State. When the advisory Council of State was formed under Sultan Abdülaziz, Süreyya took up a succession of posts on it, culminating as Secretary-general of the Council's Commission of Internal Affairs. His much-admired talents as a writer of lucid prose brought him to the attention of the palace, so that in 1885 Abdülhamid II summoned him to Court as Senior Secretary of the Palace Chancery. The Sultan and his Secretary were only three years apart in age and got along well. Süreyya Pasha occupied his influential palace post for nine years, until his unexpected demise at home on 25 November 1894, aged only 49.

The Pasha's high position at Court earned him a laudatory obituary in the capital's English newspaper:

It is with regret that we announce the death of his Excellency Sureya Pasha, first secretary of the Palace, which occurred about noon yesterday. His Imperial Majesty the Sultan was much moved by the sad news and the death of Sureya Pasha is deeply regretted by all the functionaries of the Imperial Palace. In Sureya Pasha the Sovereign loses a faithful servant who by his devotion, his loyal services, and the great tact and ability with which he accomplished his delicate duties, had gained the Sultan's confidence and esteem. Sureya Pasha was a master of the Turkish language, which he wielded with extreme elegance and ease. His style was remarkable for its purity, clearness, and precision. Before being called to the post of first secretary of the Imperial Palace, Sureya Pasha was a member, and later president, of the General Registry Council. He was promoted to the rank of Vizier about seven years ago, a promotion which he had deserved by his distinguished services. Deceased possessed the star of the *Imtiaz* in brilliants, the Grand Cordons of the *Osmanieh* and *Medjidieh*, also with the star in brilliants, the gold and silver medals of the *Imtiaz*, and the gold medals of the *Liakat*, the Fine Arts, and Crete.[77]

The next day the same paper described the state funeral accorded the Palace Secretary.

His Imperial Majesty the Sultan, who, as we said yesterday, was
deeply affected by the death of his Excellency Sureya Pasha,
sent yesterday his aide-de-camp-general Marshal Shakir Pasha
to the residence of the deceased at Nishan-Tash to convey a message of condolence and sympathy to the bereaved family. Sureya
Pasha died of heart-disease. The funeral took place yesterday
morning with great pomp. It was attended by a large number of
Palace dignitaries and superior State functionaries. The funeral
procession started from the residence of Sureya Pasha about half
past ten and wended its way to the Dolma-Baghtché quay where
the body was placed in an Admiralty steam-launch and conveyed to Sirkedji. Here the cortege was formed again and proceeded by the main thoroughfare to the St. Sophia mosque,
escorted by a detachment of troops, ushers of the Palace, gendarmes, and police and municipal agents. On the way several
halts were made before turbés [tombs], where the dervishes attending the funeral said prayers. After the prayers for the dead
in the St. Sophia mosque the body was transferred to the mausoleum of Sultan Mahmoud and deposited in a special vault.
Among those present at the funeral were: —Their Excellencies
Riza Pasha, Minister of Justice; Said Pasha, Minister for Foreign
Affairs; Khalil Rifat Pasha, Minister of the Interior; Tewfik
Pasha, Minister of Public Works; Nazif Pasha, Minister of Finance; Marshal Shakir Pasha, aide-de-camp-general of the Sultan; Tewfik Pasha, Musteshar [Undersecretary] of the Grand
Vizierate; Redvan Pasha, Prefect of the City; Nazim Pasha, Minister of Police; Mikael Pasha, Minister of the Civil List; Hashim
Bey, Musteshar of the Ministry of Justice; Rashid Effendi, first
imam of the Palace; Emin Bey, Chamberlain of his Imperial
Majesty; Nouri Bey, Imperial Commissioner to the Tobacco
Regie; . . . Behdjet Bey, director of the local Press Bureau; Hussein Hassib Bey, Governor of Pera; Kiazim Pasha, commander
of the Garrison of Constantinople; Generals Ahmed Ali Pasha
and Suleiman Pasha, . . . aides-de-camp to the Sultan, etc.[78]

The late Pasha made the newspaper again on Friday of that week:

His Imperial Majesty the Sultan has again manifested his sympathy with the family of the late Sureya Pasha. Upon an order from his Majesty the four sons of the deceased, namely, Djemil Bey, Nedjib Bey, Nebil Bey, and Abid [*sic*] Bey, were taken to the Palace on Wednesday by Djevad Bey, son of the late Osman Bey, first Chamberlain of the Sultan, and presented to his Imperial Majesty, who graciously welcomed them.[79]

In his memoir published some thirty years after Süreyya's death, the Court Chancery translator Hasan Sırrı recalled him fondly: "Because he never once sullied his reputation by underhanded dealings in the Palace Chancery, his name is ever honored by those who knew him, and his polite and kindly manner toward everyone succeeded in winning all hearts. I should like to repeat here, with feelings of the utmost gratitude, that I was greatly touched by the instances of humane kindness evidenced toward me by Süreyya Pasha, whose memory I call to mind now with the offering of a Fatiha."[80]

Süreyya Pasha's son Ahmed Edib Bey is also buried in this graveyard, as is apparently another son who, however, remains unidentified. A third son, Münir Süreyya Bey, entered the diplomatic service and served in embassies and consulates for both the empire and the republic.

TOMBSTONE

He is The Eternal One, The Everliving One
A Fatiha for the soul of the late Süreyya Pasha
Senior Secretary in the Chancery of the Imperial Palace
Illustrious Vizier
In the year 1312 [1894-1895]
Calligrapher İzzet

Talha Ağa. Chief Eunuch at Court. E98

As chief of the black eunuchs in palace service during the reign of Sultan Abdülaziz, Talha Ağa (the style *Ağa* after his name honorably indicating his status as a eunuch) bore the illustrious title *Constable of the Noble Abode of Felicity*, the latter portion of his title a reference to the Imperial Court. Bearers of this title—also shortened to *Constable of the Maidens*—wielded tremendous power and authority in the palace, supervising all female and male personnel in service at Court, overseeing vastly wealthy pious foundations, and serving as the sovereign's personal agent in any number of situations. His unmatched power as Chief Eunuch (as Europeans typically called incumbents of the post) made him the man to cultivate if one sought advancement or influence at Court. In protocol the Chief Eunuch ranked immediately below the Grand Vizier and the Şeyhülislâm and above Cabinet ministers.

We know little about the Chief Eunuchs and can only guess at Talha Ağa's background, but most likely he was born in Ethiopia to non-Muslim parents, captured by slave raiders, castrated, sold on the slave markets, converted to Islam and taught Turkish, and then, after proving his qualities in service, was presented to the palace as a gift by a wealthy man seeking influence at Court. We know he had entered the service of Abdülaziz before the latter ascended the throne in 1861, because an archival document from early 1862 already mentions his position as the new monarch's Chief Eunuch. His rise through the ranks of Court eunuchs to the highest post among palace personnel testifies to his skills not only in management, but also in cultivating his master's trust and affection.

Talha Ağa died 30 March 1876, at an unknown age, having served as Chief Eunuch to Sultan Abdülaziz for the monarch's entire reign. As a mark of the high esteem in which he was held, he was only the tenth person, and the first eunuch in Court service (as it turned out, only two Court Eunuchs would be buried here), to be honored by interment in this Imperial graveyard. His death merited mention in the city's English newspaper:

> A personage of some mark died on Thursday night—Talha Agha, for many years chief eunuch of the Sultan's harem. In virtue of an Imperial *iradé* [decree], his remains were removed yesterday with considerable pomp from the palace of Dolmabaghtché to the mosque of St. Sophia, and after the celebration of the funeral service in the mosque, were conveyed for interment to the well-known mausoleum (*turbé*) of Sultan Mahmoud, near the "Burnt Column" in Stamboul.[81]

Three days later the Chief Eunuch's estate made the news, without benefit of corroborating evidence for the sums mentioned, and with a slight inflation of his rank in Court protocol:

> The office of chief eunuch, vacant since the death of Talha Agha, has been bestowed on Djevher Agha, one of the oldest of the palace eunuchs. The late chief eunuch was wealthier than may have been generally known. His fortune is stated at £T.220,000, and, as he of course leaves no heirs, this little sum reverts to the Sultan. The salary attached to the post of chief eunuch is £T.600 a month (£T.7,200 a year), and its holder, according to the court etiquette, takes precedence of all functionaries below the Grand Vizier, with whom he ranks as an equal.[82]

Only two months after the Chief Eunuch's death, the monarch he served so long was deposed and then laid to rest shortly thereafter in the adjacent mausoleum.

TOMBSTONE

He

The Fatiha, *for the sake of God*
For the soul of the late, divinely pardoned Talha Ağa
Constable of the Noble Abode of Felicity
Who is in need of the mercy of his God, the Pardoner
4 Rebiülevvel 1293 [30 March 1876]

Parliamentary Deputies and Senators

Ârif Bey. Mayor, Parliamentary Deputy. E129

Of Kurdish descent, Ârif led the influential Pirinççizâde clan at Diyarbakir, in southeastern Anatolia. In his younger days he was editor at the local newspaper, until 1877, after which Ârif devoted himself to farming and business, becoming a wealthy landowner. Convicted of instigating the local anti-Christian pogroms of 1895, he was exiled to Mosul, but returned home before long.

While mayor of Diyarbakir, in 1908 Pirinççizâde Ârif was elected to the reopened Ottoman Parliament as one of his province's representatives. Yet he could serve only a short term as he died the following year, 1909, while in Istanbul, and hence was buried here. His famous nephew, the Turkish nationalist Ziya Gökalp, is buried in this graveyard as well.[83]

TOMBSTONE
He is The Eternal One
Recite a Fatiha, O graveyard visitor,
For within this tomb lies an Ârif
From Diyarbakir city's notable house was he
Eager for truth, this truth-discoverer
To Parliament, a deputy, he came, yet
Tarried not, sagacious one, and left this world
From heaven a voice to his grieving friends spoke the date:
"Dweller in the Garden of Nearness became Mehmed Ârif"
1327 [23 January 1909-13 January 1910]

The epitaph—a rhyming verse—includes a pleasing pun on the word *Ârif*: both the deceased's name, and meaning "a sagacious, skilled person." The chronogram of the last line totals 1,327, the date of Ârif's death in the Muslim calendar. Its phrase "the Garden of Nearness" evokes both the proximity of the dead to God, as well as the closeness of death to life.

Muhammad al-'Ajlani. Judge, Parliamentary Deputy. F141

Scion of the wealthy and prominent al-'Ajlani family of Damascus, who claimed descent from the Prophet Muhammad, this Muhammad was the son of Sheikh Ahmad Darwish al-'Ajlani, who served as *Nakibüleşraf* or "Marshal of the Prophet's Descendants" in Syria through most of the late nineteenth century. Muhammad trained in the law and became a judge in Damascus in the 1890s. He was elected to the reconvened Ottoman Parliament in 1909 (as his father had been to the first Parliament, in 1876), and so came to Istanbul, where he died in 1911, having served but two years in his elected office. Fittingly for the eminent Syrian, his tombstone is entirely in Arabic.

TOMBSTONE
In the name of God, the Compassionate, the Merciful
Fatiha
He is The Eternal One
This is the tomb of Muhammad al-'Ajlani
Notable Descendant of the Prophet, whom the Fates drove away
He died as a stranger, far from his people
With his departure his supplications have not ended
Implicitly he still continues to proclaim his wishes
Even when God the Pardoner has summoned him to his proximity
Certainly, even if my sins be huge, he cures me
The date of it my ancestor, the Chosen One, fashioned for me
23 Zilhicce 1329 [15 December 1911]

Physicians

Abdülhak Efendi. Physician. A3
Nasûhi Bey. Ambassador, Senator.

Unique in the garden, this tomb contains the remains of a renowned grandfather and grandson, each of them men of state as well as accomplished poets, the headstone at their grave referring to the elder (with whom we shall begin) and the footstone to the junior.

Scion of a family that produced four Chief Physicians to the Imperial Court, Abdülhak Efendi was born in Istanbul in 1786. Educated in the natural and religious sciences at the Süleymaniye Mosque School, he graduated from the Süleymaniye Medical School and embarked upon a career as both physician and professor of medicine. From his erudition he was also known as Abdülhak Molla, or "master," the title often given scholars. In 1828 he became Director of the newly opened Imperial School of Medicine. Favored at Court, Dr. Abdülhak received appointment as Chief Physician to Mahmud II in 1834. He ultimately occupied the post three times during his career, including during the final illness that carried Mahmud away in 1839, and twice at the Court of Sultan Abdülmecid, until his final resignation from the position in 1849 at age 63. These prestigious medical appointments alternated with his other posts in the top ranks of the empire's religious-judicial hierarchy, drawing from his training in the religious sciences, as Chief Justice of Rumelia as well as Anatolia. The fates having granted the doctor long life, in 1853 he succeeded to the honorary title *Reisülülema*, Chief of the Ulema, awarded to the doyen of the religious-judicial confraternity in terms of seniority in service.

An innovative reformer of the empire's medical establishment, Dr. Abdülhak enlisted Mahmud's support in introducing modern advances to Ottoman medicine, including the use of quarantine, compulsory smallpox inoculation, dissection of cadavers in the study of anatomy and pathology, and the first autopsy. But outside the field of medicine this brilliant savant penned histories and a body of rhyming poetry in the classical Ottoman style. The talent for writing ran in the family: his son Hayrullah (whose name was later added to Abdülhak's headstone although he was not buried here), ambassador at Tehran in the 1860s, wrote a celebrated history of the Ottoman Empire, among numerous other works, while among Abdülhak's grandsons Nasûhi Bey (buried here) became an accomplished poet and Nasûhi's famed younger brother Abdülhak Hamid (later surname Tarhan) figures among the most luminous of Turkish poets, authors, and playwrights

The first burial in the garden graveyard: Dr. Abdülhak Efendi, personal physician and friend to Mahmud II.

Dr. Abdülhak's seaside villa on the Bosphorus at Bebek included a charming garden where he hosted convivial drinking gatherings for cronies among the elite, including Sultan Mahmud. It was at his villa that he died in 1854, aged 67. Sultan Abdülmecid ordered his burial in this graveyard, beside the tomb of the doctor's longtime patron and friend, Mahmud II. And so

Dr. Abdülhak Efendi became the first person interred in this garden, a mark of the great esteem held for him by the Imperial Family.

When Dr. Abdülhak died, one Sâib Efendi penned the witty chronogram that commemorated his passing: *Uttering "God, God," to God this time went Abdülhak.* The line falls rather flat in English, but its Ottoman original sparkles with delightful alliteration that the non-Turkish-speaker can also hear when pronouncing it aloud: *Gitti Hak Hak diyerek Hakka bu dem Abdülhak.* It also offers a pleasing pun, in that the spoken (but not written) words offer a second interpretation, *Uttering "God, God," to the grave this time went Abdülhak.* The chronogram totals 1,269, but the line of verse that would have preceded and introduced it undoubtedly contained instructions to add 1 to the resulting date, so as to happily bring the total to 1,270, the year of Abdülhak's death in the Muslim calendar.[84]

HEADSTONE
God   He
There is no god but the one God, and Muhammad is his Prophet
For the sake of God—may His name be exalted—a Fatiha
For the soul of the eminent high official, Abdülhak Efendi
Who came to the world of existence on the first of the
month of Rebiülevvel
In the year one thousand two hundred and one of the Prophetic Migration
[22 December 1786],
Serving on three occasions as Imperial Chief Physician
And who, as President of the Council of Public Instruction
And formerly Chief of the Ulema
Journeyed to the Abode of Eternity
On the twenty-first day of the noble month of Şaban
In the year one thousand two hundred seventy [19 May 1854]
21 Şaban 1270 [19 May 1854], calligraphed by [name omitted]
Additionally, the deceased's son Hayrullah Efendi
Journeyed to the Abode of Eternity while at Tehran
And was buried there, in the year 1284 [1867-68]

Abdülhak Efendi's grandson Abdülhalik Nasûhi Bey was born in Istanbul in 1837 to Abdülhak's son Hayrullah Efendi, the later Ottoman ambassador to Iran who died at Tehran in his post. Nasûhi Bey began a military career but resigned his commission in 1863 in order to launch his civil career, beginning at the Translation Bureau of the Sublime Porte. From there he occupied various bureaucratic positions in the capital as well as the European provinces, going on to serve in the usual dizzying array of posts over the 1880s and 1890s, from refugee health commissions following the Russian war of 1877, to member of the Istanbul city council, District Governor at Beirut, then Governor-General, first at Aleppo and then at Harput in remote eastern Anatolia.

In 1892 Nasûhi Bey received appointment as ambassador to Shah Nasireddin at Tehran—the post his father had occupied in the 1860s, to the same monarch—followed the next year by posting as Governor-General at Adana, then again at Beirut. In 1908 he was to report to Tehran as ambassador for the second time, but with the restoration of the Ottoman Constitution that year he accepted appointment to the reconvened Senate instead. During his notable career in civil service Nasûhi Bey rose to the second-highest civil rank, *Bâlâ*, and received the usual top Ottoman decorations as well as a host of foreign orders, including the French *Légion d'honneur*.

Like his father and grandfather, Nasûhi Bey contributed to Ottoman literature, in his case poems usually humorous in nature. Most have been lost, but the few surviving verses tie into his career with irony and wit. As one example, when he had to leave charming Aleppo for rustic Harput because the mayor of Istanbul, Rıdvan Pasha, had engineered a relative's appointment to the Aleppo post, Nasûhi took his revenge in pithy verse that rhymes in the original:

> I do not say Mr. Rıdvan should occupy his coffin,
> I merely wish that he, like I, be Governor at Harput.

> I do not say Mr. Rıdvan should plummet to the fires of hell,
> I merely wish him underground, in Rıdvan's garden.[85]

> [Rıdvan also being the name of the gatekeeper of Paradise].

At his death in 1912, aged 75, the accomplished civil servant was buried beside his grandfather.

FOOTSTONE
Here is the date of death of Nasûhi Bey
Grandson of the earlier-mentioned deceased
And son of Hayrullah Efendi:
"Nasûhi is this day through justice itself among the notables in Paradise"
30 Safer 1330 [19 February 1912]

The chronogram in the last line of the verse totals 1,330, the year of Nasûhi's death in the Muslim calendar.

İbrahim Pasha. Physician, Admiral. C61

Of unknown origin or date of birth, as a young man İbrahim graduated from the Imperial School of Medicine and served with the medical corps of the Navy as an officer. After 1868 he joined the physicians on staff at the Ministry of Marine, thereafter rising through the ranks to Admiral, with the title *Pasha*, in a career that combined medicine with administration. For several years İbrahim Pasha served as Chief Supply Officer on the Naval Council. He died in Istanbul in 1897.

TOMBSTONE
All things perish, except His Face
That Vice-Admiral of fine disposition, İbrahim Pasha
Who through skill raised himself above many a physician
Made deputy to the President of the Naval Council
Served the Council as well in managing provisions
Good-natured and kind was he, courteous and respected, truly
By such good character the object of God's grace
The world is a perishing shadow, false apart from God
Proof of this lies in regarding the state of the world as warning
Raising a prayer, to the listener I spoke a date in sorrow and regret:
"May Naim become the resting place of İbrahim Pasha"
A Fatiha for his soul—29 Receb 1315 [24 December 1897]
Composer Tevfik

The epitaph, a rhyming verse by the poet Tevfik, includes the chrono-gram that mentions Naim, the fourth of the eight paradises the Koran de-scribes, and totals 1,315, the year of İbrahim Pasha's death in the Muslim calendar. The invocation in the first line is Koran 28:88.

İshak Sükûti. Physician. E128

Born to a poor family in Diyarbakır around 1864, the young İshak Sükûti completed his schooling in his hometown before coming to Istanbul, where he graduated from the Military Medical School in 1889. While still a stu-dent there he joined with others to found the C.U.P., the group of intellec-tuals and military officers opposed to what they saw as the oppressive rule of Abdülhamid II. His actions led to his arrest and banishment to the island of Rhodes in 1895, from where he subsequently escaped to Europe. Settling in Geneva, he joined other like-minded Ottoman exiles there, contribu-ting anti-government articles to the exiles' newspaper, *Osmanlı* ("The Ottoman").

Sic transit gloria: The Ottoman flag covers the casket of C.U.P. hero
Dr. Sükûti on the way to the Mahmud II graveyard.

When a split among the C.U.P. exiles led to İshak Sükûti's expulsion from the group, he accepted the Sultan's offer of amnesty, obtaining appointment as physician at the Ottoman Embassy in Rome, in 1899. Still he continued his editorials in the *Osmanlı* newspaper, anonymously, and maintained his financial support of the movement, surreptitiously. He also read widely and composed poetry.

Dr. İshak Sükûti died of tuberculosis in San Remo, Italy, in 1901, aged only 37. With the change in political climate following the reinstatement of the Constitution seven years later, in 1909 his remains were brought to Istanbul by public subscription and honored by elaborate funeral and reburial in this imperial/national graveyard. The reburial befit a founder of the powerful C.U.P. and satisfied the party's urge to preen, now that it appeared to have triumphed.

As irony would have it, nine years later, and ostensibly for eternity, he was joined here in the nearby mausoleum by his old antagonist-turned-patron, Abdülhamid II. For unknown reasons, the celebrated doctor's tombstone was erected only in 1946, long after the dramas of his lifetime had faded into history.

TOMBSTONE
Here lies
Doctor İshak Sükûti
A founder
Of the Committee of Union and Progress
1864-1901

İsmail Pasha. Physician, Cabinet Minister, Governor-General, Mayor. A16

Born to a Greek family on the Ottoman island of Chios in 1807, as a young lad the future doctor was apprenticed (or according to family accounts, sold on the slave market[86]) to a surgeon, converted to Islam, and took the Muslim name İsmail. Mastering the skills of surgery, he served for a time as military surgeon before completing his formal education as one of the first graduates of the new Imperial Medical School in Istanbul. Appointed Chief Physician to Mahmud II, the young Dr. İsmail was honored by the monarch with selection to perform the ritual circumcision of the youthful Prince

Abdülmecid. When the latter ascended the throne in 1839, he sent Dr. İsmail to Paris to further his education. Back in the Imperial capital in 1845, aged only 38, the young doctor became director of his alma mater, the Imperial Medical School, as well as Chief Physician to Sultan Abdülmecid. Throughout his life he was thereafter known by this latter medical title in Turkish, *Hekimbaşı* İsmail Pasha, to distinguish him from other dignitaries of his same given name.

During his tenure at the medical school he greatly strengthened the curriculum, but is best remembered for introducing smallpox vaccination and securing the widespread use of reliable smallpox vaccine in Ottoman lands. He also authored a treatise, at the Sultan's request in 1847, on cholera. Meanwhile, as part of his duties at Court, he conducted the ritual circumcision of two of the Sultan's sons, Prince Murad and Prince Reşad, both of whom later ascended the throne.

By his wife, a Crimean Tatar lady by the name of Nefise, Dr. İsmail had two daughters. The younger achieved great renown in Ottoman culture as the musician and poetess Leyla Saz; her husband (and so Dr. İsmail's son-in-law) Sırrı Pasha, is buried in this graveyard.

Quite apart from his medical duties, İsmail Pasha also served in the Cabinet, as Minister of Public Works and then of Commerce after 1848, followed by posts as Governor-General of various provinces around the empire, including Ioannina, Salonica, and Shkoder in the Balkans, Aydın in Anatolia, and Crete. His talents won him Imperial appointment to the Council of State, and service as Field Marshal of the Gendarmerie. In 1873 Dr. İsmail served as Prefect (Mayor) of Istanbul for three months before joining the Cabinet once again as Minister of Public Works, for but three months. In February 1874 he was appointed Prefect of the City for the second time, but while in the Foreign Minister's office to offer his thanks for the post he suffered a stroke, and retired from public life. Dr. İsmail Pasha died six years later, in 1880, aged 73.

TOMBSTONE

A Fatiha for the soul of İsmail Pasha
Well known familiarly as "Hekimbaşı"
Eminent minister and dignitary of the Exalted Sultanate
Former Prefect of the City

In the year 1297 [1879-1880]
Mısrîzâde [Calligrapher]

Süleyman Numan Pasha. Physician, General. B44

Born in 1868, the future Pasha graduated from medical school and pursued a career as a physician with the army, rising eventually through the ranks to Brigadier General and carrying out research in particular on combating malaria. During World War One he served as chief medical officer of the Ottoman army.

Following the war, along with other top leaders of the former C.U.P., which he had joined, General Dr. Süleyman Numan Pasha was exiled to Malta by the British authorities then occupying the capital. He returned to Istanbul in the early 1920s, where he died in 1925 at age 57.

In its short rhyming verse, the Pasha's epitaph invokes the Sufi concept of annihilating individual will:

TOMBSTONE
Whoever one may be, one cannot change nature's decree:
The goal of existence is union with nothingness
Behold, yet again was it proven true, for the celebrated
physician of his age
This site, O visitor, is the grave of Doctor Süleyman Numan

ETCHED BELOW THE EPITAPH
The date of Süleyman Numan Pasha's death is 28 July 1925

Royalty and Nobles

Ali Pasha, Sherif. Arab Nobleman, Adviser to Sultan Abdülaziz. D95

Second son of Muhammad bin Abdulmuin bin Aun, the Emir of Mecca (rulers of Mecca appointed by the Ottoman monarch from members of the Hashemite family, princely natives of Mecca), Sherif Ali—his title *Sherif* indicating descent from the Prophet Muhammad—was born in 1833 and brought to Istanbul as a young man. In 1862 he received appointment to the Supreme Council of Judicial Ordinances, which advised the monarch, Sultan Abdülaziz, on matters of state. Five years later, in 1867, elevated to the highest civil rank with its title *Pasha*, he joined the August Council that also advised the Sultan.

Long frail in health, Sherif Ali Pasha died in Istanbul in 1874, aged only 41. The capital's English newspaper recalled his beneficent traits while mentioning his eminent connections:

> The funeral of the late Sherif Ali Pasha, Minister without port-folio, took place with considerable pomp on Saturday last in Stamboul. The deceased, who died from a pulmonary disease from which he had been suffering for many years, was a man of great intelligence and cultivation and of most amiable dispo-sition. His brother, Abdullah Pasha, is the present Sherif of the Mussulman Holy Places in the Hedjaz, and his father was Mo-hammed-Ibn-Han [*sic*], the celebrated Emir of Mecca, who played a prominent part in the wars of Mehemet Ali Pasha of Egypt.[87]

While Sherif Ali Pasha died too soon to leave much of a mark, his family went on to assume the most influential roles in modern Middle Eastern his-tory. His son Hussein, born at Istanbul in 1854, led the Arab Revolt against the Ottomans during World War One. His grandsons—sons of Hussein—ascended the newly created thrones of Hijaz, Jordan, and Iraq after the war; the present King of Jordan descends from him.

Ten years after Sherif Ali Pasha's death, his young nephew Muhammad Bey was buried beside him.

TOMBSTONE

Sherif Ali Pasha
Son of the late Sherif Muhammad bin Aun Efendi
Emir of Mecca the Honored
Of the branch of the Prophetic Muhammadan tree
The family line of Hashemite of Adnan
Illustrious dignitary of the Exalted Sultanate

And Honored Member of the August Council
6 Rebiülahir 1291 [23 May 1874]
Calligrapher Rıza

Princess Atiye (2). Imperial Family Member. B47

The younger of two princesses of this name interred here; for the older, see Chapter 4.

Granddaughter of Sultan Murad V, Princess Atiye was born 4 December 1891 in Çırağan Palace, where her grandfather and his descendants were sequestered from 1876 until Murad's death in 1904. She was the youngest of four sisters born to the ex-monarch's son Prince Selaheddin and the lady Tevhide Zatigül.

In 1914 Princess Atiye married Osman Hâmi Bey. The couple had no children. When Parliament exiled the Imperial Family in 1924, the Princess and her husband were obliged to leave the country, but they returned after revocation of the law of exile for royal females in 1952.

Atiye with her husband and her niece Nilüfer, in exile at Budapest, 1924.

Princess Atiye died in 1978 in Istanbul at the age of 86. Her husband was buried beside her when he died four years later.

TOMBSTONE

A Fatiha for the soul of
Princess Emine Atiye
Granddaughter of Sultan Murad V
Daughter of Prince Selaheddin
Wife of the Imperial Son-in-Law O. Hâmi
1893-1978

The stone kindly shaves a bit off the Princess's years, but dynastic records verify her correct year of birth to be 1891 rather than 1893.

Edhem Pasha. Council Member, Imperial Son-in-Law. A25

The future Edhem Pasha was born in 1831 to Mehmed Emin Ali Pasha, the illustrious statesman who at the time of his son's birth was Second Chamberlain at the Court of Mahmud II, but later rose to Admiral of the Fleet, ambassador, and Grand Vizier. In 1845, when Edhem was yet a teenager, as a typical reward for loyalty of high-ranking men of state his father was given the hand in marriage of Princess Âdile, Sultan Mahmud's daughter. By that young age Edhem was already on the path to career success, entering the War Academy in 1850 with the rank of Major-General, thanks to his father's lofty connections, even though aged but 19.

Four years later the young general was rewarded by Imperial favor when, as a gesture to his father's services to the state, he was engaged to Princess Refia, 12-year-old daughter of Sultan Abdülmecid. In honor of the engagement, Edhem was immediately promoted to Divisional General. The couple had to wait three years for the bride to reach adulthood, finally marrying in April 1857 in magnificent ceremonial befitting an Imperial wedding, at the now-vanished Palace of Neşatabad on the Bosphorus.[88]

The following year the Sultan raised Edhem to the highest civil rank, and appointments began that protocol of the day considered appropriate for an Imperial Son-in-Law: to the advisory Supreme Council the year after his marriage, followed in the 1860s and 1870s by appointments to the Cabinet, the Council of State, and the General Council. In 1877 he served in the newly born Ottoman Parliament.

His marriage to the bright and well-educated Princess, however, was most unhappy, as correspondence between the Princess and her siblings tells us, and the couple grew apart. The Princess could not produce a child, and money problems besieged them. In the late 1870s, Refia developed what appears to have been ovarian cancer, from which she died in January 1880 at the age of 37. She was buried beside her mother in the Mausoleum of the Imperial Ladies at the New Mosque.

Shortly after the Princess's death, Edhem Pasha married again, this time becoming father to a son and daughter. An unspecified illness in the mid-1880s left him bedridden for some two years, however, until he succumbed in 1886 at age 55. His funeral service took place at the New Mosque, in whose adjoining mausoleum his royal first wife lay buried. Newspaper accounts tell of the illustrious contingent of statesmen, sailors, gendarmes, and police that accompanied his casket uphill from the mosque to this burial ground.[89]

Edhem's daughter Seniha lived to adulthood but his young son Mehmed Ali died the year after his father and is buried in the adjoining tomb. At the boy's death, Edhem Pasha's stepmother Princess Âdile (at the same time aunt to his first wife Princess Refia, confusingly enough), the royal poetess of the dynasty, penned a eulogy that mentioned all three departed family members; see the entry in this subsection for "Mehmed Ali Bey."

TOMBSTONE
He is The Eternal One, The Creator
A Fatiha for the soul of
The illustrious Field Marshal and Member of Parliament
Son-in-Law to His Imperial Majesty
The late Edhem Pasha
Son of the former Grand Vizier and Admiral of the Fleet
The late Imperial Son-in-Law Mehmed Ali Pasha
3 Cemaziyül'evvel 1303 [7 February 1886]

Fahir Bey. Imperial Son-in-Law. E126

Born around 1884 to a family high in state service (his maternal grandfather, the Governor-General and Cabinet minister Galib Pasha, is also buried in this garden), Fahir Bey took up work in state service himself, most notably as an official at the embassy in Bucharest. He saw his family's loyalty and service to the Imperial House rewarded when in 1909 he was engaged to Princess Şadiye, daughter of Abdülhamid II. The marriage was postponed when Abdülhamid was deposed that year and the Princess accompanied her father into exile at Salonica, but at her return to Istanbul in 1910 the couple married. It was a most happy union, as his wife wrote in her memoir, and their daughter Princess Samiye was born to the couple in 1918.

Ever of delicate constitution, however, Fahir died at the youthful age of about 38, in 1922, at the couple's villa in Nişantaşı, of scarlet fever and uremia, leaving his young widow and daughter to fend for themselves when the Imperial Family was exiled eighteen months later.

Some fifteen years after Fahir's death, Sultan Reşad's Senior Secretary

Befitting an Imperial Son-in-law, the opulent tomb of Fahir Bey (left); beside it, the complementary yet simpler tomb of his father, who died four years later.

recalled the sterling qualities of the young man, who actually had been Princess Şadiye's second choice for a husband:

> I'd known Fahir Bey since he was a boy, and he came to see me often. Grandson of Galib Pasha, the long-serving Minister of Pious Foundations renowned for uprightness and integrity, he was truly one of Istanbul's most attractive, good-natured, and cultured sons. I thought very highly of him, and had even found the means to help and oversee his education, when the opportunity arose to secure an excellent teacher for him.
>
> There's not the slightest doubt that Fahir Bey made up for the painful loss of the Princess's first candidate. Yet what can one do, good luck had smiled warmly on him but the overpowering hand of death took the unfortunate young man away at an age when one expected it not at all.[90]

Fahir's father and maternal grandfather are both buried here, his father beside him, his grandfather nearby. Some fifty-five years after Fahir's death, his royal widow was buried within the mausoleum proper at her own demise.

TOMBSTONE

The precious remains committed to this sacred sanctuary of God's mercy
Are those of Ahmed Fahir Bey
Imperial Son-in-Law to His Majesty Sultan Abdülhamid II,
whose abode is Paradise
Grandson of the late Galib Pasha,
the Former Minister of Pious Foundations
And son to Fevzi Bey
Singular hope and peerless pride of his Mother and Father
The sweet-faced and pure-hearted young man was
With his angelic virtue and integrity
An excellent person of eminent perfection
No creature did he injure, nor did any injure him
Alas and oh, before completing his thirty-eighth year, his death
Like a mournful sigh, a covetous flash

Plunged his hapless parents into grief and sorrow
And left the leaders of his family and all his acquaintances
Deeply distressed and disconsolate
May the compassion of the All-Compassionate be with him
3 Zilhicce 1340 [28 July 1922]

Fahru'l-Muhadderat. Arab Noblewoman. D91

The young lady Fahru'l-Muhadderat (full name Fahru'l-Muhadderat wa
Taju'l-Masturat, "The Pride of Virtuous Women and Crown of Modest
Ladies") was daughter to Abdullah Pasha, of the dynasty (descended from
the Prophet) that ruled as emirs of Mecca, and who himself served as Grand
Sherif of Mecca from 1858 to 1877. By the time of this unmarried daughter's death in 1884, at an unknown age but probably in her 20s, Abdullah
Pasha and his family resided in Istanbul, where the young lady's illustrious
family connections earned her an obituary in the capital's English newspaper:

> We regret to announce the loss which his Highness the Sherif
> Abdullah Pasha, brother of the Grand Sherif of Mecca, has sus-
> tained by the death of his daughter. The funeral ceremony took
> place with great pomp at St. Sophia, and the mortal remains
> were interred in the cemetery of the Imperial Family, attached
> to the Mausoleum of Sultan Mahmoud II. at Stamboul.[91]

Fahru'l-Muhadderat was buried next to her brother Muhammad, who
had died nine months earlier, at age 20, and was interred beside their uncle
Sherif Ali Pasha. Through her sister Abdiye, who married her cousin Hus-
sein (the Emir of Mecca who led the Arab Revolt against the Ottomans in
World War One, and son of the uncle Sherif Ali Pasha who is buried here),
Fahru'l-Muhadderat was aunt to the future King Abdullah I of Jordan and
King Ali of the Hijaz, and great-aunt to Queen Aliya of Iraq, while her
grand-nephew Ali bin al-Hussein is the current claimant to the throne of
Iraq.

TOMBSTONE
He is The Eternal One, The Creator
Here is the luminous tomb of Her Excellency
The lady Fahru'l-Muhadderat wa Taju'l-Masturat
Daughter of compassionate comprehension
To His Excellency the illustrious sherif of noble descent, Abdullah Pasha
The Fatiha
26 Muharrem 1302 [15 November 1884]

Princess Gevheri. Imperial Family Member, Musician. B49

Granddaughter of Sultan Abdülaziz through his son Prince Seyfeddin, and twin of her brother Prince Ahmed Tevhid, Princess Gevheri was born in her father's villa in the Istanbul district of Çamlıca in 1904. Prince Seyfeddin numbered among the gifted musicians of the Imperial Family, composing brilliant works in the Turkish classical repertoire, and the young Gevheri inherited his talent. She became an accomplished performer of traditional Turkish musical instruments, notably the kemanche (small violin, played upright) and tambur (long-necked lute).

Along with the rest of the Imperial Family, Gevheri was sent into exile in 1924, at the age of 19. She developed her musical gifts despite the distresses of exile in France and Cairo, and continued composing and performing after returning to Turkey following the revocation of the law of exile for princesses in 1952. Gevheri did not marry, and died in Istanbul in 1980, aged 76, leaving rare musical instruments (including several inherited from her father) and compositions for a museum of Turkish music, which as yet has eluded permanent establishment.

The musical Princess's tombstone mentions her surname Osmanoğlu ("Son of Osman"), adopted by the Imperial Family after the end of the monarchy.

TOMBSTONE
The composer
Fatma Gevheri Osmanoğlu
Granddaughter of Sultan Abdülaziz
Daughter of Prince Seyfeddin Osmanoğlu
1909-1980

Hüsnü Pasha. Field Marshal, State Councillor, Imperial Son-in-Law. C60

The future Hüsnü Pasha was born around 1835 as one of the many sons of the prominent Mustafa Nuri Pasha, who had been Privy Secretary to Mahmud II, then Minister of War and Governor-General of numerous provinces around the empire during his long and eminent career. With such an illustrious father, Hüsnü would have found doors open to him when he launched his own career with the army. Over time he advanced through the ranks to Divisional General.

In 1860, as supreme token of the Sultan's esteem for his father, Hüsnü was presented the hand in marriage of Princess Seniye, granddaughter of Mahmud II through his daughter Princess Atiye, who is interred in the mausoleum. The couple had no children. Three years after his marriage, the Imperial Son-in-Law (strictly speaking he was the son-in-law of a princess rather than a reigning monarch, but husbands of Imperial granddaughters could use this prestigious title) was raised to the rank of Field Marshal, and he served for many years on the Council of the Ministry of War, including as its President. He also served the palace as Director of the Salutation Procession, the royal procession to mosque each Friday.

When the Pasha died in 1899, the capital's English-language newspaper reported his obsequies:

> The funeral of Marshal Hassan Husni Pasha, brother-in-law of his Majesty the Sultan, took place yesterday and was attended by many relatives and a large number of civil and military officers. From Arnaoutkeui, where the deceased resided, the coffin was conveyed in a steam-launch to Sirkedji and thence to the mosque of St. Sophia where the service was held. The cortège was headed by sheikhs and dervishes, and escorted by a detachment of troops. The interment took place in the mausoleum of Sultan Mahmud. Among those who followed the Marshal's remains to their last resting-place were Marshals Mahmud Pasha, Ahmed Zulkefl Pasha [whose infant daughter Princess Kâmile was buried inside the mausoleum three years earlier], and Khalid Pasha, brothers-in-law of his Majesty; the two brothers of the deceased, General Osman Pasha, director of the Cavalry

Department at the War Office, and Bekir Bey, formerly chief
accountant of the Ministry of Commerce; General Hakki Pasha,
commanding the Ertoghrul Regiment; Husni Pasha, aide-de-
camp of the Sultan; Hafiz Vehbi Bey, manager of the Shirket-
Hairieh [the Bosphorus steamship company], etc.[92]

At her own death twelve years later, in 1911, his widow Princess Seniye
was buried in the Lady Nevfidan Chamber of the mausoleum rather than
in the garden, since she was of the blood-royal.

TOMBSTONE
He is The Eternal One, The Everliving One
The Imperial Son-in-Law Field Marshal Hasan Hüsnü Pasha
Director of the Noble Salutation Procession
Son of the Member of Parliament, former Minister of War
Vizier and Sheikh, and Privy Secretary
Mustafa Nuri Pasha
May God bless his soul
2 S. [Safer] 1316 [but the month should be L., Şevval,
to yield 13 February 1899]

Mehmed Ali Bey. Son of Edhem Pasha. A26

The six-year-old son of Edhem Pasha, next to whom he is buried, died in
1887, the year following his father's death (two years following his father's
death, by the Muslim calendar, as the tombstone attests). He left his
mother—the Pasha's second wife—as well as his sister, Seniha. When he
died, his grieving step-grandmother Princess Âdile, the noted poetess of
the Imperial Family, penned the following eulogy that alluded to the boy's
deceased grandfather Mehmed Ali Pasha (the poetess's late husband), and
the sorrows of his father's first marriage to Princess Refia (Princess Âdile's
beloved niece):

May God make of Mehmed Ali Pasha's grave
The garden of Paradise, the rose-bed of the garden of the heavens.
The precious ornament of his heart, his son Edhem Pasha,

Found from fate no happiness on this earth;
His esteemed wife, the Princess Refia
Would depart for the Kingdom of the Compassionate One.
The poor soul fell at last to grief and worry,
He took sick, the fires of anguish seared his heart.
Weeping and weak, withdrawn in mourning and yearning,
The doctors' treatment could offer no cure.
The end yielded its trusts, to God he journeyed,
May light of the Koran illumine his pure grave.
In the end a child remained, light of his eye,
The young master, Mehmed Ali, fresh with youth.
Fate took him too, and plunged us into pain of loss;
God grant us strength to bear these sorrows.
Assuredly, Âdile, abode of affliction is the world;
Let us gladden their souls with the Fatiha.[93]

The capital's English newspaper announced the child's death, although the paper erred in naming him the Sultan's brother-in-law rather than the son of the Sultan's (late) brother-in-law:

> The death is announced, after a long illness, of Mehmed Ali Bey, brother-in-law of His Imperial Majesty the Sultan. It occurred on Thursday last, at Scutari [Üsküdar]. The funeral took place with great pomp at Stamboul, the deceased being interred near the mausoleum of Sultan Mahmoud.[94]

TOMBSTONE
He is The Eternal One, The Everliving One
May the soul of the late Mehmed Ali Pasha
Be favored with the compassion and forgiveness of the Lord Most High
Son of the Imperial Son-in-Law Edhem Pasha
Who departed this life two years previously
While but a child his virtues . . . [illegible]
At age fifty, adversity entered his life
May God grant his pure Mother and Princess Âdile
Forbearance and consolation, health and long life and good fortune

O İsmet, the residents of Paradise recite your poetic date:
"To Heaven went Mehmed Ali Bey, and found there reunion"
18 Muharrem 1305 [6 October 1887]

The chronogram in the last line of verse totals 1,305, the year of the boy's death in the Muslim calendar.

Princess Mihrişah. Imperial Family Member. B50

Princess Mihrişah was born in August 1916 at the villa of her father, Prince Yusuf İzzeddin, the late Heir to the Throne. She never knew her father because he died six months before her birth. Her mother, the Prince's consort the lady Leman, was also mother to his two other children.

At not quite eight years of age, in 1924 Mihrişah was sent into exile along with her brother and sister (their mother remaining in Turkey), by 1929 settling in Egypt, where several members of the Imperial Family had taken refuge. In 1948 she married her divorced cousin Prince Ömer Faruk, eighteen years her senior, son of Caliph Abdülmecid II. Following the 1952 revocation of the law of exile for princesses she returned to Istanbul with her sister Princess Şükriye. The two took up residence in their father's villa in the Çamlıca district of Istanbul, their mother having maintained the mansion over the intervening three decades. Mihrişah and Ömer Faruk divorced in 1959, and in 1973 the Princess—having sold her father's villa the previous year at the death of her sister—married Dr. Şevket Aslanoğlu.

Mihrişah died in Istanbul in 1987, aged 70. As part of the restitution of this complex as a site for Imperial Family interments beginning in the 1960s, she was buried here alongside her two cousins who predeceased her, her tombstone bearing the surname Osmanoğlu that the Imperial Family adopted after the end of the monarchy. Her father and paternal grandparents are interred in the main chamber of the mausoleum.

TOMBSTONE
He is The Eternal One
A Fatiha for the soul of
Mihriban Mihrişah Osmanoğlu
Granddaughter of Sultan Abdülaziz

Daughter of the Heir to the Throne, Prince Yusuf İzzeddin
And of the lady Leman
1916-1987

Prince Osman Ertuğrul. Head of the Imperial House. B41a

Grandson of Abdülhamid II through his son Prince Burhaneddin and the
latter's wife the lady Nazlıyar, Prince Osman Ertuğrul was born in 1912 at
his father's villa in Istanbul. At age eight he went to Vienna for schooling,
and he (with his father) was in Vienna when the Turkish government exiled
the Imperial Family, in 1924. The young Prince finished his studies in Paris
and in 1933 sailed to America, settling in New York where he pursued a
successful business career.

Upon revocation of the exile law for royal males in 1974, the Prince did
not return immediately to Turkey. The government's refusal in 1949 to
allow his father to be buried in Turkey still rankled, as did the government's
referring to the revocation as a "pardon," since the Prince saw nothing to
be pardoned for. He first returned to his homeland to visit in 1992, seventy
years after he last saw it. Two years later he inherited the honorific title,
Head of the Imperial House.

After meeting the Turkish Prime Minister in New York in 2004, the 92-
year-old Prince received, as a kind of apology for past treatment, a Turkish
passport. Reflecting Turkey's renewed interest in its Imperial Family, his
return to Istanbul in July that year caused a media sensation, much to his
surprise. Subsequently he returned to Turkey for summer visits.

In 2009, aged 97 (but over 100 in the Muslim calendar), Prince Osman
Ertuğrul died at the American Hospital in Istanbul. His funeral, widely covered in the media, took place at the Sultan Ahmed ("Blue") Mosque, attended by high representatives of the government and business world as
well as thousands of simple mourners. The huge crowd accompanied the
flag-draped coffin the short distance from the mosque to this garden for
burial "near his grandfather," as was said. The Turkish press dubbed Prince
Osman Ertuğrul *son Osmanlı,* "the last Ottoman," which of course he
wasn't, and *son saraylı,* "the last palace resident" (more precisely, the last
Ottoman prince born during the monarchy), which indeed he was. He was
the final survivor of the 155 members of the Imperial Family exiled in
1924.

Osman Ertuğrul married twice. His first wife, South African Gulda Twerskoy, whom he married in 1947, died in 1985. His second wife, Zeynep Tarzi, born in Istanbul to a cadet branch of the Afghan Royal Family, married the Prince in 1991 and survived him.

TOMBSTONE

Prince Osman Ertuğrul Efendi

Grandson of Sultan Abdülhamid II

Son of Prince Burhaneddin Efendi

Born 18 August 1912   Died 23 September 2009

Osman Hâmi Bey. Imperial Son-in-Law. B48

Son of Osman Ferid Pasha of the prominent Sırkâtibizâde family, Hâmi was born in 1890 (contrary to the date stated on his tombstone) and trained in the law before marrying Princess Atiye, granddaughter of Sultan Murad V, in 1914. He was well placed for marital alliance with the Imperial Family, since in 1860 his uncle Hüsnü Pasha (also buried in this garden) had married Princess Seniye (convolutedly enough, aunt to Hâmi's cousin Ferdâne).

Living out the exile of the Imperial Family in Europe after 1924, the couple could finally return to Turkey in 1952. Childless, Osman Hâmi Bey devoted himself to philanthropic support of the Darüşşafaka ("House of Compassion"), the school for orphans and poor children in Istanbul. Upon his death in 1982 he was buried beside his royal wife, who had predeceased him by four years.

TOMBSTONE

A Fatiha for the soul of

The Imperial Son-in-Law Osman Hâmi Bey

Son of Osman Ferid Pasha

Who was son of the Privy Secretary and Doyen of

Viziers Mustafa Nuri Pasha

And of Emine Fahire Hanım, Daughter of Ali Rıza Bey

Husband to Princess Emine Atiye

Philanthropic benefactor of the Darüşşafaka Society

1900 – 2 December 1982

Sadık Pasha, Sherif. Arab Nobleman. E102

Grandson of the Arab notable Abdulmuttalib of the Hijaz, who served as Emir of Mecca three times during the nineteenth century, Sherif Sadık Pasha (his honorary title "Sherif" indicating his descent from the Prophet) lived in Istanbul, where he lost his life during the Counter-revolution that broke out in the capital in mid-April 1909. Under unclear circumstances, in the night of 13 April, the first day of the revolt, Sherif Sadık Pasha and his secretary were killed by unknown assailants in the street. As such they numbered among the first victims of the bloody uprising in the capital.

Most likely their deaths were in error, a case of mistaken identity. Later, the two were dubbed "the most innocent victims of the bloody crimes" committed during the revolt.[95] To commemorate his unjustified murder during the suppressed uprising, Sherif Sadık Pasha (but not his secretary) was laid to rest here in what was now evolving into a national graveyard for prominent martyrs in the struggle against tyranny, including the slain journalist Hasan Fehmi who had been buried here only seven days previously.

The newspapers of the day were quick to record his innocent death in the turbulent early days of the revolt:

> At ten o'clock last night, Cherif Sadik Pasha and his secretary were found murdered in the street before the offices of the Pension Fund.

> Yesterday there took place the obsequies of Sherif Sadik Pasha, who was killed in circumstances that are known the night before last. The burial took place in the environs of the Mausoleum of Sultan Mahmoud.[96]

Also interred in this graveyard are Sadık's distant cousins from the same noble Meccan family, Sherif Ali Pasha and the siblings Muhammad Bey and the lady Fahru'l-Muhadderat.

TOMBSTONE

God is Everlasting

Here stands the tomb of the late descendant of the Prophet

Sherif Mehmed Sadık Pasha
Son of Sherif Ahmed Adnan Pasha
Grandson of Sherif Abdulmuttalib Efendi
Who on 31 March of the Solar Rumî Year 1325
(22 Rebiülevvel 1327) [13 April 1909]
During the military revolt that arose in Istanbul
Set forth to provide counsel to the rebels
And was instantly martyred by gunfire during an attack
A Fatiha for his soul

Selaheddin Ali Bey. Imperial Son-in-Law. E114

Born in 1889-90, Selaheddin Ali married Princess Âdile, granddaughter of Sultan Murad V, in April 1914 in a splendid wedding attended by relatives among the Imperial Family and by ranking men of state. He was well placed for this marriage since his grandfather, Admiral Moralı İbrahim Pasha, had been Minister of Marine and Governor-General of the Aegean Archipelago. The young Imperial Son-in-Law impressed his new family as kindly and generous, an elegant dresser of the day, always in good taste, an accomplished horseman, and a gracious host at numerous dinner parties. At the end of World War One, the fall of the C.U.P., whose staunch supporter he had been, shook him deeply.[97]

Selaheddin Ali was not granted time to consider the vast changes

Selaheddin Ali Bey with his wife,
Princess Âdile, and young daughter.

befalling the country, however, for he took sick and quickly succumbed, on 26 December 1918, to influenza in the worldwide epidemic that followed the war. A commoner despite his marriage and thus not interred inside the mausoleum, Selaheddin Ali was buried in the garden beside the tomb of his father, Ali Bey, which in turn stands beside the tomb of his illustrious grandfather, the Admiral.

Aged about 29 at his death, Selaheddin Ali left his young widow and 2-year-old daughter Nilüfer. Upon their own respective deaths in 1973 and 1989, both Princess Âdile and Princess Nilüfer (who married the son of India's Nizam of Hyderabad in 1931) were buried in Paris, where they resided.

TOMBSTONE

The Imperial Son-in-Law Moralızâde Selaheddin Ali Bey

To his religion and country the young man who lies here was devoted

He lived but the springtime of his life

To his family's honorable past

He added still another pure name, and then departed

In life he loved and was loved

Of you he asks a Fatiha

Born 1305 [1889-90], died 1334 [1918, both dates in the Rumî calendar]

Princess Zehra Fatma. Imperial Family Member. A23

Grand-niece to Abdülhamid II, in whose palace of Yıldız she was born, Princess Zehra Fatma (or Fatma Zehra) came into the world on 28 May 1895 according to contemporary dynastic records but contrary to her tombstone. Her mother was the lady Tesrid, one of the five ladies of Prince İbrahim Tevfik, the accomplished musician and artist who was the only son of Abdülhamid II's brother Prince Burhaneddin (not to be confused with Abdülhamid's son by the same name). Since her mother's sister, the lady Emsalinur, was a consort of Abdülhamid's and mother to Princess Şadiye, Princess Fatma was doubly related to that Princess, who is buried in the mausoleum.

In 1917 she married Selami Alpan, son of Field Marshal Kâzım Pasha, and gave birth to two sons in the 1920s. At the dynasty's exile in 1924 she settled with her family in Haifa (where her husband died in 1945) and then Beirut. Returning to her homeland after revocation of the law of exile for females in 1952, the Princess was living in Istanbul at the time of her death in 1965, aged nearly 70. She was the first person buried in the long-disused cemetery since 1925 (apart from the four remains transferred here in 1957 and 1961), her burial heralding the new tradition of interring returned members of the Imperial Family at the Mahmud II Tomb Complex. Her tombstone bears the surname Osmanoğlu, adopted by the Imperial Family after the end of the monarchy.

TOMBSTONE

Zehra Fatma Osmanoğlu
Descendant of Sultan Abdülmecid
Granddaughter of Prince Burhaneddin
Daughter of Prince İbrahim Tevfik
Born 20 March 1896
Died 24 May 1965
A Fatiha for her soul

Scholars and Religious Figures

Ahmed Fâik. Judge. E97

Scion of a line of religious scholars at Bodrum, Ahmed Fâik was born at that future resort on the Aegean Sea probably around 1840. His father, grandfather, and great-grandfather all completed the pilgrimage to Mecca during their lifetimes. The young man's father, Ömer Lûtfi Efendi, came to Istanbul where he taught religious studies at institutions of higher education and received Imperial appointment as tutor to Prince Yusuf İzzeddin, who is buried in the mausoleum. His father's career was crowned with appointment by Abdülhamid II to the highest possible religious post, that of Şeyhülislâm, in January 1889.

Not nearly as much is known about Ahmed Fâik as about his renowned father, but we can say that he followed in his father's footsteps by training as a religious scholar himself. He became a teacher, then a judge, and was honored with advancement through the judicial ranks.

Ahmed Fâik passed away in June 1890 in Istanbul, probably around the age of 50, during his father's tenure as chief religious figure of the empire. Clearly Abdülhamid II authorized his burial here as a token of respect for his father's present and past services to the Imperial House. His tombstone pays tribute to his (and his familial) connections to the religious establishment in two ways: the turban of a trained religious scholar caps the stone (after 1828, only religious dignitaries wore turbans), and the first four lines of the epitaph are in Arabic (which Ottoman Turks would not ordinarily understand unless they had been trained in the Koran).

Had Ahmed Fâik died only fifteen months later he surely would not have been buried here, as the suspicious Abdülhamid II dismissed his father the next year, based on a highly dubious informer report implying the Şeyhülislâm might decree Abdülhamid's deposition in order to restore the Sultan's deposed brother Murad to the throne.[98]

TOMBSTONE

He is The Eternal One, The Everliving One
O Visitor of my grave, I am indeed Ahmed
I ask for myself pardon—for the dignity of Ahmed—
From the Merciful Lord
Grant him bliss and the most pleasant of lives

The Fatiha for the soul of Ahmed Fâik
Who is in Need of the Mercy of his God, the Creator
Bearer of the rank *Haremeyn*
Noble son of the illustrious and munificent Ömer Lûtfi Efendi
Currently Şeyhülislâm and Legal Counsel of Mankind
May God extend peace to him
21 Şevval 1307 [10 June 1890]

The opening four lines of the epitaph, in Arabic, play on the name *Ahmed*: in the first line, the name of the deceased; in the second line, an alternate name of the Prophet Muhammad. Another play on words is "bliss," *al-Na'im*, since this is also the name of the fourth of the eight paradises that the Koran mentions. *Haremeyn* ("the Two Holy Cities," Mecca and Medina) was a high rank of judge.

Atâ Bey. Financial Official, Teacher, Historian, Translator. D89

Born in Aleppo in 1856, Atâ Bey spent a good deal of his youth in Beirut, where his father was posted. His knowledge of Arabic, Persian, French, and Italian served him well in later years. Beginning his career in the finance and taxation branches of government, he also served as general inspector of the Imperial Post and Telegraph Office before rising to posts as governor in Anatolian provinces in the early 1900s. Subsequently serving on various governmental finance committees, in 1919 he was appointed Minister of Finance, but being nervous by nature he had spent much of his last years in bed and was unable to occupy the post, dying shortly after his appointment.

Quite apart from his work in government finance, Atâ Bey devoted significant time to his three passions of history, literature, and ethics, teaching all three at various schools of higher education. Among other works, he compiled a reader for teaching composition and literature in schools, and translated French novels into Turkish. Perhaps his greatest contribution was his translation into Turkish (probably from the French translation of its original German) of the monumental, multi-volume *History of the Ottoman Empire* by Joseph von Hammer-Purgstall, published originally in 1918, and still in use today.

TOMBSTONE
He is The Eternal One
The Fatiha for the soul of Mehmed Atâ Bey
Teacher, historian
And former Minister of Finance
1338 [26 September 1919-14 September 1920]

Derviş Pasha. Chemistry Professor, Cabinet Minister. A14

Born around 1818 to a family that claimed descent from the Prophet
Muhammad, Derviş pursued a dual career as both statesman and professor
of chemistry and physics, which gave rise to his sobriquet *Kimyager* ("the
Chemist") that distinguished him from others of the same name.

Beginning his teaching career at the War College School of Engineering,
Derviş rose to the rank of Divisional General in 1848, aged only 30. His
research was making a name for him, as the capital's French newspaper
reported that year:

> Dervish Pasha, professor at the War College, and member of the
> Council of Public Instruction, has just composed a manual com-
> pletely in Turkish on the manufacture of gun powder. This work
> has been presented to the Sul-
> tan, who received it with
> great kindness. Dervish
> Pasha studied for several
> years in Europe, and among
> the young Muslims who have
> attended our schools, he is in-
> contestably one of those to
> have obtained the most posi-
> tive and complete bodies of
> knowledge. He has already
> composed a most remarkable
> work on chemistry, and we
> have no doubt whatsoever
> that his manual on the fabri-
> cation of powder, which is to
> be published presently, will
> prove a most useful tome,
> conscientiously produced,
> and worthy, in all respects, of
> the attention of practitioners
> of the art.[99]

Science professor Derviş Pasha
rose to the highest ranks in state service,
but one suspects he was happiest in
the chemistry laboratory.

Ten years later came the chemist's appointment to the advisory Supreme Council, followed by postings in the Ministry of Public Instruction. In 1867 Derviş became Director of Military Schools, followed by appointment to ever higher posts in government service: the Council of State in 1867, appointed by Sultan Abdülaziz; promotion to the highest civil rank, *vizier*; Governor-General of Aleppo, in Syria; return to Istanbul in 1872 with Cabinet appointment as Minister of Public Instruction; Governor-General of Ankara, 1873-1874. In 1877 he was appointed Senator in the new and short-lived Ottoman Parliament.

Chemist Derviş Pasha died unexpectedly in 1879 at the age of about 60 (by the Western calendar), after a career in teaching and government service that had lasted four decades. His science courses at the War College and the Imperial School of Medicine trained a new generation of modern chemists and physicists in Turkey.

TOMBSTONE

A Fatiha for the soul of the late and divinely pardoned Seyyid
Mehmed Emin Derviş Pasha
Renowned Professor of Science
Who served the Ottoman State from the age of eighteen
to the age of sixty-three
Honored during this time with important posts including
Ambassador and Minister
Celebrated for having obtained the rank of Vizier
in the year 1284 [1867-68]
And who passed away while serving as member of the
Senate and the Military Council
14 Muharrem 1296 [8 January 1879]
Calligrapher Emin

Muallim Naci. Poet and Author. E105

The future celebrated litterateur, named Ömer at his birth around 1849 in Istanbul, was raised by an uncle in Varna (today's Bulgaria) after his father died. He completed his education from tutors, studying Arabic and Persian and achieving some mastery of calligraphy. At age 18 in 1867, he was appointed as a teacher in the high school the government opened that year in Varna.

The young teacher continued his education with private instruction in classical Ottoman prosody as well as in French. He began to write and publish verse, taking the pen name "Naci" from the story he read in these years featuring a character by that name. And so the young Ömer morphed into *Muallim Naci*, "Teacher Naci."

Leaving teaching, Naci secured work as Private Secretary to the high-ranking bureaucrat Said Pasha, following him in posts around the empire in the 1870s and early 1880s. Even so he continued composing verse and publishing it in the influential Istanbul newspaper *Tercüman-ı Hakikat* ("Translator of Truths"), in 1883 leaving Said Pasha's employ to launch himself as the newspaper's literary columnist. His fame as a poet and literary commentator spread, thanks particularly to his delightful skill at composing *nazires*—the witty poems, published in his literary column, that imitated and paralleled classical Ottoman poetry. This latter talent did not sit quite well with his boss at the paper (whose daughter he had married), so around 1885 Muallim Naci left to found his own periodical, write for other papers, and teach literature at various schools. In these years he produced a copious and skilled array of poetry, literary criticism, biographies, letters, memoirs, plays, translations from Arab and French literature, and a famed dictionary long used in schools. His engaging compositions and winning verses in simple language won many followers. Honors followed: the gold medal of the International Congress of Orientalists for services to the

Muallim Naci's fame as an author and poet earned him burial here.

Turkish language; decoration by Abdülhamid II for his rhyming verse on Ertuğrul Gazi, progenitor of the Ottoman dynasty; and investiture by the Sultan with the grand title, "Chronicler of the Sultans of the House of Osman."

Inspired by the latter honor, Naci embarked upon the ambitious project of compiling an official history of the Ottoman monarchs. Before he could compose the text, however, he suffered a fatal heart attack on 12 April 1893, aged only 44. Grieved at his sudden passing, Abdülhamid II honored the eminent litterateur by ordering his burial in this Imperial graveyard, settling the burial expenses from the Imperial purse.

Naci's old newspaper described the funeral procession the following day from his home to the courtyard of Aya Sofya Mosque for the prayer service, then to this graveyard for burial:

> His remains, traced with God's pardon, made their way around six o'clock for the appropriate memorial services, accompanied by noble elders of the religious orders, gentlemen of the Imperial Household, and a company of Imperial guards, policemen and municipal police officers and sergeants, representatives of the gendarmerie, municipal officials, the deceased's family and loved ones, a delegation from the Ottoman press, and many other persons as well, all preceded by high public officials, and by dervishes reciting the Profession of God's Unity and the affirmation *Allahu Ekber* ("God is Most Great).[100]

The prominent author's death warranted an obituary in the capital's English newspaper as well:

> Professor Nadji Effendi, a distinguished Mussulman man of letters and historian, who was highly appreciated in Ottoman literary circles, died suddenly on Wednesday in his residence at Stamboul, succumbing to heart disease. Some days before, Nadji Effendi had an attack of influenza which weakened him considerably. On Wednesday he was suddenly taken ill and expired before the arrival of the physician summoned by Ahmed Midhat Effendi, his father-in-law, who was with him. The

funeral, which took place yesterday, was largely attended, the expenses being paid by the Privy Purse of his Imperial Majesty the Sultan, who was deeply affected by the death of Professor Nadji Effendi. The body was interred, by Imperial order, within the precincts of the Mausoleum of Sultan Mahmoud.[101]

Muallim Naci's legacy endured as champion of the joys of classical Ottoman poetry—at which he excelled in beautiful language, simply expressed, elegantly rhymed, and artfully arranged to suit the meter—at a time when European influence portended dramatic change in literary taste among the Ottoman reading public. Fittingly, the rhyming couplet that opens the poet's epitaph was composed by the deceased himself.

TOMBSTONE

He

Right-minded am I, one with the Court where I proffered
sincerity of heart
In not one breath did I part from proclaiming God's Oneness; God is One

Here is the spiritual resting place of His Excellency Muallim Naci
Chronicler of the Sultans of the House of Osman
Born in the year 1266 [1849-1850]
Died in the year 1310 [1893]

Necib Efendi. Chief Justice, Religious Scholar. C71

Born around 1810 to a family that claimed descent from the Prophet Muhammad, the young Necib devoted his studies to religion, memorizing the Koran early on. In the 1840s and 1850s his abilities brought him the post of imam in the London and Paris embassies, where he studied European languages.

Returning to Istanbul when the ambassador at Paris, Mustafa Reşid Pasha, was appointed Grand Vizier in the late 1840s, Necib Efendi served the Pasha's household as librarian and teacher. From there he climbed the career ladder of the religious-judicial confraternity, serving as judge or inspector in increasingly important posts. By 1866 he had risen to Chief Justice of Anatolia, and in 1872 to Chief Justice of Rumelia, a post to which he received appointment four times, and in which he was confirmed again in 1891, out of deference to his personal qualities, even though he was by then quite elderly and infirm. At the same time he was still a member of the prestigious Council of State, to which Sultan Abdülaziz had appointed him back in 1868, and from which he eventually only retired due to advanced age.

After a protracted illness Necib Efendi died at his home at Küçük Çamlıca on the Asian side of the Bosphorus, 22 July 1891, probably in his eighties. At the time he held the honorary title Chief of the Ulema, inherited by the longest-serving religious scholar in high government service. The English-language newspaper of the day described his obsequies:

> The funeral of the late Nedjib Effendi, chief of the ulemas, took place yesterday at Stamboul. From Scutari [Üsküdar], the body was taken to Sirkedji in a steam launch, and thence to St. Sophia, and buried in a private vault near the mausoleum of Sultan Mahmoud. Among those who attended the funeral were: — Their Excellencies Zihni Pasha, Minister of the Evkaf; Arif Pasha, military commander of Constantinople; Redvan Pasha, Prefect of Stamboul; Sherif Abdoullah Pasha; Hassan Pasha, former vali of Aleppo; Nazim Bey, Minister of Police; . . . Colonel Youssouf Izzet Bey, aide-de-camp of His Imperial Majesty the Sultan, and many other functionaries from the Sheikh ul-Islamate.[102]

TOMBSTONE
He is The Eternal One
A Fatiha for the soul of
Mehmed Necib Efendi
Son of Ahıskalı Salih Efendi
Descendant of the Prophet
Who journeyed to the Abode of Eternity
Having served as Chief Justice of Rumelia on four occasions
Zilhicce 1308 [July 1891]

Sırrı Pasha, Giridli. Governor-General, Author. C68

Born in 1844 to a notable family on Crete—hence his epithet *Giridî* or *Giridli* ("the Cretan")—the young Sırrı came to Istanbul to complete his education, during which he mastered Arabic and Persian. At the tender age of sixteen he began his career back on Crete, as secretary to a law court, moving on to serve in increasingly important secretarial posts in provincial governments around the empire. His star rising, in the 1870s Sırrı Pasha left secretarial work to begin serving as administrator of subdistricts in various provinces. After 1879 he reached the upper bureaucratic ranks with appointments as Governor-General of provinces as diverse as Trabzon, Diyarbakir (twice), and Baghdad, in the latter province winning for himself a reputation for useful projects that yielded at least one rhyming poem:

> When His Excellency the worthy Sırrı Pasha
>   Nine months served to govern that locale,
> Through copious zeal of that eminent chief
>   There opened this year the Hille Canal.[103]

of which the last two lines formed a chronogram that adds up to 1,308, the Muslim calendar year in which Sırrı Pasha opened the canal in question.

Quite apart from his job duties, Sırrı took up the pen for pleasure and interest, producing poetry, letters, and calligraphy, as well as some twenty works of commentary on the Koran. His exquisite and quite distinctive penmanship in the Ottoman script won admirers, while his caustic temper earned him a reputation in other quarters.

In 1869 Sırrı married Leyla Hanım—daughter of the Court physician to Sultan Abdülmecid, İsmail Pasha, who is also buried in this graveyard—and the couple had four children. As Leyla Hanım developed into the charming and multi-talented musician, poetess, and memoirist by which she is still known today (under the name Leyla Saz), the couple grew apart, living separate lives after Sırrı's appointment to Baghdad in 1890, since Leyla refused to leave the Imperial capital for that remote outpost. Heart problems forced Sırrı to retire to Istanbul in 1894 in search of medical care, but treatment failed to cure him, and he died in the capital in 1895, aged only 51. The capital's English newspaper printed two short death notices on the prominent civil servant and writer:

Sirri Pasha, formerly governor-general of the province of Diarbekir, who had been ailing for some time past, died yesterday evening at his residence at Mahmoud Pasha, Stamboul.

Deceased was a well-known author in Turkish literary circles, and he leaves several works of a religious character. Sirri Pasha had successively held the office of governor-genral of Angora, Bagdad, Adana, Trebizond, Sivas, and other provinces.

The funeral takes place today.[104]

The funeral of the late Sirri Pasha, ex-governor-general of Diarbekir, took place yesterday. The burial service was held in the St. Sophia mosque and the body, as desired by his Imperial Majesty the Sultan, was interred within the precincts of the Mausoleum of Sultan Mahmoud. The funeral expenses were defrayed by the Sovereign's Privy Purse.

Among those who accompanied the deceased to his last resting place were: —His Excellency Munif Pasha, formerly Minister of Public Instruction; Reshid Bey, Councillor of State; Eumer Fehim Effendi, president of the civil section of the Court of Cassation; . . . Said Bey, translator at the Palace, and many others.[105]

TOMBSTONE

He is The Eternal One, The Creator
A Fatiha for the soul of the late
Sırrı Pasha of Crete
Who secured an eminent position
Among learned men of the Islamic Community
Through his religious writings
And among dignitaries of the Ottoman State
Through his capable administration
24 Cemaziyül'ahir 1313 [12 December 1895]
Born in the year 1260 [1844]

Thanks to his family connections
Subhi Pasha entered state service,
but clearly he leaned more toward
museology, numismatics, and Sufism.

Subhi Pasha. Scholar, Cabinet Minister. A18

Born in 1818 to a leading Ottoman family in Tripolizza, in the Peloponnese peninsula (today's Greece), and son of the future Sami Pasha who is also buried in this graveyard, the very young Abdüllâtif Subhi fled with his family to Egypt during the Greek Revolution of the 1820s. Educated by private tutors, he entered service in the Palace Secretariat of Muhammad Ali, governor of Egypt. Coming to Istanbul in the 1840s, Subhi rose through the ranks of government service, thanks in no small measure to his prominent father, coming to hold the title of Pasha and becoming Minister of Pious Foundations, then Minister of Public Instruction, and Governor-General of Syria, under Sultan Abdülaziz.

His star continued to rise under Abdülhamid II after 1878, as Subhi served in the Cabinet in the same posts he had previously occupied. Meanwhile his family's prominence received recognition by the marriage in 1879 of his much younger brother Necib to Princess Mediha, the Sultan's sister.

Quite apart from his official duties, reflecting his passion for education Subhi Pasha helped establish the High School of Commerce, the School of Fine Arts, and the Imperial Museum. His vast intellectual interests led him to publish a history of Islam, and delve into numismatics, publishing a study of Islamic coinage. He was also a practicing Sufi.

Subhi Pasha died in office as Minister of Pious Foundations on 16-17 January 1886, aged about 67, only 5 years after his father Sami Pasha, near whose sepulchre he was buried. His death notice in *The Times* of London honored the Pasha's scholarly pursuits:

The death of his Excellency Subhi Pasha on the 16th of January at Constantinople, at the age of 72 [in Muslim calendar years], leaves a wide gap among the survivors of the Ottoman renaissance. From his father he inherited a princely fortune, which he devoted liberally to the promotion of literature and science. His rich Oriental library was freely open to scholars, and his fine numismatic cabinet attracted Europeans. Among his writings are some on numismatics and statistics, and he was an honorary member of the English and French societies devoted to statistics. During the troubles of his country he sold his collections, and he is said to have died in debt. By command he was buried in the Imperial vaults of the mosque [*sic*] of Sultan Mahmoud.[106]

TOMBSTONE
O He

In good nature and generosity and learning
Mankind knew no equal to Subhi Pasha
God's mercy upon him

While Minister of Pious Foundations that worthy and
dignified gentleman
Set out for the All-highest Throne
God's mercy upon him

To the path of Divine Blessing he kept inwardly and outwardly
Verily he was of the two wings
God's mercy upon him

Making known his approaching death, he did not withdraw
And drew up his testament in accordance with canonical law
God's mercy upon him

May the brothers of the Faith who visit his grave
Fittingly utter this prayer
God's mercy upon him

Weeping, his neighbor Lûtfi spoke this date:
"Oh! Subhi Pasha has perished,
God's mercy upon him"

11 R. [Rebiülahir] 1303 [17 January 1886]

Subhi Pasha's epitaph consists of rhyming couplets in highly erudite language suitable to the learned scholar he was, and redolent of the Sufi hymns
he would have known in life. The rhyme precedes and incorporates the repeating Arabic phrase that ends each couplet. The references to the path of
Divine Blessing, inwardly and outwardly, and the two wings, invoke
Sufism and the Pasha's mastery of both formal science and the spiritual
path. The poet Lûtfi's chronogram in the last couplet cleverly includes the
invocation of God's mercy and totals 1,303, the year of Subhi Pasha's death
in the Muslim calendar.

Tevfik Efendi. Marshal of the Prophet's Descendants. C65

Tevfik Efendi served as *Nakibüleşraf* (Marshal of the Prophet's Descendants), the titular head of those who claimed descent from the Prophet
Muhammad. The Ottoman monarchs traditionally appointed a worthy candidate to this post, which brought with it a government salary and house
for his residence, at least as of the nineteenth century. Duties included reg-
istering births, deaths, and marriages among members of these descendants,
and participating in high ceremonial functions. There were several such
Marshals throughout the Ottoman state at any given time, the most important being that of the Imperial capital.

The incumbent holder of the title at Istanbul through the latter forty years
of the nineteenth century, Tevfik Efendi, was well-poised to receive the appointment, since his father, Abdurrahman Efendi of Harput in southeastern
Anatolia, had been a prominent sheikh of the Nakshibendi order of
dervishes. His father's moniker as *Kürt Hoca* or the Kurdish Khoja
(teacher) indicates that the family came from a Kurdish, or possibly mixed
Arab-Kurdish, background.

Tevfik's date of birth is unknown, but he was likely born in the 1820s.
Initially he pursued a successful judicial career, serving at one point as

Chief Justice of Rumelia. By at least 1865, however, he had received his appointment as Marshal of the Prophet's Descendants. Archival records show that along with the generous salary and provision of a house for his residence (in this case, at Kızıl Toprak on the Asian shore of the Bosphorus), Tevfik Efendi received other evidence of Imperial favor through the decades, including orders and decorations.

Having served in the post for at least thirty-six years when he died in 1901 at an advanced age, Tevfik received the permission of his patron Abdülhamid II for burial in this prestigious graveyard. His death rated a brief notice in the capital's English newspaper:

> The Nakıb-ul-Eshref, Tewfik Effendi, died last night in his residence at Kizil Toprak.[107]

TOMBSTONE
O Most Compassionate of Merciful Ones
A Fatiha for the soul of
The Marshal of the Prophet's Descendants
Seyyid Mustafa Tevfik Efendi
Formerly Chief Justice of Rumelia
Son of the seyyid Abdurrahman Efendi
The Instructor at the Imperial Court
Who was well-known as the Kurdish Khoja
28 Muharrem 1319, 4 Mayıs 1317 [17 May 1901]

Glossary

Ağa. Title of respect accorded mostly to eunuchs

Bey. Title of respect accorded to men

Chronogram. Line of verse composed of words chosen for the numerical values of the letters; when added together, the sum of the values equals a date the composer had in mind

Consort. The highest-ranking concubines of a sultan, limited to four in number at any given time; beneath the consorts in Court hierarchy came the middle rank of concubines, the *ikbal*s, followed by the lowest rank, the *gözde*s

C.U.P. Committee of Union and Progress, the military-backed organization that dominated the government between 1908 and 1918

Efendi. Title of great respect for men of considerable standing; standard title of an Imperial prince; also accorded to women usually in tandem with another title, e.g., *Sultan Efendi* for a princess

Empress Mother. Mother of the reigning sultan; *Valide Sultan* in Turkish, hence occasionally called Validé Sultana by Westerners of the day

Ghazi. Title granted to a victor or hero in a war against non-Muslims

Governor-General. Governor (*Vali*) of a province

Gözde. "Chosen One," the lowest of the three ranks of Imperial concubine

Grand Vizier. Prime minister, or head of the Ottoman government, appointed by the sultan

Hajji. One who has performed the hajj or pilgrimage to Mecca

Hanım. Title of respect accorded women

Hanımsultan. "Lady Princess," title of daughters of princesses

Hazinedar. "Treasurer," high-ranking post for female managers of the harem and for Court Eunuchs

İkbal. "Fortunate One," the middle of the three ranks of concubine

Illiyin. The highest of the eight paradises mentioned in the Koran

Kadınefendi. "Ladyship," title of great respect reserved for the four Imperial consorts

Kalfa. Title whose meaning varies according to gender: for men, master-builder on construction projects; for women, supervisor in the Imperial Harem

Konak. Mansion, villa

Naim. The fourth of the eight paradises named in the Koran

Padishah. Emperor; alternative title for the sultan

Pasha. Title accorded the highest-ranking men in the civil bureaucracy and
the military

Rumelia. Collective name for the Ottoman European provinces

Senior Chamberlain. Highest-ranking official in the palace chancery, overseeing interactions between the Court and the outside world

Şeyhülislâm. Chief Muslim religious dignitary of the empire, charged with
oversight of canon law and Islamic institutions

Seyyid. Title indicating descent from the Prophet Muhammad

Shahanshah. "King of kings," a title of the sultan

Sheikh. Head of an order of dervishes; head preacher

Sherif. Title indicating descent from the Prophet Muhammad; title of the
governor of Mecca

Sirkeci. District at the Stambul side of the Golden Horn Bridge; site of pier
for steamers bringing coffins for burial at the Mahmud II tomb

Stambul. Historic central district of Istanbul, within the city walls that ring
the peninsula bounded by the Golden Horn, the Bosphorus, and the Sea
of Marmara

Sublime Porte. Offices of the Ottoman government

Sultana. Title used in the West for an Ottoman princess, but never used at
the Ottoman Court

Sülüs. A style of calligraphy

Tuğra. Monogram device of the sultan, weaving together his and his father's names

Ulema. The class of educated religious scholars, including judges and pro-
fessors

Usta. Female supervisor of women servants in the palace harem

Vali. Governor-General of a province

Validé Sultana. *see* Empress Mother

Veliahd. Title of the Heir to the Throne of the Ottoman Empire

Vizier. Highest rank in the civil bureaucracy, bringing with it the title of
Pasha

Yalı. Seaside villa, traditionally built of wood along the Bosphorus

Notes

Abbreviations
BOA = Başbakanlık Osmanlı Arşivi (Prime Ministry Ottoman Archives), Istanbul
EE = *The Eastern Express* (newspaper published in Istanbul, as were *JC* and *LH*)
JC = *Journal de Constantinople*
LH = *The Levant Herald*
TL = *The Times* of London

Chapter 1. The Mahmud Quandary
1. *Pennsylvania Inquirer and Daily Courier* (Philadelphia), 22 Aug. 1839.
2. *TL*, 25 July 1839.
3. Eldem 2005, 34.
4. Gautier 1854, 306.
5. *Pennsylvania Inquirer and Daily Courier* (Philadelphia), 22 Aug. 1839.
6. Ibid.
7. The clever chronogram works much better in Turkish, pleasing readers by its alliteration and its punning on the word "mahmud." The letters total 1,256, so that since Mahmud II died in the Muslim calendar year 1255, either the verse follows a line instructing the reader to subtract 1 from the total, or it commemorates the year Mahmud's tomb was completed (1256).
8. Lûtfi 1290-1306, 6:31-32.
9. Vatin and Veinstein 2003, 425-430.
10. *Takvim-i Vekayi*, 26 Şaban 1256 (23 Oct. 1840).
11. Wharton 2011, 19-33.
12. Özgüven 2003, 357.
13. Akın 1989, 21.
14. BOA, C.SM. 105/5268; Hat 1424/58266 and İ.DH. 32/1523.

Chapter 2. More Than a Tomb
1. Lûtfi 1290-1306, 6:43; Büngül ca. 1970, 2:47-50.
2. *The National Magazine*, May 1855.
3. For example H. Barth, *Constantinople* (Paris: Renouard, 1903), 160.
4. *San Francisco Daily Evening Bulletin*, Apr. 19, 1869.
5. Waters 1895, 140.
6. de Amicis 1878, 301-302.
7. Gautier 1854, 306.
8. Waters 1895, 140.
9. BOA, İ.MTZ(05) 4/106.
10. BOA, DH.MKT 2454/5.
11. Helena (Mont.) *Independent*, 26 June 1874.
12. *St. Louis Globe-Democrat*, 28 Jan. 1877.

13. Twain, Mark. *The Innocents Abroad or The New Pilgrims Progress.* (New York: Signet, 1980), 270-271.
14. *The Star and Banner* (Gettysburg, Pa.), 8 Nov. 1850.
15. *Takvim-i Vekayi,* 26 Şaban 1256 (23 Oct. 1840).
16. *Ceride-i Havadis,* 21 Şaban 1256 (18 Oct. 1840).

Chapter 3. The Cemetery as Window
1. Pardoe 1839, 134.
2. BOA,Y.PRK.ZB 28/110
3. BOA, A.MKT.NZD 368/45.
4. BOA, Y.PRK.ZB 14/65.
5. Mehmet Zeki Pakalın, *Osmanlı Tarih Deyimleri ve Terimleri Sözlüğü,* 401.
6. Abdülaziz Bey 1995, 279 n. 4.
7. Tezcan 2006, 184.
8. Findley 1989, 55.

Chapter 4. The Dynasty in the Tomb
1. Brookes 2008, 27.
2. Şehsuvaroğlu 1949, 140.
3. *The Graphic,* 24 June 1876, 611, whose report of immense crowds conflicts with one author's much later claim (Ayvazoğlu 2003, 46-47) of few mourners in the streets; but the quoted eyewitness account, published two weeks after Abdülaziz's funeral, carries more weight as evidence.
4. Öztuna 2008, 212.
5. Özdemir 1996, 250.
6. Tevfik 1943, 95.
7. Osmanoğlu 1994, 11.
8. Ibid., 13
9. Layard 2009, 44-45.
10. Türkgeldi 1951, 129. The Şerif Pasha who uttered the verse also composed the rhyming elegy to his late wife, Princess Emine (see her entry in Chapter 4).
11. Refik 1918, 16.
12. Türkgeldi 1951, 129.
13. *New York Times,* 12 Feb. 1918.
14. Özdemir 1996, 263.
15. *JC,* 19 July 1848.
16. *JC,* 14 Aug. 1850.
17. Uluçay 1992, 120-121.
18. Sakaoğlu 1999, 323.
19. Slade 1867, 86-88.
20. *TL,* 17 May 1853 (correspondent's report dated 2 May).
21. *TL,* 24 May 1853.
22. BOA, DUİT 5/142, 10 Ca 1338.
23. Uluçay 1992, 112.
24. *JC,* 6 June 1848.

25. Özdemir 1996, 262-63.
26. Lûtfi 1290-1306, 7:18.
27. Kelly 1987, 249.
28. Pardoe 1839, 161-162.
29. Özdemir 1996, 258.
30. *TL*, 18 July 1839.
31. Osmanoğlu 1966, 63.
32. *Ceride-i Havadis*, 11 Muharrem 1259 (11 Feb. 1843).
33. Özdemir 1996, 258-259.
34. BOA, DUIT 7/1.
35. *JC*, 9 Oct. 1848.
36. BOA, Y.EE 149/13.
37. *LH*, 23 Oct. 1899.
38. *LH*, 24 Oct. 1899.
39. Sakaoğlu 2008, 400.
40. Ibid., 398.
41. Uluçay 1992, 127.
42. Saz 1994, 201.
43. *TL*, 17 Sept. 1842.
44. Uluçay 1992, 123.
45. Özdemir 1996, 265-266.

Chapter 5. From Garden to Graveyard

1. Demirel 2009, 510.
2. Ayvazoğlu 2003, 50.
3. *LH*, 11 Apr. 1895.
4. *LH*, 13 Apr. 1895.
5. *TL*, 11 Oct. 1872.
6. *LH*, 11 Sept. 1876.
7. Davison 1986.
8. *LH*, 17 Jan. 1891, 19 Jan. 1891, 20 Jan. 1891, 29 Jan. 1891, 30 Jan. 1891.
9. *LH*, 4 June 1894.
10. *EE*, 3 May 1883.
11. *LH*, 9 Oct. 1899.
12. Ibid.
13. *LH*, 9 Nov. 1901.
14. *LH*, 22 June 1896.
15. Süreyya 1996, 412-413.
16. Ibid., 444.
17. Galib 1977, 130.
18. http://www.chronicledergisi.com/yasak-sehir-ve-sakinleri/, accessed 23 Dec. 2011.
19. *TL*, 2 Mar. 1858.
20. Süreyya 1996, 522.
21. İnal 1930-42, 452.
22. *LH*, 13 Jan. 1905.

23. *LH*, 1 Feb. 1904.
24. Süreyya 1996, 932.
25. *LH*, 4 Mar. 1891.
26. *TL*, 8 and 11 Sept. 1871.
27. *TL*, 11 Oct. 1872.
28. Ali Vasıb 2005, 51; and "Mora'dan Moda'ya Cimcozlar," accessed 30 Nov. 2011 at http://www.chronicledergisi.com/moradan-modaya-cimcozlar/
29. *LH*, 20 Aug. 1908.
30. *LH*, 26 Nov. 1877.
31. Süreyya 1996, 1389-1390.
32. *EE*, 19 Nov. 1883.
33. Layard 2009, 40 and 514-15.
34. *LH*, 24 Feb. 1896.
35. Layard 2009, 66 and 417-18.
36. *LH*, 30 Oct. 1907.
37. Eldem 2005, 286.
38. Pakalın 2008, 17:72.
39. Süreyya 1996, 1478.
40. Galib 1977, 91.
41. *LH*, 11 June 1886 and 12 June 1886.
42. *LH*, 1 Apr. 1892.
43. *LH*, 22 Aug. 1891.
44. *LH*, 29 May 1893.
45. *LH*, 3 June 1887.
46. Süreyya 1996, 302.
47. *LH*, 21 Aug. 1891.
48. *EE*, 23 Oct. 1884.
49. *LH*, 20 Mar. 1889.
50. Eldem 2005, 218.
51. Pakalin 2008, 18:5.
52. Uşaklıgil 2003, 363
53. *TL*, 19 Aug. 1898.
54. Ayvazoğlu 2003, chart preceding p. 53.
55. Süreyya 1996, 1066-67.
56. *LH*, 13 June 1902.
57. *LH*, 10 June 1910 and 11 June 1910.
58. *LH,* 13 June 1910.
59. *LH*, 10 Apr. 1909.
60. In *House With Wisteria: Memoirs of Halidé Edib* (Charlottesville, Va.: Leopolis, 2003), 228.
61. *İkdam*, 26 Mar. 1325 (8 Apr. 1909); quoted in Baydar 1955, 20-21.
62. *Volkan*, 30 Mar. 1325 (12 Apr. 1909); quoted in Baydar 1955, 22.
63. Süreyya 1996, 397.
64. *LH*, 27 and 29 Oct. 1900.
65. *LH*, 15 Mar. 1875.
66. Süreyya 1996, 520.

67. *LH*, 15 Jan. 1902.
68. *EE*, 25 Sept. 1882.
69. Süreyya 1996, 593.
70. *LH*, 29 June 1887.
71. *LH*, 4 July 1887.
72. *LH*, 7 Oct. 1899.
73. Keller 1935, 109 and 113.
74. *LH*, 6 Oct. 1899.
75. Süreyya 1996, 1354.
76. *LH*, 4 Dec. 1905.
77. *LH*, 26 Nov. 1894.
78. *LH*, 27 Nov. 1894.
79. *LH*, 30 Nov. 1894.
80. Örikağasızâde 2007, 61.
81. *LH*, 1 Apr. 1876.
82. *LH*, 4 Apr. 1876.
83. Jongerden, Joost. *The Settlement Issue in Turkey and the Kurds: An Analysis of Spatial Policies, Modernity and War* (Leiden: Brill, 2007), 247-251.
84. İnal 1930-42, 23.
85. Ibid., 1106.
86. Saz 1994, 217.
87. *LH*, 26 May 1874.
88. Described in detail in Saz 1994, 172-181.
89. Akyıldız 1998, 24-37.
90. Uşaklıgil 2003, 97.
91. *EE*, 17 Nov. 1884.
92. *LH*, 14 and 15 Feb. 1899.
93. Özdemir 1996, 283-284.
94. *LH*, 8 Oct. 1887.
95. Baydar 1955, 28.
96. *LH*, 14, 15, 16 Apr. 1909.
97. Ali Vasıb 2005, 51 and 94.
98. Altunsu 1972, 216-217.
99. *JC*, 26 Jan. 1848.
100. *Tercüman-ı Hakikat*, 13 Apr. 1893; quoted in Ayvazoğlu 2003, 91.
101. *LH*, 14 Apr. 1893.
102. *LH*, 22 and 23 July 1891.
103. İnal 1930-42, 1735.
104. *LH*, 11 Dec. 1895.
105. *LH*, 12 Dec. 1895.
106. *TL*, 5 Feb. 1886.
107. *LH*, 18 May 1901.

Bibliography

Abdülaziz Bey. 1995. *Osmanlı Âdet, Merasim ve Tabirleri*. Istanbul: Tarih Vafkı.

Akın, Günkut. 1989. "Divanyolu Küresi." *Tarih ve Toplum* 72, 21-24.

—. 1994. "Mahmud II Türbesi ve Sebili." *Dünden Bugüne İstanbul Ansiklopedisi* 5, 263-265. Istanbul: Kültür Bakanlığı and Tarih Vakfı.

Akyıldız, Ali. 1998. *Mümin ve Müsrif bir Padişah Kızı Refia Sultan*. Istanbul: Tarih Vakfı.

Alderson, A. D. 1956. *The Structure of the Ottoman Dynasty*. Oxford: Clarendon.

Ali Vâsıb Efendi. 2005. *Bir Şehzadenin Hâtırâtı: Vatan ve Menfâda Gördüklerim ve İşittiklerim*. Istanbul: YKY.

Alparslan, Ali. 1994. "Mustafa İzzet Efendi." *Dünden Bugüne İstanbul Ansiklopedisi* 5, 562. Istanbul: Kültür Bakanlığı and Tarih Vakfı.

Altunsu, Abdülkadir. 1972. *Osmanlı Şeyhülislâmları*. Ankara: Ayyıldız.

Arberry, A. J. 1974. *The Koran Interpreted*. New York: MacMillan.

Artan, Tülay. 1993. "The Kadirga Palace: An Architectural Reconstruction." *Muqarnas* 10: 201-211.

Ayvazoğlu, Beşir. 2003. *Divanyolu: Bir Caddenin Hikâyesi*. Istanbul: Ötüken.

Baydar, Mustafa. 1955. *31 Mart Vak'ası*. Istanbul: Anıl.

Brookes, Douglas Scott. 2008. *The Concubine, the Princess, and the Teacher: Voices from the Ottoman Harem*. Austin: University of Texas.

Büngül, Nurettin Rüştü. ca. 1970. *Eski Eserler Ansiklopedisi*. Istanbul: Tercüman.

Çakıroğlu, Ekrem (ed.). 1999. *Yaşamları ve Yapıtlarıyla Osmanlılar Ansiklopedisi*. Istanbul: YKY.

Davison, Roderic. 1986. "Halil Şerif Paşa: The Influence of Paris and the West on an Ottoman Diplomat." *Osmanlı Araştırmaları* 6:1, 47-65.

De Amicis, Edmondo. 1878. *Constantinople*. Trans. Caroline Tilton. London: Low, Marston, Searle.

Demirel, Muammer. 2009. "Bezmiâlem Valide Sultan School: Darülmaârif." *Middle Eastern Studies* 45:3, 507-516.

Eldem, Edhem. 2005. *Death in Istanbul: Death and Its Rituals in Ottoman-Islamic Culture*. Istanbul: Ottoman Bank Archives and Research Centre.

Findley, Carter Vaughn. 1989. *Ottoman Civil Officialdom: A Social History*. Princeton.

Galib, Mehmed, and Ali Rıza. 1977. *Geçen Asırda Devlet Adamlarımız*. Istanbul: Tercüman.

Gautier, Théophile. 1854. *Constantinople of Today*. Trans. Robert H. Gould. London: David Bogue.

İnal, İbnülemin Mahmut Kemal. 1335. *Evkaf-ı Hümayun Nezaretinin Tarihçe-i Teşkilâtı ve Nüzzarın Terâcim-i Ahvali*. Istanbul: Evkaf-i İslamiye.

—. 1930-42. *Son Asır Türk Şairleri*. Istanbul: Orhaniye.

İşli, Necdet. 2010. "II. Mahmud'un Hazire Kataloğu." In Coşkun Yılmaz, *II. Mahmud: Yeniden Yapılanma Sürecinde İstanbul*. Istanbul: Avrupa Kültür Başkenti.

"İstanbul (Tarihî Eserler): Türbeler." 1950. In *İslam Ansiklopedisi*, 1214/133. Istanbul: Millî Eğitim Basımevi, 1950-.

Kara Pilehvarian, Nuran. 2000. *Fountains in Ottoman Istanbul*. Istanbul: YEM.

Keller, Mathilde. 1935. *Vierzig Jahre im Dienst der Kaiserin*. Leipzig: Koehler & Amelang.

Kelly, Laurence. 1987. *Istanbul—a Traveller's Companion*. London: Constable.

Kuneralp, Sinan. 1999. *Son Dönem Osmanlı Erkân ve Ricali (1839-1922)*. Istanbul: Isis.

Kuran-Burçoğlu, Nedret. "Osman Zeki Bey and His Printing Office the *Matbaa-i Osmaniye*." http://www.islamicmanuscripts.info/reference/articles/JSS-Sup-15-Printing/JSS-Supp-15-5-Koran-Burcoglu-2004-035-057.pdf, accessed 17 October 2011.

Laqueur, Hans-Peter. 1993. *Osmanische Friedhöfe und Grabsteine in Istanbul*. Tübingen: Wasmuth.

Layard, A. Henry. 2009. *The Queen's Ambassador to the Sultan; Memoirs of Sir Henry A. Layard's Constantinople Embassy, 1877-1880*. Ed. Sinan Kuneralp. Istanbul: Isis.

Lûtfî, Ahmed. 1290-1306 [1873-1889]. *Tarih-i Lûtfî*. Istanbul: Matbaa-ı Âmire.

Moltke, Helmut von. 1893. *Briefe über Zustände und Begebenheiten in der Türkei aus den Jahren 1835 bis 1839*. Berlin: Mittler.

Önkal, Hakkı. 1992. *Osmanlı Hanedan Türbeleri*. Ankara: Kültür Bakanlığı.

Örikağasızâde Hasan Sırrı. 2007. *Sultan Abdülhamit Devri Hatıraları ve Saray İdaresi*. Istanbul: Dergâh.

Osmanoğlu, Ayşe. 1994. *Babam Sultan Abdülhamid (Hâtıralarım)*. Istanbul: Selçuk.

Osmanoğlu, Osman Selaheddin. 1999. *Osmanlı Devleti'nin Kuruluşunun 700. Yılında Osmanlı Hanedanı*. Istanbul: İSAR Vakfı.

Osmanoğlu, Şadiye. 1966. *Hayatımımın Acı ve Tatlı Günleri*. Istanbul: Bedir.

Özdemir, Hikmet. 1996. *Âdile Sultan Dîvânı*. Ankara: T.C. Kültür Bakanlığı.

Özgüven, H. Burcu. 2003. "Mahmud II Türbesi, Sebili, Çeşmesi ve Haziresi." *Türkiye Diyanet Vakfı İslam Ansiklopedisi* 27, 357-358.

Öztuna, Yılmaz. 2008. *Bir Darbenin Anatomisi*. Istanbul: Babıali Kültür Yayıncılığı.

Pakalın, Mehmed Zeki. 2008. *Sicill-i Osmanî Zeyli*. Ankara: Türk Tarih Kurumu.

Pardoe, Julia. 1839. *The Beauties of the Bosphorus*. London: George Virtue.

Pazan, İbrahim. 2009. *Son Saraylı: Şehzade Osman Ertuğrul Efendi.* Istanbul: Babıali Kültür Yayıncılığı.

Refik, Ahmed. 1918. "Sultan Abdülhamid'in Na'şı Önünde." In Abdurrahman Şeref, *Sultan Abdülhamid-i Sani'ye Dair.* Istanbul: Hilâl.

Sakaoğlu, Necdet. 1999. "Bezmiâlem Sultan." In *Yaşamları ve Yapıtlarıyla Osmanlılar Ansiklopedisi* 1:322-323. Istanbul: YKY.

Saz, Leyla. 1994. *The Imperial Harem of the Sultans.* Istanbul: Peva.

Şakir, Ziya. 1943. *Çırağan Sarayında 28 Sene: Beşinci Murad'ın Hayatı.* Istanbul: Anadolu Türk Kitap Deposu.

Şehsuvaroğlu, Haluk. 1949. *Sultan Aziz: Hususî, Siyasî Hayatı, Devri ve Ölümü.* Istanbul: Hilmi.

—. 1953 (reprint 2005). *Asırlar Boyunca İstanbul: Sarayları, Camileri, Abideleri, Çeşmeleri.* Istanbul: Cumhuriyet Gazetesi.

Slade, Adolphus. 1867. *Turkey and the Crimean War: A Narrative of Historical Events.* London: Smith, Elder and Co.

Süreyya, Mehmed. 1996. *Sicill-i Osmanî.* Istanbul: Tarih Vakfı.

Tanman, Mehmet Baha. 2006. "Nineteenth-Century Ottoman Funerary Architecture: From Innovation to Eclecticism." In *Islamic Art in the 19th Century* 60:37-55. Leiden: Brill.

Tevfik, Rıza. 1943. *Kendi Ağzından Rıza Tevfik.* Istanbul: Remzi.

Tezcan, Hülya. 2006. *Osmanlı Sarayının Çocukları.* Istanbul: Aygaz.

Türkgeldi, Ali Fuat. 1951. *Görüp İşittiklerim.* Ankara: Türk Tarih Kurumu.

Uluçay, M. Çağatay. 1992. *Padişahların Kadınları ve Kızları.* Ankara: Türk Tarih Kurumu.

Uşaklıgil, Halid Ziya. 2003. *Saray ve Ötesi.* Istanbul: Özgür.

Vatin, Nicholas, and Gilles Veinstein. 2003. *Le Sérail ébranlé : essai sur les morts, dépositions et avènements des sultans ottomans (XIVe-XIXe siècle).* Paris: Fayard.

Vatin, Nicolas, and Stéphane Yerasimos. 2001. *Les cimetières dans la ville : statut, choix et organisation des lieux d'inhumation dans Istanbul intra muros.* Istanbul-Paris.

Waters, Clara Clement. 1895. *Constantinople: The City of the Sultans.* Boston: Estes and Lauriat.

Wharton, Alyson. 2011. "The Identity of the Ottoman Architect in the Era of 'Westernization.'" *Armenian Architects of Istanbul in the Era of Westernization.* Istanbul: Hrant Dink Foundation.

Ziyrek, Ali. 2004. "Batı Mimari Üsluplarının Osmanlı Türbe Mimarisine Yansıması." Unpublished thesis, Mimar Sinan University, Istanbul.

Index

Page numbers in italics refer to illustrations

OTHER TITLES IN THE
PRINCETON SERIES ON THE MIDDLE EAST

Cyrus Schayegh and William Blair, Editors
Department of Near Eastern Studies, Princeton University

Al-Jabartī's History of Egypt
edited with an introduction and commentary
by Jane Hathaway
> "The most accessible and comprehensive primary source
> for the history of Egypt under Ottoman rule."
> —*Book News*

HC 978-1-55876-446-0   PB 978-1-55876-447-7

*The Book of Strangers: Medieval Arabic Graffiti on the
Theme of Nostalgia*
edited and translated by Patricia Crone and Smuel Moreh.
> "An exemplary translation... readable and well
> documented"—*TLS*

HC 978-1-55876-214-5   PB 978-1-55876-233-6

*Harem Ghosts: What One Cemetery Can Tell Us
about the Ottoman Empire*
by Douglas Scott Brookes and Ali Ziyrek

HC 978-1-55876-610-5   PB 978-1-55876-611-2

*The Heritage of Central Asia:
From Antiquity to the Turkish Expansion*
by Richard N. Frye
> "A handy book. … Frye surveys the true history ...
> beautiful."—*Washington Post*
> "Incontestably one of the best studies of the history of
> Central Asia."—*Journal of Indo-European Studies*
> "Outstanding academic book of the year"—*Choice*

HC 978-1-55876-110-0   PB 978-155876111-7

CPSIA information can be obtained
at www.ICGtesting.com
Printed in the USA
FFOW02n2227210915
16984FF

9 781558 766112